STUDENT ACTIVITIES IN TODAY'S SCHOOLS

Essential Learning for All Youth

EDWARD JAMES KLESSE

SCARECROWEDUCATION

Lanham, Maryland • Toronto • Oxford

2004

Published in the United States of America
by ScarecrowEducation
An imprint of The Rowman & Littlefield Publishing Group, Inc.
4501 Forbes Boulevard, Suite 200, Lanham, Maryland 20706
www.scarecroweducation.com

PO Box 317
Oxford
OX2 9RU, UK

British Library Cataloguing in Publication Information Available

Library of Congress Cataloging-in-Publication Data

Klesse, Edward J.
    Student activities in today's schools : essential learning for all youth / Edward
James Klesse.
       p.   cm.
    Includes bibliographical references and index.
    ISBN 1-57886-087-3 (pbk. : alk. paper)
    1. Student activities. I. Title.
LB3605 .K54 2004
371.8′9—dc22   2003023553

To Dale and Jan

*Two wonderful people who
have always helped me.*

CONTENTS

CONTENTS

TABLES

FOREWORD

"Not extra, not extra! Read all about it!" That quote was used in a marketing campaign for student activities but it could easily be another title for this book. One of my staff members came up with it after years of hearing me say that student activities should not be thought of as *extra*curricular. Even though many people still refer to school-sponsored student activities as extracurricular activities, it has been a goal of mine to bury that term. Why? Because students learn valuable skills from participating in student activities, such as goal setting, responsibility, communication, problem solving, decision making, teamwork, group process, and organizational ability, just to name a few. These are indeed *leadership skills*, but they are skills that we all use in life. Reports indicate that business leaders value these skills. Why else? Because who would want to advertise that a program valuable to students, their parents, and the community is considered an extra and that in times of budget cutting should get the proverbial axe? Any other reason? Because these are school-sponsored programs and students should be learning from their participation; therefore, school-sponsored student activities should be thought of as *co*curricular. Students who participate in school-sponsored student activities generally do better academically than those who don't. The term *extracurricular activity* should be reserved for out-of-school activities in which young people participate. And finally, it is a good bet that students who feel connected to their schools through their participation in student activities will not be prone to violence against their classmates or teachers. Those are a few reasons why I feel that student activities are so important that they should not be referred to as extra; as the title of the book suggests, they are part of essential learning for all youth.

Dr. Edward Klesse has produced the first book in many years that serves as a comprehensive review of the student activities program in schools. It covers the what, why, and how of administering the program and the benefits of participation. It should be required reading for principals, activity advisers, aspiring teachers, parents, and community leaders. These groups of people need to know how the student activities program can be a positive force in the lives of students, reflect positively on the school, and be of service to the community.

When I was taking undergraduate education courses, it was never mentioned that I might be asked to serve as a student activity adviser. Too many first-year teachers are given adviser responsibilities without having had any training. This book will help them. And, I hope it will be assigned reading at colleges and universities nationwide for those students planning to become educators. In addition, parents need to know how important activities can be in their children's lives. Activities participation can change a young person's life, be the difference in whether school is enjoyable or dreaded, and help that young person get into the college of his or her choice.

Perhaps after reading this book you might accept the challenge of finding a way to ensure that all students are participating in an activity that interests them. Interest inventories could be given to students and matched to clubs and organizations already being sponsored. Additional groups could be formed as necessary to match students' needs. It would then be crucial to track which activities a student was involved in; if the tracking showed no activities for a particular student, then follow-up would be necessary to discover the reasons for the student's noninvolvement. This, of course, takes time and resources—but I believe it would be time and money well spent. Schools might hire a director of student activities to carry out such tasks as part of his or her responsibilities. If this is not possible, perhaps the student council or a parents group could work with school officials to assist in this endeavor.

Academics + Activities = Excellence is a formula we should all remember; *Student Activities in Today's Schools: Essential Learning for All Youth* is part of the equation.

—Rocco M. Marano
Director of Student Activities
National Association of Secondary School Principals

For additional resources regarding student activities, contact the National Association of Secondary School Principals. NASSP is a professional organization of approximately 35,000 middle level and high school principals, assistant principals, and aspiring principals from the United States and more than sixty countries. NASSP is the sponsor of

- National Honor Society
- National Junior Honor Society
- National Association of Student Councils

For more information concerning NASSP services and programs, please call (703) 860-0200 or contact www.principals.org.

ACKNOWLEDGMENTS

Thank you to the following for their help gathering and locating information:
Rocco Marano, Barbara Nicol, Carrie Storm, Linda Foody, Carolyn Bush, Andy Costanzo, John Waters, Harry Bettencourt, Daniel Keever, George Meyer, Harry Bull, Grace Lannert, T. C. Hardesty, and Tom D'Onofrio.

Thank you to the following for their help with chapters 7 and 15:
Jan D'Onofrio, Marsha Hirsch, Jason Andrews, and Elena Zongrone

Thank you to Linda Smetana for word-processing help and her patience with my handwriting.
Thank you to John Lynch for his guidance.
Thank you to Rocco Marano for agreeing to write the foreword.
Thank you to Ellen Boesenberg and Elizabeth Cissi for their technical and editorial assistance.
Thank you to Thomas Koerner for his encouragement, assistance, advice, and faith.

INTRODUCTION

During the early history of public high schools in the United States at the end of the nineteenth century, school-sponsored extracurricular student activities were not an officially sanctioned part of the school experience. Although school officials were either indifferent or opposed to these activities, students took the initiative to set up clubs and participated in activities that satisfied personal interests or addressed social concerns. In the early decades of the twentieth century, these student-initiated clubs were tolerated and gradually came to be viewed as worthwhile for students' learning. With the publication in 1918 of the influential *Cardinal Principles of Secondary Education*, extracurricular student activities were recognized for the benefits they conferred on students' social and personal development (Buss 1998). From the heyday of progressivism in the United States in the 1920s through the mid-1950s, most schools encouraged student extracurricular activity; as educators came to view these activities as an important part of the school experience, "extracurricular" activities became "cocurricular" activities. Gholson (1985) refers to the period since the 1950s as the *fusion phase*, in which formerly noncredit activities have been incorporated into the curriculum as credit-bearing courses. This more integrated approach dissolves the distinction between school and nonschool programs and seems better suited to meeting the needs of the diverse student population, as evidenced by the large numbers of students who participate in activity programs. Buss (1998) declares this extra curriculum to be one of the important education innovations of the early twentieth century. And so it is.

1

WHAT ARE STUDENT ACTIVITIES?

The Mighty Bull Dogs of Midland High School are coming to Washington to see that one of their own is ushered into the White House with the sweet sounds of Texas ringing in his ears. As the parade marking the 54th presidential inauguration makes its way down Pennsylvania Avenue this Saturday, 187 of the students in the marching band from President-elect Bush's adopted Texas hometown plan to be in the lineup, trumpeting tunes like "The Yellow Rose of Texas," "Red River Valley," and "The Eyes of Texas."

But pulling together a perfect performance hasn't been easy. The Midland High School band didn't receive its official invitation to the quadrennial celebration until Jan. 3rd. Since then, students, parents, teachers, and community members have been scurrying to raise the $1,000 per student needed to make the trip. And the band has been using every spare minute to practice. (Bowman 2001, 25)

Student activities provide an important means of educating our young people. Participation in student activity organizations provides students with an opportunity to learn and practice the personal and leadership skills necessary for success as adults and citizens.

Student activities are:

- Educational in nature
- Based on genuine student interest areas
- Usually conducted during student time rather than on school time
- Student led
- Opportunities for students to learn through feedback and evaluation
- Sponsored by the school
- Opportunities for developing pupil abilities and broadening student horizons
- Emotional, physical, intellectual, and social involvements that require an individual commitment by young people

---

1

- Centered in the purpose of education
- A microphone for the student voice
- A process in which the final product is sometimes not as educationally important as the process of achieving it and the learning outcomes for each participant
- Concerned with the entire student—intellectually, socially, physically, spiritually, and culturally
- Legally recognized and organized by school officials
- Positive attitude builders for young people, the school, its traditions, and its purposes (Henrico County Public Schools n.d.)

The success of the student activities program in any school depends upon the quality of the adult and student leadership, and upon the extent of shared leadership between faculty and students.

Many students identify with their school through participation in a club or on a team. In many cases, their participation helps them achieve academic success. Some students need involvement at school that allows them to apply what they learn in class in order to make sense of "academics." Others need a creative, physical, or artistic outlet to apply or to express themselves. Student activities—working in conjunction with academics—help many students develop new skills and competencies that can be applied both in and outside school (Lannert 2000). Although certainly not limited to the following list, the goals of student activities are to:

1. provide opportunities for students to gain leadership skills and an appreciation for responsibility and accountability;
2. provide ways in which students may broaden their interest and develop new experiences;
3. provide a "learning laboratory" as an extension of the daily classroom experiences;
4. provide opportunities for student involvement and student recognition within the total school program;
5. foster healthy student-student, student-teacher, student-administration, and student-community interaction;
6. provide a channel of communication through which students can contribute to the school program;
7. provide a vehicle by which social skills can be developed to aid students in society; and
8. develop an interest in current issues that involve all segments of the student population. (Henrico County Public Schools n.d., 12)

To achieve these goals, an organization might have a variety of programs from which the students might choose, such as those shown in table 1.1.

Central to the activities program is the leadership of the student council or student government. Student councils often focus on promoting spirit, improving school climate, or planning projects in their buildings but also can plan activities for their community. They can work with other student activity organizations and the administration to address problems, needs, and concerns, and to unify the student body through schoolwide activities. An example of such a program is the "Campaign for Respect" at Warren Central High School in Indianapolis, Indiana. The objective of this student-run program was to change attitudes toward other students, authority figures, the community, and themselves (Wolff 1998). The slogan was, "Respect: Learned, Earned, and Returned," and the keys to program success were to:

Table 1.1   Student Activities, Henrico County (Virginia) Public Schools

HIGH SCHOOL

VHSL*	Service	Honorary
Athletics	Key Club	Quill and Scroll
Forensics	Keyettes/Jr. Keyettes	Thespians
Debate	Interact	BETA Club
Drama	Hi-Y	Science Honor Society
Yearbook	Y-Teens/H-Teens	Language Honor Society
Newspaper	SODA	Math Honor Society
Literary Magazine	SOHO	(Mu Alpha Theta)
Cheerleaders	Triangle I and II	National Honor Society
Creative Writing	Rebellettes	Tri M (Music Honor Society)
	Key Links	Art Honor Society
	Jr. Civitan	
	Red Cross Student Club	

Performing	Cocurricular	Interest
Band	French Club	Pep Club
Band Front	Spanish Club	Intramurals
Choral	German Club	Media Club
	Latin Club	FCA
	Science Club	Ecology Club
	Computer Club	Video Yearbook Club
	History Club	Photography Club
	FHA/HERO	Chess Club
	FBLA	S.A.D.D.
	OECA	Student Safety Club
	TSA	International
	Battle of the Brains	
	VICA	*Student Leadership*
	Art Club	*Organizations*
	Jr. Classical League	SCA/SGA
	Drama Club	ICC
	Landscaping Club	Senior Class
	Photography Club	Junior Class
	Sociology Club	Sophomore Class
	Math Club	Freshman Class

MIDDLE SCHOOL

Student Leadership Organization	Athletics
SCA/SGA	Interscholastic Athletics (regulated by middle school athletic council)
	Intramurals
	Cheerleaders

Performing	Service
Band	Key Club Builder Club
Strings	Red Cross

Honorary	
Jr. BETA Club	

Interest	Cocurricular
Activity Period Interest Groups	Drama
Bridge Club	Forensics
Model Club	Yearbook
Foreign Student Club	Newspaper
Sports Car Club	Magazine
Sports Officiating Club	French Club
Cross Word Club	Spanish Club
Needle Craft Club	German Club
Sports for Teens Club	Latin Club
Trivia Club	Science Club
Great Books Club	Computer Club
Youth Advisory Club	FHA
Builders Club	Olympics of the Mind
Astronomy Club	Art Club
Calligraphy Club	Ecology Club
Pep Club	Peer Tutoring
Media Club	"A" Club
Legal Club	
Aerobics Club	

* Virginia High School League requires that all participants be enrolled in five classes and successfully complete five courses each semester to maintain eligibility for their activities.

(Henrico County Public Schools n.d., 13–14)

- Include students in the planning and activities. If students feel that they are a part of the process, they will be more willing to participate.
- Solicit faculty and administrative support. No respect campaign will be successful unless teachers and administrators serve as role models and support the program.
- Solicit community support. WCHS [Warren Central High School] students quickly discovered that parents and community members were eager to support the Campaign for Respect.
- Develop monthly themes and provide meaningful correlating activities. An example is shown in table 1.2.
- Expect respect, yet continually encourage, praise, and reward respectful behavior. In a perfect world, students would automatically show respect in every situation. Realistically, students need to be encouraged, praised, and rewarded when their behavior is exemplary. (Wolff 1998, 23–25)

Table 1.2 Sample Theme Activities by Month

December: Respect for Family	May: Respect Your Future
Theme song: "We Are Family" (Sister Sledge) Activities: • Angel Tree Campaign • Children's Christmas Party • Breakfast with Santa • Operation Christmas Child • Salvation Army bell ringers • Toy drive • Visit nursing homes • Respect letters to family members	Theme song: "Greatest Love of All" (Whitney Houston) Activities: • Senior Week activities • Career Day (dress up as you would for your future profession) • Kiss a Senior Good-bye (respect messages written by underclassmen and delivered with a Hershey's kiss to graduating seniors)

Source: Wolff 1998, 24

A change in school climate does not take place quickly. Hard work, patience, and persistence are required by all stakeholders over a period of time. However, the benefits to all staff, students, and community members make the effort worthwhile (Wolff 1998).

Students often work on school safety issues such as "The Student Pledge against Gun Violence." A national day of concern was established for October 8, 1998, to help organize young people to become part of the solution to the gun violence problem in schools and in society. "The key feature of the day of concern will be an opportunity for students to sign a voluntary promise that they will never carry a gun to school, will never resolve a dispute with a gun, and will use their influence with their friends to keep them from resolving disputes with guns" (Student Pledge against Gun Violence 1998, 42). The pledge tally total for each individual school was then reported to the Student Pledge against Gun Violence national office in Northfield, Minnesota. The national program was begun in 1996 in Minnesota by Mary Lewis Grow, who is now the national coordinator of the project (www.pledge.org).

Many students volunteer throughout the holidays as well as throughout the school year in their communities. Students regularly conduct food drives to assist needy individuals and community organizations. The Whippany Park National Honor Society in Teaneck, New Jersey, added a twist to the traditional food drive project. The honor society created a grocery shopping list, complete with the cost of each item. Students and staff indicated the items they wished to purchase and donated the cost. Donations could be made in the name of the student or staff member or in the name of another person. The honor society members collected more than $700 the first year and almost $1,000 the second year. The money was used to purchase more than a ton of groceries. "Although we were pleased with the donations (Whippany Park is a small school), we were most delighted with the spirit of caring the drive inspired. Not only were students making donations from their savings or hard-earned paychecks, but parents, teachers, administrators, and staff also contributed" (Guzo 1995, 44). The steps to their successful drive included:

1. Decide the organization(s) to which the donations will go.
2. Check your calendar for the time you will run your drive.
3. Decide where you will make your purchases.
4. Have two or three members visit the food store a few weeks before the drive.

5. Create the shopping list. We use a simple spreadsheet: food item, size, price, amount to be bought, and benefactor's name.
6. Plan the length of the drive.
7. Design the gift card.
8. Have an advertising plan.
9. Establish an assignment sheet.
10. Inform the staff of the upcoming food drive. (Guzo 1995, 45)

Student groups often take up the challenge of supporting a culturally diverse climate in their school. This is accomplished through a variety of activities such as spirit/dress-up days, assemblies that celebrate specific cultures, and diversity week. All the planned student activities are a means of sharing cultures and having fun while appreciating the diversity of the school and its students (Laird and Laird 1998).

Assistance with the transition of students between school buildings is an activity in which many student leadership groups participate. Many schools have student-led or organized programs that help ease the stress of adjusting to a new school for many unfamiliar students and staff. One such program, PantherQuest, can be found in North Central High School in Indianapolis, Indiana.

The PantherQuest [transition] project evolved in conjunction with traditional efforts by the school's guidance office to welcome and inform incoming students and their parents of the opportunities awaiting them in high school. Supported by the leadership expertise of student government sponsors, teachers, and guidance counselors, a student-driven team is set up each spring to work with parents, teachers, and administrators to help with the transition experience. The Leadership Team fine-tuned a program to welcome the 800 students expected in the freshman class through a series of one-day orientation camps for approximately 150 students daily. North Central holds four separate daylong camps before the start of the school year to meet the student demand. By dividing the freshmen into teams led by dynamic students and faculty members, the freshmen learn about their new building, their school culture and traditions, important issues facing high school students, and how to have fun in their new environment. (Grinkmeyer 1998, 26)

Panther Quest administrators believe the orientation helps freshmen feel more comfortable with their teachers, administrators, peers, and the school building. The program utilizes four key components to accomplish this goal: teams, games, information, and fun.

Many schools sponsor vocational student organizations as part of their student activities program. These organizations rely heavily on an experiential, hands-on approach. Students involved in one of these organizations may consider that field as a future career option. Specifically, these organizations support student-career experience by:

1. Providing classroom instruction on a specific field or career.
2. Encouraging students to work in this field and offering a class credit for it.
3. Sponsoring student competitive events that combine written and oral testing to measure results. For example, students may be asked to develop a new ad campaign for a local business.

The objective is for students to interact with industry leaders in a particular field of interest, to be recognized and rewarded for their competence, and to have the opportunity to experience a career by doing it (Gehrmann 1998). Students are also taught leadership skills and are encouraged to use those skills in their vocational student organization. Examples of vocational student organizations are:

- Business Professionals of America (BPA)
- Distributive Education Clubs of America (DECA)
- Future Business Leaders of America (FBLA)
- Future Homemakers of America/Home Economics Related Occupations (FHA/HERO)
- Health Occupations Students of America (HOSA)
- National Future Farmers of America Organization (FFA)
- Technology Student Association (TSA)
- Vocational Industrial Clubs of America (VICA)(Gehrmann 1998, 19)

Each of these organizations offers advantages to students. The National Future Farmers of America (FFA) organization summarizes the benefits of belonging to its organization:

Its mission is: FFA makes a positive difference in the lives of students by developing their potential for premier leadership, personal growth, and career success through agricultural education.

To accomplish this mission, the FFA:

- Develops competent and assertive agricultural leadership
- Increases awareness of the global and technical importance of agriculture and its contribution to our well-being
- Strengthens the confidence of agricultural students in themselves and their work
- Promotes the intelligent choice and establishment of an agricultural career
- Encourages achievement in Supervised Agricultural Experience Programs
- Encourages wise management of economic, environmental, and human resources of the community
- Develops interpersonal skills in teamwork, communications, human relations, and social interaction
- Builds character and promotes citizenship, volunteerism, and patriotism
- Promotes cooperation and cooperative attitudes among all people
- Promotes healthy lifestyles
- Encourages excellence in scholarship (Breeding 1998, 28)

FFA members accomplish these strategies when they practice and apply the lessons of the classroom in the real world.

Students can make a difference in the lives of others through involvement in programs such as TREND, a national alcohol and drug prevention leadership program. TREND, in partnership with the Heifer Project International (HPI), gives needy families throughout the world an animal that, in turn, provides the family with food, transportation, labor, and/or income. Families care for the animals and agree to pass on one or more of their animal's offspring to another family in need (Shaller 1999). Over one million families in one hundred countries have participated in the HPI program. TREND chapters and other student organizations raise funds to benefit HPI and purchase animals. HPI uses the money to purchase the designated animals, which are then donated to needy families. "Aside from the benefits of providing a service for those in need, the fun of Cowabunga comes from the creative efforts involved in planning an 'amoosing' event to raise money to buy an animal" (Shaller 1999, 24).

Groups sometimes take up a cause that has special meaning to their school or organization. Following the death of a DECA (Distributive Education Clubs of America) member, the club at Ironwood High School in Glendale, Arizona, focused on drawing attention to the dangers of "red light running." They devised the "Wall of Support." With a $1 donation, local businesses could have their business cards attached to a red stop sign and placed on a display board. The money raised was deposited into the student's Memorial Scholarship Fund. The scholarship honors a DECA student each year. Through this project, the club honored the memory of one of their members and alerted the community to the seriousness of the "red light running" issue. U.S. Department of Transportation statistics indicate that 89,000 crashes a year are the result of drivers who run red lights, inflicting more than 80,000 injuries and nearly 1,000 deaths, at an estimated cost of $7 billion per year (Solter and DeFamio 2000).

What do high school students learn through their participation in student activities? They learn how to:

- Make business telephone calls
- Produce informational handouts
- Use the computer for communication, publicity, and public relations
- Make professional labels, business cards, and name tags
- Use parliamentary procedure
- Prepare an agenda and conduct a meeting
- Effectively use a word processor, database, and spreadsheet
- Prepare a budget and compile a financial statement
- Balance a checkbook
- Maintain a ledger of financial records and/or a computer bookkeeping system
- Organize a filing system
- Create and utilize a point system for evaluation purposes
- Publicize events and programs
- Develop time and work schedules
- Set long-term and short-term goals
- Plan, organize, and carry out a project
- Organize projects through a daily planner and priority list
- Express oneself confidently, logically, and clearly in front of others
- Give and receive constructive criticism
- Communicate with a large group
- Compile a systematic record of a school year in scrapbook form
- Produce a slide show
- Handle pressures coming from others
- Say "no"
- Write a business letter, letters of appreciation, and thank-yous
- Make deposits
- Effectively manage one's time

- Research, develop, and lead a seminar
- Plan a yearly calendar
- Deal with authority figures
- Arbitrate and mediate conflict
- Work effectively in a group
- Evaluate options, weigh consequences, and make a decision
- Solicit, measure, mold, and create public opinion
- Motivate others
- Develop group solidarity
- Prepare a presentation for adoption by a legislative or administrative group
- Choose, plan, and implement a fundraising or sales project
- Deal with ornery, negative, and irresponsible people (Murphy 1997, 24)

Students also learn how to plan and evaluate a project. Guiding questions for every project are as follows:

- What are you planning to do?
- Why do you want to do this project?
- When and where will the activities take place?
- Who will benefit from the project?
- Who needs to approve the project?
- When will the basic planning be done?
- What funds are needed? When will the money be needed?
- What kind of publicity is needed? When is it needed?
- What committees are necessary? List the committees, tasks, chairpersons, and deadlines.
- Who deserves special thanks? Who will write the thank-you notes and when?
- Will the project be worthwhile? How will you know? (Chmielewski 2000, 22)

Every project should be evaluated after it is finished and records should be kept of the planning process. The records can be reviewed in future years to plan the same projects.

Successful student activities programs are not limited to secondary schools. Middle school activities programs can sponsor a variety of activities. These activities should be fun, such as the traditional parties and dress-up days, and include lunchtime activities and holiday contests. Activities such as helping to sponsor Red Ribbon Week or a bike safety assembly and rodeo educate students. Students are encouraged to build a positive school attitude through positive social interaction. Weekly activities such as a "positive person" campaign help students see that their individual actions do make a difference in the school. The prizes given to the most positive persons help to reinforce the desired behavior and actions (Dowty 1996).

A Spirit Club is a way in which all students can join a student activity and participate as equals. The school becomes a happier, healthier place to learn when students feel good about themselves and others, and care about their school. A Spirit Club encourages this value and teaches responsibility, social skills, and the ability to plan and organize (Farr 1997). An effective Spirit Club tries to make all students feel like winners. Meetings are held during the school day when all students are able to attend.

Adolescents are often motivated and inspired by technology and its relevance to their lives. A parent/student computer club uses technology as a way to get parents and students together. The club requires students and their parent or guardian to attend together regularly as a team and is open to all students. "There is nothing more valuable than developing a structure so that students, parents, and teachers are all helping each other in a supportive environment" (Whitaker and Hays 1998, 16).

Middle school/elementary school partnering programs are in place in many school districts across the United States. One such program in Marietta, Georgia, teams seventh-grade students with first-grade students. The first-grade students experience a sense of stability, are exposed to positive role models, and receive academic help and social attention. The seventh-grade students develop interpersonal skills, learn to behave responsibly, and learn more about themselves and others. Both schools involved in the program experience community involvement. The activities between the two schools are variable and span the entire school year (Abrams 1999).

Other middle schools plan activities such as "The Acts of Kindness Experience," which teaches students the values of caring, sharing, and giving. Landisville Middle School (Lancaster, Pennsylvania) annually plans a day that involves all students in environmental and community activities that help and benefit others (Feifer 1998). This event helps students think about how they can help others and improve the world. Some of the activities have included:

- Making care packages for children in area hospitals and shelters
- Constructing and decorating ornaments and cards for recipients in our community
- Learning about ways to protect animals in our environment
- Making coloring books, homemade sidewalk chalk, and videos for children
- Practicing phrases in sign language to videotape a signed greeting
- Participating in a Red Cross–sponsored activity that sensitizes students to the aging process
- Making cards and placemats for residents in area hospitals and hospices
- Creating a video sing-a-long for local retirement facilities
- Visiting residents of area nursing homes
- Beautifying the school campus (Feifer 1998, 16–17)

The "Acts of Kindness Experience" is an event that is a positive and enjoyable experience for all participants. The event has helped students to think about others, contribute to the community, and experience the joys and rewards of volunteerism.

Another area frequently addressed by middle level student activities is the transition to middle school. Most schools develop a program that encompasses activities over many months that will help new students become successful middle school students. The goal is to make middle school the "land of no surprises" (Kaiser 1995, 18).

Student councils and other student organizations regularly plan and implement school and community service programs that benefit all involved. Middle school student activities allow students to explore and develop leadership skills such as communication, problem solving, decision making, goal setting, teamwork, and conflict resolution. These skills transfer to other learning experiences; when used with an integrated curriculum, such skills increase student success. Student leaders assist principals and teachers to foster positive, safe classroom environments (Sherrill 1999).

Student leadership classes at the middle level can help students become less dependent on the teacher and more actively involved learners. Middle school students are capable of and need opportunities to practice leadership skills. The leadership class at Herbert Green Middle School in Placerville, California, is organized around five distinct topics:

- Foundations of Success
- Personal Development
- Tools for Group Effectiveness
- Contributions to Change
- Making a Difference (Watters 1996, 22)

Each topic is composed of daily student skill lessons that take three to five weeks to complete. In this course, students learn about themselves and how to plan and run successful student activities in their school.

Student activities help keep kids involved in their school and help them make positive lifestyle choices through social influence. This is especially important when peer pressure encourages some students to begin smoking. One-third of teen smokers will eventually die of a tobacco-related disease if they become regular smokers. For many young people, the decision to use or not use drugs, alcohol, and tobacco occurs during the middle school years. The decision can have far-reaching consequences, as almost 90 percent of adult smokers started smoking before age nineteen. "Over the three-year period from ages 12 to 15, the proportion of teens who have smoked cigarettes in the previous month soared from 2 to 21 percent, and the number of teens who say that they smoked marijuana jumped from 1 to 34 percent" (Adair 2000, 44).

Students are more likely to participate in cocurricular activities in high school if they have done so in middle school. In terms of participation in cocurricular activities, McNeal (1998) found that athletics contain the highest portion of student participants (56 percent), academics 36 percent, and fine arts 28 percent. More boys (66 percent) compared to girls (46 percent) participate in athletics, as well as higher-SES (social economic status) students (66 percent) compared to average-SES students (56 percent) (McNeal 1998).

Generally, African Americans and Latinos are as likely or less likely than whites to participate in all types of cocurricular activities. However, African American students have higher participation rates in cheerleading and vocational activities. Asian American students have higher participation rates for academic activities, newspaper/yearbook activities, and student service/government organizations. Participation rates of retained students and students from single-parent households are lower while participation rates of higher-SES and higher-ability students are higher across all activities, with the exception of vocational clubs, where retained, lower-SES, and lower-ability students are more likely to participate (McNeal 1998).

There is a clear-cut distinction in participation patterns between girls and boys. Girls have lower participation rates in high-status athletic activities (except for cheerleading). But girls participate in fine arts activities at a rate of 34 percent compared to boys, whose rate is 21 percent, academic organizations (41 percent compared to 31 percent), newspaper/yearbook (13 percent compared to 8 percent), and student government (25 percent compared to 14 percent) (McNeal 1998).

Blacks are 1.2 times more likely to participate in athletics, 1.4 times more likely to participate in cheerleading, 1.3 times more likely to participate in fine arts, and 1.4 times more likely to participate in newspaper/yearbook than are Whites, holding other covariates [variables] constant. Similarly,

Asian Americans are significantly more likely than Whites to participate in academic clubs (1.3 times), newspaper/yearbook (1.3 times), and service/student government (1.5 times). (McNeal 1998, 186)

Latino students are as likely to participate in various activities as whites. It seems that racial and ethnic minorities seek to participate in specific cocurricular activities more than whites, except for vocational activities, indicating that they may be more committed to and involved in school (McNeal 1998).

It is estimated that boys are 2.2 times more likely than girls to participate in athletics. However, girls are more likely to participate in other high school cocurricular activities than boys.

Compared with their female counterparts, boys are .1 times more likely to participate in cheerleading, .6 times as likely to participate in fine arts, .7 times as likely to participate in academic *activities*, .6 times as likely to participate in newspaper/yearbook, .5 times as likely to participate in *student* service/ government, and .8 times as likely to participate in vocational *activities*. Another significant finding is that students of higher SES are an estimated 1.4 times, 1.3 times, and 1.4 times, respectively, more likely to participate in athletics, newspaper/yearbook, and *student* service/government than are lower SES students, controlling for other covariates [variables]. In fact, higher SES students are significantly more likely to participate in each category of co-curricular activities except vocational *activities*. (McNeal 1998, 188)

Lower-SES and ability/achievement students participate at a lower rate than would be expected. "In essence, any advantage that minority students appear to hold over their comparable White counterparts is more than offset by the minority students' likely lower social class and achievement level" (McNeal 1998, 189). Therefore, the "elimination of certain activities (e.g., athletics and fine arts) may be the most detrimental to racial minorities. A pay-to-play system will likely further exacerbate the relative disadvantage already experienced by students of lower socioeconomic standing" (McNeal 1998, 190).*

In order to increase student participation in activities, many schools have adopted alternative or block schedules. Block scheduling allows projects and activities additional time to be developed and completed than does the standard forty-minute high school class period (Lenz 1997b). Student activities also fit nicely into a block in the school day (Shanahan 1997). The block schedule adopted by Drake High School in San Anselmo, California, allows students to attend club meetings twice per month during the school day. This change helped to increase the number of clubs from five to twenty and has allowed a much greater number of students to become involved. Student representative assembly meetings are held once a quarter and student council meetings once a month, as well as a monthly rally or assembly that the entire school attends.

"Since we have changed to a block schedule, students report feeling more a part of our school and participation in cocurricular activities has increased dramatically. Teacher support for student activities has increased because we do not need to pull kids from class for meetings and we do not change

* The data for McNeal's study were then from the NELS: 88 database. "NELS is a nationally representative database; data collection of eighth graders began in 1988, and occurs every 2 years thereafter" (McNeal 1998, 4). The data used for this study were from the 1988 and 1990 databases and consisted of almost 15,000 cases.

the schedule to accommodate rallies and assemblies" (Lenz 1997b, 28). When a student activity period is used, it can be designed to:

- Involve more students in the decision making process
- Give students a positive forum to voice concerns
- Inform students of upcoming policy changes and help students be informed stakeholders with a say in any proposed modifications
- Give student senate representatives the opportunity to be directly involved in school matters (without having to be enrolled in the leadership class)
- Keep students notified of important dates and upcoming events
- Allow students to be more active (Klima 1997, 25)

The student activity period at Palisades Charter High School in Pacific Palisades, California, meets every other Thursday during an extended class period. The time is used to provide students with information and as a place to discuss school policies, procedures, and planned events and activities (Klima 1997).

In addition to helping more students become involved in their school, some schools are attempting to get more parents involved. Parental involvement generally decreases through the middle school and high school years. Factors contributing to this decline include:

- High schools are larger and often less personal
- Parents take a less active role as their teenagers become more independent
- Programming in the high school is much more content specific
- Involvement in high school PTAs is replaced by involvement in booster organizations that support specific activities such as sports teams or the band (Graf and Henderson 1997, 37)

Increasing parental involvement in student activities can be achieved by having parents serve on committees such as a prom fashion show, a senior boat ride, a student art show, a holiday talent show, a fine arts musical, or a SADD (Students against Drunk Driving) project (Graf and Henderson 1997).

As families are increasingly likely to be geographically dispersed, children may lack a close relationship with their grandparents, aunts, and uncles. Divorced and single-parent families also contribute to the problems of family isolation. Consequently, children may grow up with little exposure to older generations. Another consequence of geographic dispersion is that older individuals in the community may experience isolation and often wish to find a way to make a positive contribution. These seniors are a tremendous political community resource for school districts all across the country.

The Community Consolidated School District 15 in suburban Cook County, Illinois, started a Senior Exchange program in 1992. "The first such program in Illinois, Senior Exchange gives residents age 55 and over an opportunity to help the schools while also earning money to pay the portion of their property tax bill that supports District 15. The program theme is 'Building Our Future Together'" (Conyers 1996, 14). Seniors tutor students in reading, writing, math, or other academic subjects. They also work in computer labs, resource centers, and other areas of the school building. Participants are paid an hourly rate based on the minimum wage (Conyers 1996). Many schools actively seek seniors to be volunteers to share their knowledge and skills with students at all grade levels.

Many schools also have "Golden Age" or "Golden Years" programs that provide senior citizens free admission to athletic events, musicals, and other activities. Also, programs like the one in the Henrico County Public Schools in Virginia provide free tuition in adult education classes (Henrico County Public Schools n.d.).

Some schools have also started programs with senior citizen centers. In Hellgate Middle School, the students taught computer skills to senior citizens from the Grizzly Park Retirement Center. Outcomes of this project include the following:

- The interaction between Hellgate Middle School and the Grizzly Peak Retirement Center has brought widely divergent groups of the community together in a manner that would not likely happen by chance.
- It has given students of the middle school an authentic sense of personal worth based on significant contributions to their community.
- It has expanded the students' learning environment beyond the limits of the school's walls to include much of the surrounding community.
- It has broadened the base of school support within the community by initiating interaction between senior citizens and intermediate school children, thus exposing the senior population to a new personal value to be realized by supporting the community's educational system. (Lundt and Vanderpan 2000, 21)

In a similar program, seventh-grade students became teachers in a Computer Partners Program, which offers computer classes to senior citizens. The goals and objectives for the students and the seniors in this program are shown in table 1.3.

Table 1.3 Computer Partners Program Goals and Objectives

Students:	*Seniors:*
1. Establish a one-to-one personalized relationship with a senior.	1. To be viewed by the student as older peers who are also learners.
2. Develop a positive attitude toward older people.	2. Receive students' patient, personalized attention, thus eliminating their fear of technology.
3. Increase self-esteem through the opportunity to teach skills to someone older than themselves.	3. Become more familiar with the educational facilities and programs that their tax dollars support.
4. Improve time management skills necessary to be able to participate in and out of class.	4. Acquire computer skills.
5. Strengthen their own computer skills.	5. Experience a feeling of accomplishment and enhanced self-worth.
6. Develop a better understanding of the role of their own teachers.	6. Receive recognition from students, teachers, school administrators, and peers.
7. Receive recognition from their peers, adults, and their community.	7. To be put at ease by youthful teachers.
8. Discover seniors are patient, appreciative students.	8. To view students positively.
9. Recognize the value of a senior friend and communicate this to their parents and their community.	9. Meet new friends from the senior center and the school.
10. Learn how to work as a team.	

Source: Kurth 1996, 44–45

14

In 1993, with strong support and leadership from Lieutenant Governor Kathleen Kennedy Townsend, Maryland students who entered ninth grade were required to perform seventy-five hours of community service in order to earn a high school diploma. Almost 100 percent of Maryland's high school graduates performed the seventy-five hours, and the requirement redefined the meaning of community service in the state of Maryland (Megyeri 1999). However, service learning takes students beyond community service. Service learning requires students to apply their newly developed skills, abilities, and talents in the community. Classroom learning is applied to real-life situations and problems and is followed by a formal reflection. Students learn a variety of useful leadership skills that lead to personal growth, development, and empowerment. They also gain a sense that they can and do make a difference, which contributes to positive self-concept. "Service learning also forms a natural bridge between schools, parents, and communities" (Andrus 1996, 15). The service-learning projects performed by students may be part of a club or class activity or projects may be school based and long term or short term. However, regular reflection must always be part of the student and program experience for all participants.

The discussion of what skills and academic course work helped with the planning and implementation of the service learning is important to build the relationship of classroom learning to real-life experience. Young people should be asked to answer questions such as the following as part of their reflection:

- What happened to me?
- What difference did I make?
- What does this experience mean for me? For my community?
- What have I learned and how does this learning relate to the academic areas I am studying? (Andrus 1996, 16)

For teachers, the use of service learning in the classroom should increase student motivation and student achievement. However, establishing meaningful service-learning programs that engage students and contribute both to authentic student learning and to community improvement has not always been easy. "The difficulty of evaluation is another concern" (Nebgen and McPherson 1990, 91). Did the programs make a difference for the community and for the student in the short term and in the long term?

"It takes time and vivid examples to develop creative ways to infuse service into the curriculum and to expand participants' definition of community to include home and school and the global as well as the local community" (Nebgen and McPherson 1990, 91). High schools are organized into academic departments that offer courses in short blocks of time. This makes it difficult to find time to plan and develop curriculum units based on service learning. And finally, "schools and districts are often evaluated by the public on the basis of standardized tests, which do not assess the meaningful outcomes of service learning—a sense of community membership, willingness and capacity to participate in the community, compassion and caring for others" (Nebgen and McPherson 1990, 91).

One of the primary benefits of service-learning programs is a positive school climate. "A school that feels good about itself has spirit" (Fortin 1997, 46). School leaders can improve school climate by making all students feel welcome and safe. Table 1.4 provides a graphic organizer for staff and students to consider when planning service-learning activities.

Table 1.4   School Climate and Maslow's Hierarchy of Needs

Self-Actualization

Peak experiences that happen rarely in
the life of a school. May include state
championships, special recognition, etc.

Self-Esteem

School Self-Esteem = School Spirit
Students can care about the school only when
they feel they are part of the school.

Belonging

Do people feel like they belong?
Is school a place that accepts all students?
What activities can be provided to increase a sense of belonging?

Safety Needs

Is the school environment safe, both physically and emotionally?
Do students feel safe regardless of economic status, ethnicity, or gender?
What can students and staff do to improve the emotional safety of the school?

Basic Needs (food, shelter, etc.)

What projects are done within the school to support families in need?
What new activities might be taken on to serve the basic needs of students?

Source: MOTIVATION AND PERSONALITY 3/E by Maslow, © Reprinted by permission of Pearson Education, Inc.,
Upper Saddle River, N.J.

In closing:

Cocurricular activities vary from school to school. They are determined more by tradition, expectations, and policies of local schools and their respective publics than by written educational philosophies. Change, flexibility, and adaptability characterize the cocurricular component of the educational program perhaps more than the more traditional classroom component of American education. (Gholson and Buser 1983, v)

When we help to build something, we experience it as ours. We gain authority and confidence to act. We have motivation to learn what we need to learn. (Boyte and Skelton 1997, 12)

2

WHY DO SCHOOLS HAVE STUDENT ACTIVITY PROGRAMS?

In 1918, the Commission on the Reorganization of Secondary Education proclaimed seven aims of education: "(1) health; (2) command of fundamental processes; (3) worthy home membership; (4) vocation; (5) citizenship; (6) worthy use of leisure; and (7) ethical character" (Buss 1998, 88). The commission believed that these aims could be achieved through the combination of an academic curriculum and an activities curriculum. Furthermore, the student activities offered were a significant means of "accomplishing the goals of health, citizenship, and worthy use of leisure time" (Buss 1998, 88). In Goodlad's 1984 report, *A Place Called School,* our goals for education are outlined that closely parallel the 1918 seven aims for education in America. The 1984 goals are:

A. Academic Goals
  1. Mastery of basic skills and fundamental processes
  2. Intellectual development
B. Vocational Goals
  1. Career education-vocational education
C. Social, Civic, and Cultural Goals
  1. Interpersonal understandings
  2. Citizenship participation
  3. Enculturation
  4. Moral and ethical character
D. Personal Goals
  1. Emotional and physical well-being
  2. Creativity and aesthetic expression
  3. Self-realization (Buss 1998, 88, adapted from Goodlad 1984, 51–56)

A U.S. Department of Education study (1992) showed "that participants in cocurricular activities have more consistent attendance, better academic achievement, and higher aspiration than non-participants" (*Breaking Ranks* 1996, 4). Table 2.1 provides a summary of the findings.

Table 2.1 Indicators of Success
Percentage of Public School Seniors Reporting Selected Indicators of School Success by Participation and Nonparticipation in Cocurricular Activities

Indicators	Participants	Nonparticipants
No unexcused absences	50.4%	36.2%
Never skipped classes	50.7%	42.3%
Have a GPA of 3.0 or above	30.6%	10.8%
Highest quartile on a composite math and reading assessment	29.8%	14.2%
Expect to earn a bachelor's degree or higher	68.2%	48.2%

Source: U.S. Department of Education, National Center for Education Statistics, National Education Longitudinal Study, Second Follow-up 1992 (*Breaking Ranks* 1996, 5)

Student activity participation also has the potential to help students reach broadly defined education goals.

> For example, governance-related activities, like student councils, foster interpersonal understandings, develop citizenship participation skills, and encourage critical thinking about moral and ethical issues. Athletic and sport-related activities promote physical fitness and interpersonal understandings. Music, speech, and drama provide opportunities for creative expression, emotional development, self-realization, and career awareness. Class or subject-oriented clubs contribute to intellectual and vocational growth as well as self-awareness. Service-related activities help students realize interpersonal, citizenship, enculturation, and moral and ethical goals. (Buss 1998, 89)

In summary, the student activity program is authentic and provides experiences that classroom learning alone cannot.

Schools that foster positive interactions among students and between students and teachers are more likely to have engaged, high-achieving students. One factor that has a strong effect on school success is the cultivation of a relationship between a caring school climate and student engagement. When young people believe teachers care about them, they care about each other. When they get a lot of encouragement at school, they are much less likely to come unprepared to class or feel bored. Engaged students earn better grades (Scales 1999). Conversely, students who believe their schools don't care about them tend not to care about their schools, either. They may believe that teachers who don't expect the best must not care for them. However, when teachers and parents bond, teachers' confidence in the children increases. Students feel more connected to their schools, try harder, and get better grades (Scales 1999). Adolescents who develop a positive identity feel more connected to school and supported by their parents, peers, and teachers. As a result, they are more competent and engaged in their class work. They are also likely to attend school regularly, behave well, and achieve success. A personalized education where students are known by adults in the school is the single most important factor that keeps kids in school (Shore 1995).

Schools can involve students and build spirit in many ways. They can do so in traditional ways, such as through class competitions, pep rallies, attendance at athletic events, and through painting faces, wearing spirit ribbons, and cheering at games. The "school spirit" activities recognize each student as a member of the school community. The goal is to value each student and create an inclusive environment (Aimone 2000). Wenatachee (Washington) High School's IGNITE! Freshman Orientation and Transition Program recognizes each student. Groups containing ten incoming freshmen are matched with two upper-class students who provide a personalized orientation to the high school before the school year begins. The mentors remain with the freshmen throughout the year, giving advice or information about high school programs, and inviting them to join activities. Such activities build school spirit through their welcoming attitude and the value they place on all students (Aimone 2000).

The mandates and regulations that govern school systems tend to make them impersonal, indifferent, and generally insensitive to the individuals within them. Consequently, "education appears to be a limited experience that takes place within a box called a classroom" (Hansen and Childs 1998, 14). A public display throughout the building of student talent encourages participation in nonacademic pursuits as well as academic pursuits. The cafeteria, for example, might exhibit artwork that students can view during their lunch periods (Hansen and Childs 1998).

The most "spirited" schools are those with a large percentage of students with a sense of belonging and ownership. The challenge is to plan a variety of activities to allow all students to get involved, thereby developing positive feelings about themselves and a positive relationship to the school. Recognition of students is important. It can start with something as simple as learning more students' names. Class competitions can also involve large numbers of students in team-building activities (Burton 1997). Students then feel the activities program belongs to them and, in turn, the school becomes an extension of them. "It's all about TEAM—Together Everyone Achieves More" (Namey 2000, 10). The sport or activity doesn't matter; what does matter is the team building and getting everyone involved. How do you create team spirit and pride? Do the following:

1. *Believe in Each Other*. First, get the key people together. We discuss ways we can support each other without getting in the way of practices and the preparation that each group must do for the week. This clears the way for students to participate because they now feel that they can do something without getting anyone upset.
2. *Share Common Goals and Objectives*. This starts you into the second step—deciding what to do and when to do it. It is important that everyone feels that they have an equal voice. Everyone must feel that they are being heard and their ideas are being considered.
3. *Cooperate*. This leads into the third step—cooperation. It is working together. No one should be looking for the credit or the spotlight. No one should see his or her role as greater than anyone else's role. (Namey 2000, 10–11)

The program is based on the premise that building school spirit builds school esteem. The plan is not based on a single activity, team, or event. "Tying school spirit to winning sports seasons will eventually fail. School spirit should be the result of a careful plan with activities each month that celebrate the uniqueness of your school" (Building School Spirit 2000, 14). By working with the leadership class, spirit club, student council, activities coordinator, and administration prior to the start of the school year, an overall plan is created, the purpose of which is to boost school "self-esteem." A sample plan is shown in table 2.2.

School spirit is about more than cheers, songs, and wins, however. It is also about community

Table 2.2   School Self-Esteem Activities

September:
- Posters up at school welcoming students
- A "gift" to welcome students as they arrive
- A faculty welcome gift
- Donate a day to help faculty before school starts
- A personalized welcome card to every new student
- An opening day assembly
- Lunchtime activities
- "Welcome Back" dance
- Pep assemblies
- Student of the Week—anything of interest
- "We're Great" bulletin board (newspaper clippings)

October:
- Spirit Week—honor all fall sports and general ASB officers
- Class spirit chain
- Homecoming parade
- Homecoming assembly
- Homecoming dance
- More lunchtime activities
- Masquerade Day—best costume

November:
- Kids night out
- Ski swap
- Food drive
- Turkey draw
- Catch 'em being good

December:
- Winter sports assembly
- Jingle Bell Ball
- Winter assembly
- Toy drive
- Holiday babysitting
- Alumni basketball game
- Winter snow-in
- Faculty stockings in teachers' lounge

January:
- Welcome cards for transfer students
- New Year's Ball
- All-school pizza sale
- Basketball hoop shoot
- GPA class competition
- Finals hot line
- Theme game
- Faculty appreciation breakfast—half-day pot luck
- Peer tutoring

February:
- ASB/faculty secret pals
- Distribute first semester academic recognition pins
- Interhigh exchange
- Sweetheart Ball
- Wal-o-grams
- Blood drive on Valentine's Day
- Citizen of the Week—American Heritage Week
- Student Council Week

March:
- Star Dress-Up Day
- Lip synch
- Fall orientation for freshmen
- St. Patrick's Day celebration
- Spring sports pep assembly

April:
- Academic pep assembly
- Spring fling
- Easter egg hunt lunchtime activity
- Campus clean up—surprise
- Elections—recruit
- Support Staff Appreciation Week

May:
- Teacher Appreciation Week
- School improvement project
- Recognition assembly—spirit award
- Calendar activity planning meeting
- Sandwich seminar (outside)
- Opinion poll (spirit temperature check)

June:
- Student/faculty softball game
- Distribute academic recognition pins
- Senior awards ceremony
- Memories assembly—slide show
- Finals hot line
- ASB picnic at lunch with games

Source: More than Pom Poms and Pyramids: A coach's guide to a quality cheerleadership program, Association of Washington School Principals. (Building School Spirit 2000, 14)

and believing in the power of teamwork and each individual's unique contribution to the whole. It is understanding that each person's unique contribution is important and helps build a sum that is greater than its individual parts. A strong school tie can be a powerful force in anyone's life. School spirit helps individuals believe that they are an important piece of a bigger picture, something to be proud of and excited about (Colburn 2000). Uniqueness certainly must be valued and celebrated, but it is important that students and faculty also feel connected. School spirit is the vehicle in our schools through which students (and adults) learn to believe in something bigger than themselves and to feel connected to their school and their community.

The sense that everyone needs to contribute to the raising of school spirit is especially strong in small communities (Colburn 2000). In small and large schools, "themes" are a great way to create a sense of community spirit and unity within the student body. Themes make connections among students and to school events. Using a theme, either yearlong or a series of single events, makes each individual event memorable. Yearlong, schoolwide themes might be:

- Get Connected
  - Create an atmosphere in the school where each person feels he or she has something to contribute and is a part of the community.
    - Starter idea: Cut out large paper puzzle pieces for each person in the school. Write a name on each one and put them on walls in the school. From the first day of school, promote the idea that everyone is an important piece of the puzzle at your school.
- Make Your Mark
  - Promote the idea that each student is responsible for what he or she does and can leave a legacy at the school.
    - Starter idea: Give out pencils with the theme to all students and faculty members on the first day of school.
- Special Event Themes
  - Homecoming Week—SOAR. With the SOAR theme, student groups can adopt ideas surrounding flight for various activities such as parade floats or hall decorations. Ideas include:
    - The student council teaches goal setting to the entire school over the PA system, then asks each student to write one goal on a cut-out of a flying object (plane, bird, spaceship).
    - Display students' goals on the walls and hang them from ceilings throughout the school.
    - Create a wall to display the successes of alumni and announce these at the game on Friday.
    - Have the game ball delivered by local skydivers.
    - If you have a homecoming court, give toy planes as favors. Find a nice aviation memento for the king and queen.
- Pep rally themes
  - Pep rally themes can be specific to the team you are playing or more general.
    - Team-specific example:
      - "Capture the Tigers" features a jungle theme with safari hats and shirts, decorations in the school with a jungle motif, a skit in which your mascot nets a tiger, etc.
    - General example:
      - "Friday Night Fever: A Disco Pep Rally" features students wearing 1970s clothing, disco music over the PA system all day, a disco ball in the gym, a disco song by the pep

band, cheerleaders and football player wearing retro uniforms to the pep rally, etc. (Colburn 2000, 7)

Another means to involve students in the community of the school is to offer a class in leadership development. Such a class involves students with leadership potential with other students and staff, which benefits the entire school and community.

At Broken Arrow High School (Oklahoma), "teachers, coaches, and activity advisers identify those students whom they feel would benefit from a class that encourages the development of their individual strengths while working with school and community members" (Lannert 2001, 10). In the class, participants apply problem-solving skills to the school and the community as individuals and as a team.

The class follows these guidelines:
- Leadership class focus:
- Encouraging responsibility and reliability
- Nurturing creativity
- Igniting school/community spirit
- Enhancing esteem/confidence
- Opening students' horizons
- Meeting the needs of others
- Understanding leadership roles

Needs to be met:
- Help others fit in and feel accepted
- Deal with and relate to others
- Plan and organize
- Accept and work with differences
- Be a citizen and prepare oneself for the real world
- Be a valuable volunteer

Class impacts:
- Enhanced actions and outlook
- Being active in school and taking ownership of their education
- Being a role model for students in the younger grades (by modeling appropriate behavior)
- Demonstrating that high school students are capable of interacting in a positive and caring manner to community members and business leaders. (Lannert 2000, 11)

Leadership students feel empowered to work toward having a positive effect on others. Class projects allow students to interact with and make a difference in their schools and their communities. In addition to leadership skills, students also form personal bonds and discover new facets of their own personalities.

Some high schools have instituted Character Education or Character Counts! programs as a unifying theme for the year. Ellet High School (Ohio) students created cardboard pillars listing the six character traits of the Character Counts! program. The pillars were placed at the school entrance as a daily reminder for students of the program's qualities—responsibility, respect, citizenship, caring, fairness, and trustworthiness (Baltrinic 1998).

Character Counts! programs would become the link between our school and the cluster elementary schools through the initiative of the National Honor Society and a leadership team made up of officers of the main service organizations on campus. Last year was the first time the leadership team organized to form a community outreach program that would have significant impact. Officers from NHS, student council, senior class, and Key Club worked together to provide character presentations for the elementary schools in the district. The leadership team, which consisted of 16 seniors, broke into groups of 2–3 students to create skits and lessons on the Character Counts! program. Each group focused on one of the pillars of character (Baltrinic 1998, 28).

Tom Lickona, director of the Center for the 4th and 5th Rs, developed five structures that use student government as a vehicle for learning about democratic participation, solving school problems, and developing students' character and democratic citizenship. (Lickona 2000)

The structures referred to by Tom Lickona are:

1. *Special-Focus Student Council with a Delegate System*—to ensure representation and a voice for all students.
2. *Linked Primary Level and Intermediate Level Student Councils*—the two groups can tackle problems jointly or separately in the same building. Each council meets separately with the elementary principal but the vice-president of the Intermediate Level Student Council chairs the Primary Level Student Council and acts as a link between the two groups.
3. *The Cross-Grade Community Meeting*—a weekly meeting of all fourth and fifth graders in the school to tackle K–8 building problems or concerns in a fair and effective way.
4. *Multiple Student Councils*—the principal sets up three student councils: the School Issues Committee, the School Spirit Committee, and the Community Service Committee. Each group of students was taught how to run a meeting by utilizing parliamentary procedure.
5. *The High School Congress*—elected student delegates from seminars (similar to homerooms). Students make up the majority of the Congress, but it also includes elected representatives of the faculty, administration, and parent body. (Lickona 2000)

Participatory student government gives students responsibility for real problems and develops three aspects of character—moral knowing (because students must decide what is right and fair), moral feeling (because students must consider the rights and responsibilities within the school), and moral behavior (because students have opportunities to take action) (Lickona 2000). Finally, participatory student government develops democratic character; the skills, abilities, and attitudes needed by future citizens are developed by this hands-on problem solving. It also sends the message: "This is *our* school. If we've got a problem, we should fix it" (Lickona 2000, 6).

Some schools have started peer leadership teams that make a difference for students, families, and community. Bonneville Junior High School (Utah) is one of them. Peer leaders address primarily three areas: drug and alcohol prevention, character education, and service learning.

Peer education programs have a positive effect on academic and attitudinal growth. Both the leader and the receiver benefit from the experience. Students are trained in leadership, citizenship, communication, life skills, and drug and alcohol prevention. Students are involved in a very complex program reaching children, teenagers, families, school faculty, and other members of the community. (Grier 1996, 34)

Student leaders can play an important role by helping fellow students welcome refugee and immigrant students to their schools, as well as students transferring from other schools. "In the United States the population of students of color reached 30 percent in 1990, 34 percent in 1994, and will grow to 40 percent or more by 2010" (Holland 1999, 9). Today in our high schools, the use of derogatory language that degrades specific groups on the basis of gender, race, ethnicity, sexual orientation, religion, economic status, and physical and mental disability, appears to have increased. Words that threaten violence have increased in frequency and intensity as well (Wessler 2000–2001). The use of slurs and other degrading language have desensitized many students, who no longer understand or hear the real meaning of the words they use. Often, the only students who truly realize the impact and meaning of these words are the boys and girls who are the targets of the slurs, jokes, and put-downs.

The impact on these students is powerful and destructive, and in many cases will lead to the following:

Escalation—violence is never the beginning of anything. Rather, violence is the end of something that has escalated over time and turned into a pattern of harassment.

Fear—slurs and degrading language of all types carry an implicit threat of violence.

Rage—some students bend and bend but eventually break and strike back at the tormentor.

Loss of spirit—students from traditionally targeted groups understand that words of hate will eventually break your soul. Too many children lose hope. (Wessler 2000–2001)

Diversity can be the source of pride or prejudice, depending on how the lessons are reinforced in students' lives. As middle school teacher Angela Bennett stated, "I think when we don't know anything about each other, there tends to be fear. Or we ignore each other, or we perpetuate stereotypes" (Holland 1999, 6). However, supporting diversity can be an important approach for effective learning.

If you take your curriculum and tie it to those lessons (about tolerance), then you get a double effort. You get learning and standards but also the balance of teaching the values of respect and understanding and tolerance, whether its respect for senior citizens, respect for the people who came before us, or respect for the colleagues who sit next to us," said Steven Cohen, a recently retired middle school principal. (Holland 1999, 8)

Many student leaders have the courage and empathy to speak up for what is right and are not afraid to take a stand. They can be considered our greatest resource for addressing the problems of incivility, prejudice, and violence in the United States (Wessler 2000–2001). Cocurricular activities can help, too, as the following example from Monica Larrieu, a bilingual resource assistant, illustrates:

Three years ago, Larrieu started a chess club to reduce lunchtime disputes in the Gunston cafeteria. She got the idea after one of the school's worst troublemakers, a Venezuelan student, told her that he had been a chess champion in his native country. Larrieu put the boy in charge of Gunston's chess club, which now has 60 members—many of them students from low-income families and special education classes. Participants have become model diplomats, Larrieu said. "They came up with the rules themselves. They shake hands (after matches) and there is no name calling." (Holland 1999, 9)

Many schools have also turned to mediation programs to resolve conflicts, using tactics such as peer resolution instead of various forms of adult intervention. Certain kinds of conflicts, such as those involving racial hatred and sexual assaults, are usually mediated by adults under established policies of peer mediation programs. Under mediation programs, conflict is considered a normal part of human social life, but it is used as a catalyst for learning. It provides a unique opportunity for education—a teachable moment (Henze 2000). Schools must also make the effort to connect with people committed to supporting their work. All parents and family members want the best for their children. Minority and low-socioeconomic families are no different, and they view education, in particular, as the chance to achieve a better economic future (White-Hood 1994).

Do schools have student activities available to students? Consider the information in table 2.3.

Who participates in the available student activities? Table 2.4 shows the percentage of public school seniors participating in selected cocurricular activities by socioeconomic status of student and affluence of school.

The recent literature related to emotional intelligence identifies five areas of emotional and social competencies that children need to succeed in life: self-awareness and impulse control; persistence; zeal; self-motivation; and empathy and social skills. For students, this translates into three broad areas of competencies:

- Self-awareness: recognizing one's feelings, temperament, and style
- Self-management: impulse control, organization, and outlook
- Relationships: social skills and team mindedness (Shelton 2000, 30)

We also know that emotions affect learning. The general principles are summarized as follows:

1. Emotions simply exist; we don't learn them and they are difficult to change.
2. Most students already know emotions are complex and the ways they are experienced by themselves and others.

Table 2.3   Percentage of Public School Seniors Reporting Availability of Selected Cocurricular Activities by Affluence of School*

Activity	All Public Schools	Less-Affluent Schools	More-Affluent Schools
Any Cocurricular Activity	99.8%	99.8%	99.9%
Publications	99.4%	99.3%	99.6%
Performing Arts	98.8%	98.7%	99.1%
Sports	98.7%	98.6%	99.1%
Honor Societies	98.1%	97.4%	98.8%
Student Government	96.5%	94.9%	97.6%
Academic Clubs	95.9%	94.6%	97.0%
Vocational/Professional Clubs	93.3%	93.4%	93.7%
Service Clubs	89.2%	87.2%	90.7%
Hobby Clubs	87.5%	85.4%	89.2%

*School affluence was defined by the percent of the student body receiving free or reduced price lunches; schools at 20 percent or more students receiving free lunch were considered less affluent; those with less than 20 percent, more affluent.
Source: U.S. Department of Education, National Center for Education Statistics, National Education Longitudinal Study, Second Follow-up 1992 (*Breaking Ranks* 1996, 5).

Table 2.4 Participation of Public School Seniors in Selected Cocurricular Activities by Socioeconomic Status (SES)*

| | | Low-SES Students | | High-SES Students | |
Selected Activity	All Students	Less-Affluent Schools	More-Affluent Schools	Less-Affluent Schools	More-Affluent Schools
Any Cocurricular Activity	79.9%	74.7%	73.0%	86.8%	87.6%
Sports	42.4%	34.3%	33.2%	48.6%	53.1%
Performing Arts	27.5%	25.0%	20.7%	32.0%	29.2%
Academic Clubs	26.2%	20.2%	20.5%	36.2%	32.3%
Vocational/Professional Clubs	20.8%	29.2%	25.6%	16.0%	11.8%
Honor Societies	18.1%	10.3%	10.0%	30.8%	29.9%
Publications	17.0%	17.6%	9.5%	22.4%	20.0%
Student Government	15.5%	12.6%	9.9%	17.5%	20.9%
Service Clubs	15.2%	10.0%	9.4%	25.0%	21.1%
Hobby Clubs	8.5%	8.2%	6.9%	9.4%	9.6%

* Low and high SES are defined as the bottom and top quartile, respectively, of a composite measure of parent education and occupational status and of family income.
Source: U.S. Department of Education, National Center for Education Statistics, National Education Longitudinal Study, Second Follow-up 1992 (*Breaking Ranks* 1996, 5).

3. Activities that emphasize social interaction and that engage the entire body, such as games, provide the most emotional support for an individual.

4. Memories are contextual. School activities that draw out emotions—team participation and role-playing, for example—may provide important contextual memory prompts that have parallels to closely related events in the real world.

5. Emotionally stressful school environments are counterproductive to schools because they can interfere with a students' ability to learn. (Sylwester 1994)

A major factor that enhances or limits a student's quality of life is self-esteem. The word *esteem* is defined as "to appreciate the value of" and self-image determines one's sensitivity to the needs of others, problem-solving ability, and the ability to handle responsibility and make judgments (Fiscus 1995). People who have a positive self-image have a great deal of self-confidence. Seven areas of competence to be positive and self-reliant are:

1. Identification with role models whom you would like to emulate—people who are productive, self-sufficient, and reasonably happy.

2. Identification with a sense of responsibility for "family" processes—knowing that your actions and words affect others and have real consequences. This develops a sense of social responsibility and a feeling of belonging.

3. Confidence in personal resources for problem solving—becoming a self-confident person involves developing the abilities and attitudes that allow you to work through problems with the belief that problems can be solved through your own initiative.

4. Development of intrapersonal skills—applying intrapersonal skills in order to communicate with yourself.

5. Development of interpersonal skills—for example, being able to initiate and carry on a conversation.
6. Situational skills—skills that aid in determining the nature of a situation and how best to respond to it.
7. Judgment skills—the ability to recognize, understand, and apply good judgment in your environment. (Fiscus 1995)

But is self-esteem enough? According to Roy F. Baumeister, a psychologist at Case Western Reserve University in Cleveland, recent research indicates that "while self-esteem has some positive effects, we have yet to see it produce improvements in school performance or better grades" (Colvin 2000, 29). Students must be motivated and possess self-esteem before they can function. The self-esteem comes from achievement, not the reverse. Robert J. Stevens of Pennsylvania State University has summed the relationship up as follows: "There's nothing that boosts self-concept more than being able to do something" (Colvin 2000, 31). Most educators believe that being supportive of kids and making them feel comfortable about themselves and secure in their surroundings, while also setting high goals for academic achievement and citizenship, are not inconsistent goals.

Students who are actively involved in the learning process learn and retain more than those who are not actively involved. Student-centered instruction ensures that students are not passive learners but active participants in shaping their academic and social experiences (Weasmer and Woods 2000).

> Activity programs are the perfect complement to the classroom—not because students learn how to become more proficient in sports or debate or music, but because they learn how to become productive citizens in these hands-on laboratories. It is through cocurricular activity programs that students learn respect for others, specifically teamwork, loyalty, compassion, tolerance, courtesy, fairness, integrity, and humility, as well as respect for self through self-esteem, discipline, courage, responsibility, honesty, ethics, poise, and pride. (Kanaby 1996, 9)

Through cocurricular activities, students learn how to work cooperatively, and how to win and lose graciously. Of paramount importance, activity programs are the venues for learning respect for self and others. Sportsmanship embodies the concepts of citizenship and character development. The purpose of sports and school activities is to transmit to young people qualities of citizenship and character development. Students' interests in sport and activity programs make them willing learners. They become involved because they enjoy what they are doing. The outcomes and experiences gained through these activities relate to real-life circumstances that they will confront regardless of their career choices (Kanaby 1996).

Actions speak louder than words. Children are more influenced by what we do than by what we say. One of the strengths of the public school system is that it serves community needs. In order to best serve the community, public schools must educate a wide spectrum of students (Gerzon 1997).

> Students involved in activity programs learn how to be honest and forthright with themselves and others. This trait will manifest itself later through acceptance of responsibility for actions in our society as workers, parents, and human beings. Through sports and activities, students learn to seek and to find, to strive and to fail or succeed, to never yield and to accept the outcome, and to feel good about themselves. These are core educational learnings, and they are all contained within the high school activities curriculum—a curriculum that is found in one word: citizenship. (Kanaby 1996, 11)

In the words of another author,

A young person's involvement in positive and constructive activities, structured and unstructured, is an essential component of healthy development. Whether offered in schools, community organizations, or religious organizations, constructive activities contribute to positive growth and development and promote the development of other assets. When young people spend time in such activities, they have the opportunity to develop and master skills, interact and develop relationships with peers, and have important relationships with adults other than their parents or guardians. (Shaller 2000, 25)

Sports and activities provide opportunities for teaching and learning respect for self and others. They also place participants in competition—a situation that can help students develop skills and abilities necessary for success as an adult (Kanaby 1996). A high school in Pueblo, Colorado, surveyed its ninth graders to determine what type of transition program should be offered to them as eighth graders to facilitate success in the high school.

They responded by calling for more visits to the high school (65 percent); information about cocurricular activities (68 percent); information on how to improve study skills (51 percent); more assistance to plan and develop their class schedules (47 percent); and, more time with their teachers (41 percent). These responses, combined with the input of teachers at both levels, guided the development of our transition program. (Pantleo 1999, 31)

A high school–organized cocurricular fair was an important part of the program. High school staff and students involved eighth-grade students in the activities and provided them with information about club and athletics, recruiting many of them.

Some districts have used one or more of the following transition approaches:

- Ninth Grade House: The teachers in the house get to know the students and see them frequently during the day.
- A ninth-grade advisory/mentoring program: Students are assigned an adviser/mentor and meet with them several times during their eighth-grade year.
- Activities throughout the summer: The summer activities keep incoming ninth-grade students in contact with rising tenth graders, providing a link to the school.
- Transition Team: The team begins meeting early in the fall of the eighth-grade year to plan activities, both social and informative, to assist in student adjustment to grade nine. Activities continue throughout the students' first year in the high school. (Hertzog and Morgan 1999)

The transition from the elementary school to the middle school can be a difficult time for many adolescents. The familiar school setting is gone and the size and perceived anonymity of the middle school may be overwhelming to young adolescents. Elementary school friendships may evaporate as middle school students, in teams, may not easily interact with former schoolmates. Lacking the skills to cope with these stressors can have significant effects on all phases of student adjustment, and affect achievement, aspirations, and feelings of self-worth (Shoffner and Williamson 2000).

Developing coping skills during this transition can facilitate future transitions, such as the move to the high school. Some middle school transition suggestions during the summer are as follows:

- Provide information regarding the opening of the school year early in the summer.
- Make assignments of students to teachers or teams before the close of the school year in June.
- Establish a buddy or big brother/big sister system with older students.
- Provide opportunities for students and parents to meet with teachers, counselors, and administrators prior to the start of the school year at an open house or social gathering. (Shoffner and Williamson 2000)

Some middle school transition suggestions during the school year:

- Address early concerns over how to operate lockers and find your way around the building.
- Provide an opportunity for parent groups to continue the high level of support that most elementary students have received.
- Provide classroom guidance lessons for use by teams, teacher advisers, or school counselors that deal with the common transition issues of middle school (study skills, peer pressure, etc.)
- Schedule a time for counselors and/or administrators to meet all new students in classrooms or activities at the start of the school year.
- Work with all persons involved to evaluate the effectiveness of the transition activities provided. (Shoffner and Williamson 2000)

What are students concerned about when they move from elementary school to middle school and from middle school to high school? A student-generated list might include:

- Adjusting to grading differences; different honor roll standards
- Less explaining, less reminding, and less guidance from teachers
- Stress of tests and examinations
- Adjusting to new rules and new expectations
- Not having enough time to spend with friends or family
- Complex schedules; more and different students, some of whom "disrupt" the learning process

Teachers might list these as student concerns:

- More teachers to deal with
- More peer pressure
- Fear of new, larger, more impersonal school
- Merging with students from several elementary/middle schools
- Longer-range assignments
- Lack of parent involvement
- Inability to complete work on time

Parents might list these student concerns:

- Unreasonably high expectations and standards
- Teachers' unwillingness to extend extra help
- Punitive policies on class attendance
- Teachers' and administrators' inflexibility (Cooke 1995, 9)

In one research study of nearly 100,000 sixth through twelfth graders from across the country, the data showed that 75 percent of students revealed that they felt their schools don't have a caring climate. From sixth through eighth grade, the percentage of students who felt that they had a caring climate at school dropped from 38 to 24 percent; it drops only one additional percentage point by the twelfth grade (Scales 1999). A caring environment is one in which students believe teachers care about them, students care about one another, and students get encouragement at school. Student-to-student interpersonal conflict is the most disruptive factor in a high school but is often overlooked in the quest for safer schools. It is necessary to teach students how to handle conflict constructively in order to create a culture that promotes caring and reduce the potential for violence. When tensions exist in schools, student anxiety and stress lead to concerns about threats and violence. What is needed is the development of supportive relationships to overcome the impersonal nature of large high schools. "Rather than leaving these relationships to chance, school personnel can help students learn to support one another. A combination of student mentoring and peer conflict mediation integrated into the high school can provide the framework for such an undertaking" (Stader and Gagnepain 2000, 29).

Students have become active in preventing violence through their willingness to talk more openly. They realize that kids with weapons in schools can create tragic consequences. In the Fort Collins (Colorado) schools, hallway posters urge students to tell someone if they see threatening behavior—an indication that there has been a cultural change in how "snitching" is viewed. "The code used to be snitching was the lowest form of human behavior for kids" (Butterfield 2001). However, Secret Service psychologists have determined that the assailant in almost 75 percent of school shootings since 1984 told someone (usually another student) about his or her plans prior to carrying them out (Butterfield 2001).

Ten years ago, students in Charlotte, North Carolina, started a program called Students Against Violence Everywhere (SAVE). It has become a national program that promotes the use of nonaggressive methods to settle conflicts. It shows students the consequences of violence and suggests cocurricular activities that help them promote peaceful community relations (Robinson 1999). The program has grown to nearly 400 registered SAVE chapters in the United States and Canada. The program promotes:

- Training of secondary students in peer mediation and conflict resolution
- Teaching young people how to respond if they encounter guns
- Teaching students how to avoid unhealthful and risky adolescent behaviors
- Giving back to the community through community service activities and projects (Robinson 1999)

To break the cycle of violence in our schools, schools also need to address the following:

1. Broken Social Bonds—the most powerful restraints on violent behavior are healthy human attachments.
2. Stress and Conflict—in manageable doses, stress is a normal product of living. Most children handle it reasonably well; they are resilient and thrive in spite of challenges. Others are overwhelmed and behave in self-destructive or antisocial ways.
3. A Culture of Violence—societies placing clear, consistent, reasonable sanctions on acts of

aggression do not mass-produce violent children. The United States has strong laws against violence, but they are inconsistently applied and compete with pervasive proviolence messages.

4. Unhealthy Brains—with so much learned violence, educators often overlook neurologically triggered aggression. Only an intact, rational, sober brain can control angry impulses. Alcohol and other drug abuse chemically alter brain states, leading to loss of self-control, angry outbursts, and deadly violent acts. (Brendtro and Long 1995)

Schools must also meet the developmental needs of students by encouraging:

- *Attachment*: Positive social bonds are prerequisites to prosocial behavior
- *Achievement*: Setting high expectations means refusing to accept failure
- *Autonomy*: True discipline lies in demanding responsibility rather than obedience
- *Altruism*: Through helping others, young people find proof of their own self-worth (Brendtro and Long 1995, 56)

Most crisis incidents in schools originate from problems outside school, but escalate to violence because participants resort to confrontations to solve disagreements. Peer-helping programs are one means of reducing potential conflicts among students. They operate by having students help other students by listening, providing information, and referring those students to a professional. The students offering the help are usually trained and supported by a school counselor or a teacher. In addition to mediation, these programs may offer tutoring, cross-age tutoring or teaching, and other types of youth leadership. Through their work, peer helpers often improve the school climate, contributing to its health and security in addition to helping individual students. Some programs encourage leadership skills and the value of service. Most programs enhance relationship skills and improve communication between students and adults. Students who feel that their school cares about them are more likely to care about their school (Tanaka and Reid 1997).

Another avenue to deal with potential violence and disruption in schools is through a conflict resolution program. Conflict resolution programs help individuals to deal with conflict and to utilize conflict resolution techniques. Destructive behaviors such as fighting and making threatening remarks are replaced by constructive behaviors such as talking, cooperating, and peer mediation.

> In peer mediation conferences, disputants sit face-to-face in the company of a trained peer mediator and present their viewpoints in a supportive environment. During the peer mediation process, the mediators and disputants define the problem between the disputants, delineate solutions, and evaluate potential outcomes. The peer mediation process differs from other programs facilitated by peers such as peer counselors or peer helpers because it involves a clearly defined formal process with distinct roles for each party. (Robinson, Smith, and Daunic 2000, 24)

After-school hours are also a concern to parents and school officials, as many students go home to electronic caregivers: a television, a VCR, a computer with Internet access, or a telephone. "One out of every ten known violent crimes committed against juveniles on school days occurs between three and four P.M." (Kolbe and Berkin 2000, 40). The ramifications often spill over into the school. Students involved in after-school activities avoid being unsupervised at home or in a location where a violent crime might be committed. They also have "extra time" and an "extra opportunity" to contribute in a positive manner.

Consider what students might learn by working on a new school publication after school.

In roundtable discussions, they planned each issue's content and determined who would create it. Poetry, fiction, essays, and art were solicited in school-wide campaigns. They determined, however, that students wanted "more than just poetry and art." The staff decided the publication should be "like a real magazine." They wanted interviews, photographs, and special feature stories on major school events, e.g., building a pond and small wetlands area in the school courtyard, and the school's rooftop egg-drop competition. To more closely resemble a "real magazine," students eventually changed the publication's size from 5 ½″ x 8 ½″ to 8 ½″ x 10″. (LoCastro 2000, 4)

Students gained leadership, decision-making, and social skills as they engaged in meaningful activities. These skills can then transfer to their English, reading, computer, and mathematics classes. They also learned interpersonal skills such as how to work as a diverse group and increased their self-confidence. Students also had the opportunity to develop and sharpen the English language arts skills of speaking, listening, reading, and writing as they worked on the paper.

In addition to learning firsthand the importance of identifying their audience, a student who works on a school magazine has opportunities to sharpen writing, reading, and speaking skills. . . . Students also build spoken English skills when going out in the school's hallways to interview students or speak with a teacher or administrator to request and subsequently conduct a feature story interview. (LoCastro 2000, 5)

Working on a school magazine requires students to learn and use desktop publishing and word processing skills. Students also use math skills to plan a layout and crop the selected photographs to make them fit the allotted space on a page. They also must decide how to make a picture that is $3″ \times 5″$ fit in a space that is not $3″ \times 5″$. By allowing any student who meets the school's academic and behavioral performance standards to join, a diverse group of students with all levels of academic and social ability become club members. Students also gain social skills working with each other in a relaxed after-school environment. Their self-confidence grows as they have the opportunity to master skills in a nonthreatening, supportive environment. Finally, "instead of going home to an empty house or hanging out with friends who need more supervision than they get, students in productive after-school activities, such as a student magazine, have an opportunity to master skills that will help them in the present and the future" (LoCastro 2000, 7).

Long after the particulars of any activity are forgotten, the following competencies should stay with our students for a lifetime:

- Speaking with conviction
- Writing with clarity
- Organizing with results
- Leading with courage
- Caring for the community (Brown 1996, 19)

When students work in groups (for example, to plan a dance, or a school or community project), they must practice group decision making. Selecting from among two or more possible choices, they utilize one of the following four decision-making strategies:

- Autocratic—one person is the group's decision maker
- Democratic—the group votes to make decisions and resolve differences
- Consensual—the group comes to a resolution that is acceptable to all members
- Laissez-faire—decision making is made by the group if and when they choose. (Fiscus 1995)

And students exercise leadership when they act or speak in ways that move the entire group closer to any of the following goals:

1. The accomplishment of the task
2. The resolution of internal group problems
3. The ability of the members to work together effectively as a group (Fiscus 1995, 14)

In summary, leaders serve the group, and should act in ways that benefit the organization to achieve its goals. Successful leaders use their vision for the group to lead it in a positive direction. Involvement in student activity teaches leadership skills on a daily basis (Fiscus 1995).

In closing:

Adolescents make choices that have fateful consequences both in the short term and for the rest of their lives—choices affecting their health, their education, and the people they will become. (Jackson, Davis, Abeel, and Bordonaro 2000, x)

To help students succeed, each of them can count on at least one adult in the school who serves as the student's advocate, plays a significant role in the student's life, and does not allow the student to "fall through the cracks." (Sternberg 2000, 71)

3

WHAT ARE THE SHORT-TERM AND LONG-TERM BENEFITS OF SCHOOL ACTIVITIES FOR STUDENTS?

America's Promise exists to provide young people with access to five fundamental resources that they will need to grow up into confident, self-supporting, and contributing members of society. The five America's Promise Fundamental Resources are:

1. An ongoing relationship with a caring adult—a parent, mentor, tutor, or coach
2. Safe places and structured activities during nonschool hours
3. A healthy start
4. A marketable skill through effective education
5. An opportunity to give back through community service (Powell 1999, 13)

For young people, giving to others also helps them learn about themselves. When young people realize that they can do something for others, it boosts their self-esteem and gives them a sense of importance. They begin to realize that the world needs and appreciates their gifts and talents, leading them to develop those gifts and talents more fully. They may even discover latent abilities and talents that they didn't know they possessed (Powell 1999).

Cocurricular activity participation by secondary students provides many of the same benefits described by General Colin Powell. These activities are integral to the education of young people and have legitimate links to course work and the purposes of middle level and high schools. They support the goals of teaching students to become responsible and fulfilled adults and contain opportunities for the development of character, critical thinking, social skills, and talents (NASSP 1996). Cocurricular activities also allow students to find peers and adults who have interests and talents similar to their own. Participating students are given the opportunity to excel as individuals, to be part of a group, and to learn about the importance of teamwork, responsibility, commitment, and hard work through their experiences (Educational Research Service 1999).

Participation in cocurricular activities helps adolescents avoid risky behaviors such as dropping out, teen parenthood, delinquency, smoking, and drug and alcohol abuse through three mechanisms:

1. Time displacement: You can't be in two places at once. If you are engaged in constructive student activities, you don't have time to get into trouble.
2. Commitment building: By developing ties to the school and a stake in its success, you become committed to traditional career pathways and existing institutions.
3. Group pressure: Participation on teams and clubs promotes a sense of belonging and positive peer pressure. (Zill, Nord, and Loomis 1995)

Cocurricular activities can provide students with a safety net that might provide the final, vital connection that fosters a sense of belonging, whether the students are average, gifted, or at risk (Gerber 1996).

Cocurricular activities augment a good educational program and support the academic mission of the school. "Students who participate in activity programs tend to have higher grade point averages, better attendance records, lower dropout rates and fewer discipline problems than students generally" (National Federation 1998, 2).

Students who participate in cocurricular activities are more successful academically and also develop their personalities in the process. The leadership skills and competencies developed through participation enhance the cognitive abilities learned in the classroom. Cocurricular activities allow students to apply their academic learning to social interactions and vice versa (Allison 1979). Participation is a means of promoting student competency as lifelong learners and contributing citizens.

> Students who take part in extracurricular activities such as band, school plays, academic clubs, and sports generally do better in high school, and even beyond, than those who don't, according to an ongoing long-term study of more than 1,000 former Michigan sixth graders. The activities are linked to better grades, lower rates of truancy, stronger feelings of attachment to a school, and higher rates of college attainment according to the Michigan Study of Adolescent Life Transitions. (Galley 2000, 8)

The study also revealed that students participating in any cocurricular activities were also more likely to have obtained a college degree than those who had not participated.

Cocurricular activities may contribute to students staying in school and finding personal meaning in the middle level and high school years. Students participating in cocurricular activities are better able to extend and enrich cognitive skills learned in the classroom through competitions and real experiences. Cocurricular activities may also develop artistic, musical, and psychomotor talents; leadership skills; and future career and occupational skills (Haensly, Lupkowski, and Edlind 1985–1986).

As students participate in cocurricular activities such as drama club, they begin to see their abilities and strengths. "They must practice their own part to perfection so that it blends into the ensemble, thereby providing their equal share to the performance; a share that certainly cannot be absent" (Neel 1996, 18). Students begin to learn that "practice makes perfect." No group is better than its weakest player. Students who become apprentices in theater productions receive training from more experienced peers that is often more thorough and demanding than the training that an advisor would provide. The peer trains the student, gives him or her hands-on experience, and slowly relinquishes responsibility, so that by the time the older student graduates there is another ready to become a peer mentor (Aubrey 1996).

> Not only do goal-directed activities help to develop skills in young people, they may also foster positive character traits. Both individual and group activities can teach the importance of vigilance, hard work, attention to detail, repeated practice, patience and persistence in the face of setbacks. Group activities encourage cooperation and teamwork, sacrificing personal convenience for group goals, seeing the other's viewpoint, and learning how to follow and lead. All of these qualities can be of benefit to young people in their studies, their jobs, and their personal lives, as well as help them become responsible and successful adults. (Zill, Nord, and Loomis 1995, 4)

Cocurricular activities can lead to success in later life—in college, in the workplace, and in society (National Federation 1998). Industry often requires its employees to possess "people skills," the ability to accept responsibility and follow directions, poise, and high personal ideals, in addition to positive attendance records and high academic averages in core courses. These skills are cultivated in cocurricular activities (Good Grades 1993).

Involvement in student activities develops leadership skills and the ability to plan, manage, organize, implement, and evaluate. They also stress the importance of accountability, commitment, dependability, reliability, and trustworthiness—all of which are elements of the fourth "R"—responsibility. According to June Jacoby, middle level principal, "Students learn by doing. Through a carefully designed and implemented student activities organization, leadership skills that affect the entire school and community are taught, including planning, organizing, communicating, meeting deadlines, and teamwork" (Baker, Jacoby, and Gugliuzza 2000, 42). A well-designed and well-organized student activities program is just as important as the school curriculum because it benefits:

- Students—by recognizing them and giving them the opportunity for involvement to help them grow and develop.
- School—by becoming more than just a building. It will return to the "gathering place" where positive activities are enjoyed, thereby creating good attitudes toward education and increasing spirit and enthusiasm for school programs.
- Community—by sharing in the many experiences and close working relationships with the school. Positive attitudes and support are readily gained when residents, parents, and business in the area work together. The Chamber of Commerce, the Optimist Club, the Rotary Club, and many other civic organizations benefit from interaction with the students, given the opportunity. In return, the school receives more positive support from the community. (Thomson 1983, 3)

Many young people need to learn how to interact effectively with others. Interpersonal and group skills are the result of conscious effort. Students must be taught these skills and they must be motivated to use them. Cooperative groups will not be productive if group members lack interpersonal and small-group cooperative skills. "In order to coordinate efforts to achieve mutual goals, students must (1) get to know and trust one another, (2) communicate accurately and unambiguously, (3) accept and support one another, and (4) resolve conflicts constructively" (Johnson and Johnson 1989–1990, 30). Participation in activities teaches the important skills that contribute to employability and career success. The social skills learned during one's school years often affect one's quality of life as an adult.

Jack Canfield (1990) developed a ten-step system to help teachers strengthen students' self-esteem and increase their chances for future success. The elements of the system are as important as the social skills discussed above. The elements are:

1. *Assume an attitude of 100 percent responsibility.* I introduce the following formula: E (events) + R (your response to them) = O (outcomes). I tell them that it is not what I say to Peter but what Peter says to himself afterward that ultimately affects his self-esteem.
2. *Focus on the positive.* In order to feel successful, you have to have experienced success.
3. *Learn to monitor your self-talk.* Each of us thinks about 50,000 thoughts per day, and many of them are about ourselves. We all need to learn to replace negative thoughts.
4. *Use support groups in the classroom.* It's possible for a kid to come to school for a whole day and never once be the center of positive attention.
5. *Identify your strengths and resources.* An important part of expanded self-esteem is the broadened awareness of one's strengths and resources.
6. *Clarify your vision.* Without a vision, there is no motivation.
7. *Set goals and objectives.* Until our visions are broken down into specific and measurable goals—with timelines and deadlines—we are not likely to move forward very quickly.
8. *Use visualization.* The most powerful yet underutilized tool in education is visualization.
9. *Take action.* To be successful, you yourself have to "do the doing."
10. *Respond to feedback and persevere.* I try to inspire students with stories of people like themselves who have gone on to do great things, often by working against the odds; for example, Wilma Rudolph, the great track star, was told as a youth that she would never walk again. (Canfield 1990, 48–50)

Many teachers follow all or part of this model in their daily instruction of students. It puts the focus on the student, not the subject. Activity advisors help students every day with the above ten suggestions. Most studies of the benefits of cocurricular activities do not establish whether participating leads to success, whether successful students are more likely to participate, or whether both theories are correct. However, students involved in activities are often more interested in academic courses, have the opportunity to practice leadership and fellowship skills, socialize with students, and interact with teachers outside the classroom. They are recognized for their involvement and achievement, and have a good outlet for their leisure time. Cocurricular programs are often a good training ground for adolescents who may participate in similar organizations as adults (Buss 1998).

Many people ask, "Why student activities?" "Can they be justified?" "Is it educationally beneficial?" Every person needs opportunities that can only be provided in the school setting through student activities. These are not "extracurricular" activities; they are cocurricular educational vehicles. One project done by a student organization may provide the single most significant learning experience of a young person's life. A positive, well-developed student activities program can serve many purposes. Some of those that are most cited include:

1. Encouraging Responsibility through Participation: Students who gain and display responsibility are the foundation of tomorrow's democracy. Self-respect, honesty, and admiration of peers as

well as teachers, administrators, and family are developed through active participation in a positive program.

2. Developing Healthy Attitudes: Every student can have a healthy attitude given the right experiences, and student activities can be the instrument in opening doors to make this possible. *To be what we are and to become what we are capable of becoming* is the motto that students will adopt if the activities program is a success.

3. Establishing a Total Program: It is essential to make all student organizations and all students feel a part of the total student activities program. To realize this objective, the Student Council must encompass a wide scope of varied activities to fill the many interests of students. Students need and want a feeling of belonging. The thought that every student could find some activity worthwhile is the goal of Student Council.

4. Promoting Leadership: Leadership development is so very important in the total growth of our young people. We can all benefit by utilizing the ideas of students and gain their support by seeking their input in solving relevant school problems. Providing young people with a positive climate in which to plan, speak, and be heard is a step toward positive leadership. (Thomson 1983, 2–3)

There are now more than 30 million young people in the United States between the ages of twelve and eighteen. They are reported to be less violent, less self-destructive, and take better care of themselves, and to take fewer drugs than in past decades (Males 1998). High school activity programs are extremely cost effective, requiring only 1 to 3 percent (in many cases, less) of a school's overall budget. Young people learn lifelong lessons as important as those taught in the classroom in such activities as student council, sports, music, speech, drama, and debate. Participating in these high school activities often predicts a student's later success in college, career, and becoming a contributing member of society. The Phi Delta Kappa/Gallup Poll (1998) of the public's attitudes toward the public schools indicated that 63 percent of those surveyed judged cocurricular activities to be very important (National Federation 1998). A 1985 survey by the National Federation of State High School Associations conducted by Indiana University in cooperation with the National Association of Secondary School Principals surveyed high school principals and nearly 7,000 high school students in all fifty states. The survey, funded by a grant from the Lilly Endowment in Indianapolis, found that:

- 95 percent believed that participation in activities teaches valuable lessons to students that cannot be learned in a regular class routine
- 99 percent agreed that participation in activities promotes citizenship
- 95 percent agreed that activity programs contribute to the development of "school spirit" among the student body
- 76 percent said they believe the demand made on student's time by activities is not excessive
- 72 percent said there is strong support for school activity programs from parents and the community at large. (National Federation 1998, 4)

Students who participated in several activities had greater academic achievement and also expressed greater satisfaction with their high school experience than students who did not participate. Students learned valuable lessons that are applicable to practical situations—teamwork, sportsmanship, winning and losing, and hard work. Students learned self-discipline and self-confidence, and developed skills useful for handling competitive situations (National Federation 1998).

Consider the following, written by Joshua Adler, president of the Whitman Group:

The seemingly simple task of gaining a Scholastic Matchmakers customer beyond our old high school took three years of trial and error. Throughout this difficult but exciting period, I came to realize the importance of many of the skills and values I had developed through my high school leadership activities. For example, although I have rarely had the opportunity to wrestle a customer to the ground (as much as I have occasionally wanted to), four years of intense wrestling practice gave me the discipline and internal drive to put in the long hours of Whitman Group work after an already long day of difficult college classes and singing rehearsals. Debate taught me to think and talk on my feet, to speak persuasively, and to do thorough research. All my activities, including singing, gave me the self-confidence necessary to take risks with my time and money (and other people's time and money!) and to believe I could triumph after repeated failures and dead-ends. (Adler 1995, 40)

The values of persistence, patience, thoroughness, organization, self-motivation, and vision contributed most to Joshua Adler's success. All these values are part of the life skills that are learned by all participants in student activities to some degree.

Are we teaching emotional intelligence through student activities participation? Emotional intelligence is defined by Daniel Goleman as a cluster of skills that includes "self-control, zeal and persistence, and the ability to motivate oneself" (O'Neil 1996, 10). This short list of skills is remarkably similar to the skills Adler describes as learning in his student activities participation. Emotional intelligence differs from the traditional conceptions of intelligence that focus on cognitive skills and knowledge. It is the enactment of social skills—being able to get along with other people and manage one's emotions in relationships, and being able to persuade or lead others. Emotional intelligence includes awareness of your feelings, using them to make good life decisions as well as being empathetic, knowing what the people around you are feeling. It includes the ability to manage distressing moods and control impulses and to remain motivated, hopeful, and optimistic in the face of setbacks in reaching your goals. "The good news about emotional intelligence is that it is virtually all learned. . . . So if a child learns to mange his anger well, or learns to calm or soothe himself, or to be empathic, that's a lifelong strength" (O'Neil 1996, 8–9).

Every child should be taught the essentials of handling anger and resolving conflicts in a positive way. Obviously, educators and activity advisors must model emotional intelligence in caring, respectful interactions with students. Why is emotional intelligence so important? It "may be the best predictor of success in life, redefining what it means to be smart (Cobb and Mayer 2000, 14). "IQ contributes, at best, about 20 percent of the factors that determine life success. That leaves 80 percent to everything else. There are many ways in which one's destiny in life depends on having the skills that make up emotional intelligence" (O'Neil 1996, 6).

Another way of being smart may be that of successful intelligence. Sternberg (1996, 19) defines successful intelligence "as the acquisition and use of what you need to know to succeed in a particular environment, which you are not explicitly taught and which usually isn't even verbalized." People who are high in successful intelligence show certain characteristics over and over again:

1. They know their strengths and weaknesses, and how to make the most of their strengths while finding ways to correct or at least to compensate for their weaknesses.

2. They are goal setters. Some of them are visionaries; others are not. But they all know they need to work toward explicit measurable goals.

3. They are highly motivated, but they know when to quit as well as when to persevere. They know there is no substitute for working very hard toward a goal, but they also know that sometimes a tactical retreat is better than a strategic debacle.

4. They follow through. They know that one of the best ways to lose credibility is to make all sorts of promises and then fail to keep them.

5. They are high in self-efficacy. They believe in their ability to accomplish what must get done. A common mistake is to believe that self-esteem is important for success. It isn't.

6. They figure out who owns what problems, and take responsibility for the problems they own.

7. They can translate thought into action. Successful intelligence, ultimately, is measured by what you accomplish. (Sternberg 1996, 19–20)

The best students excel in academic intelligence as well as successful intelligence, which involves translating good thinking into effective action. To be academically intelligent, you don't necessarily need to act. The criterion for successful intelligence, however, is real-world accomplishment—not a test score. Getting good grades and high test scores is not a bad thing, but it is not the only thing that matters (Sternberg 1996).

What matters is how much you have learned from your experiences, not how much experience you have had. Service-learning projects can be meaningful experiences. In schools, they render needed services and engender student learning that is supportive of successful intelligence, personal growth, and development. Thoughtfully developed and executed service-learning projects can teach students:

- About needs in their communities and responses to the needs
- About raising, managing, and giving money
- To get others involved and work in groups
- To measure the impact of their effort to make a difference
- To use skills developed in classes "in the real world"
- To be active citizens (O'Neill 1996, 24)

The American Alliance for Rights and Responsibilities found that approximately 25 percent of public school districts nationwide require students to participate in some form of service learning. In Maryland, participation in service learning is a requirement for graduation; students can earn elective credit for service learning in other states. Many student activities, clubs, and organizations include service in their missions (O'Neill 1996). Seven "best practices" for service-learning programs sponsored by student activities are:

1. Meet a recognized need in the community. In the best service learning, students are responsive to their communities; "making a difference" is most meaningful when students address real needs.

2. Achieve curricular objectives through service learning. Many educators have found that service learning adds relevance and purpose to what they teach. Even though the student activities–sponsored service projects may take place outside school hours and doors, students can research, talk, and write about their experiences in their classes.

3. Reflect throughout the service-learning experience. Plato said, "The life which is unexamined is not worth living." Reflection on the service activity is key to making a project a reciprocally beneficial service-learning experience.

4. Develop student responsibility. The best practice of service learning is second nature to student activity sponsors. What is true for student activities in general is also true for service learning: students are most eager to participate in activities when they have a say in what happens, how it happens, when it happens, and what role they will play.

5. Establish community partners. Inviting community partners to help design and participate in service learning lends value to the activities and encourages students to get involved as part of a larger community effort.

6. Plan ahead for service learning. To guarantee that both service to the community and learning for the students result from the project, students, sponsors, and community partners need to think through the details of a project.

7. Equip students with knowledge and skills needed for service. Acquiring and using skills and knowledge in service settings will be novel for most students. It may even be scary. To serve effectively, students may need to practice skills particular to the service setting, such as speaking up when working with hearing impaired senior citizens or asking open-ended questions when tutoring. (O'Neill 1996, 24–25)

Youth service is a community-building activity when it brings young people of diverse racial and ethnic backgrounds to work together toward a common goal or objective. Youth service is also a self-building activity. Students become valued, competent resources and gain self-satisfaction and respect when they work to provide community service as opposed to being clients of social institutions like schools. Their experience can transform them in a short period of time. Youth service can instill a sense of civic responsibility in young people as they become a part of the community through their service learning. They develop a lasting commitment to do their part in the future as well (Commission on National Community Service 1993).

> The health of our democracy depends on its students gaining a sense of their connection to the larger community. One of the best ways to create such ties is through service learning, which enables young people to contribute their efforts to activities that are useful to the community and helps them reflect on what they learn from their participation. (NASSP 1996, 94)

Will students be prepared for the world of work when they leave school?

> Businesses surveyed [by the Westchester Education Coalition, Westchester County, N.Y.] expressed a need for employees who can work as team members, who have skills in verbal and written communication and problem solving, who are motivated and technologically capable, who can do an increasing number of different kinds of jobs with less supervision, and who know how to set and achieve goals. (Rhoder and French 1999, 534)

Students who have the chance to apply the information and skills learned in classrooms have a much better chance of developing the skills and competencies needed by businesses. Student activities provide an excellent vehicle to make this connection.

Student activities also provide young people opportunities that help them to develop character, critical thinking, social ability, and specific skills. They help schools teach students to be responsible. Cocurricular activities should always be evaluated by educators in terms of how they support the school's broader objectives. It is imperative that connections to learning exist if activities are to be truly cocurricular (NASSP 1996). All activities supported by the high school need to be evaluated to determine the degree to which they support the school's mission and goals. This requirement applies equally to all athletic teams and clubs sponsored by the school. A comprehensive high school should seek to engage as many students as possible in cocurricular activities. Students who are not engaged will miss a valuable part of their education by not participating. The cocurricular program, therefore, should offer a variety of activities that will appeal to a wide range of student interests (NASSP 1996).

A problem inherent in almost all of the studies on student activities is student self-selection with participant and nonparticipant categories. The differences that already exist among participating and nonparticipating students may account for the effects of involvement rather than the influence of the activity itself. Students who participate in cocurricular activities tend to perform better academically, have greater achievement, and have higher academic aspirations. Nonparticipating students' academic goals and accomplishments tend to be lower (Holland and Andre 1987). Students who participate in service-related activities and athletics are more likely to aspire to a college education, while students who do not participate in activities are much less likely to aspire to that goal (Buss 1998). What explains these effects? Consider the following suggested by Otto (1982):

1. When students participate in activities, they acquire attitudes, skills, and capabilities that serve them well academically.
2. Participation gives students visibility and expands their network of contacts with important people; in other words, accomplishment is based on who you know, not what you know.
3. Participation in activities, especially sports, elevates the students' peer status and self-esteem, which, in turn, raises aspirations.
4. Some students are born achievers; they start in high school with extracurricular activities and they continue achieving into adulthood.
5. Students assess their achievement potential, set their goals, then receive encouragement from their peers based on past performance in activities and in the classroom. While participating, they acquire important learning that reaps benefits in later life. (Buss 1998, 94)

Two important outcomes of participation in the cocurricular program are that students' educational success is reinforced by school personnel and achievement-oriented peers and that students acquire knowledge, skills, abilities, and resources that help them translate personal goals into action (Hanks and Eckland 1976). Cocurricular programs can be viewed as preparation of adolescents for participation in comparable adult organizations. In the school setting, skills and habits needed later in voluntary associations are formed and practiced (Hanks and Eckland 1978).

In closing:

Young adolescents are continuously struggling to form a positive self-concept, and their success in school is a key part of how they see themselves. They value guidance and assistance from adults some of whom may be advisers, teachers or coaches. (Crockett 1995)

What I didn't understand at the time I had Eugene in class, and what I would not understand until I met him again years later, was that I had been successful with Eugene. I just couldn't see it at the time because my definition of success was a short-term one. (Urban 1999)

4

WHAT ARE THE SHORT-TERM AND LONG-TERM BENEFITS OF STUDENT ACTIVITIES FOR SCHOOLS?

In light of recent incidents of school violence, I believe that student activities can play an important role in creating a school climate in which students feel involved and favorable toward school, teachers, and administrators. Our goal should be to have all students involved. The only way that we will reach this goal is through a systematic approach in which we track all students' participation in activities just as we track all students' academic progress. Educators can use surveys to ascertain what areas students may be interested in, and students who are not involved can be encouraged to participate in activities that correspond to their interests. Some students will not participate until someone reaches out to them. You might have to convince them, for example, that their talents could be used for a drama production or for posters advertising the homecoming dance. I realize that involving all students in activities is a lot of work, but in the long run, everyone will be better off if we can help students achieve academically and socially balanced skills. Academics + Activities = Excellence. (Marano 2000b, 8)

Research has shown that low levels of participation in student activities are characteristic of at-risk students (Klesse and D'Onofrio 1994). "Compared to those [students] who reported spending 1–4 hours a week in extracurricular activities, students who reported spending no time in school-sponsored activities were 57 percent more likely to have dropped out by the time they would have been seniors; 49 percent more likely to have used drugs; 37 percent more likely to have become teen parents; 35 percent more likely to have smoked cigarettes; and 27 percent more likely to have been arrested" (Zill, Nord, and Loomis 1995, 52).

Students develop a sense of personal accomplishment and extend interpersonal skills when they engage in cocurricular activities. Through these activities, adolescents have opportunities to assume meaningful roles and responsibilities. The sense of effectiveness that all students gain from these experiences can be an important factor in their growth and development. This is especially true for those students growing up in difficult home situations (Wagner 1999). Students learn that they worked hard and succeeded because of their effort with the help of caring adults and peers. They say to themselves, "If I can overcome obstacles in my cocurricular activities, I can do the same in my life."

Team sports are especially important as a means to overcome racism and the increase of school-based hate groups because sports activities create bonds that cut across racial lines. Approximately three-quarters of all white and African American student athletes say they became friends with someone outside their own racial or ethnic group while participating on a team (Lapchick 1996). Students who are involved in athletics develop a strong sense of school ownership and pride. Every student and staff member should feel that they are a part of the school community. To accomplish this goal, the cocurricular program and sports activities available to students should be reviewed through an assessment of the needs of all potential participants (Stephens 1994). Students need positive activities that focus on leadership, involvement, and recreation, activities that are challenging and interesting. Otherwise, they may find less productive—or even destructive—ways to spend their time.

Consider the following:

- Violent acts can occur in any school, even though they are more likely in some schools than others.
- A proactive response is superior to a reactive response.
- A violent act is never over when it is over: it lives on in the feelings of those affected by it.
- There are two kinds of school safety—actual and perceived; they are related, but not necessarily the same.
- School safety is relative; it can be thought of on a continuum from minimum safety to maximum safety.
- School violence is a district and community problem. (Watson 1995, 58)

School violence includes those daily occurrences of pushing, shoving, and verbal abuse and sometimes involves weapons. Under these conditions, teachers cannot teach and students cannot learn.

One way to help reduce student violence and to help teach students to resolve their differences peacefully is peer mediation. Establishing a safer and more healthful environment in schools allows all students to grow socially and emotionally, laying the foundation for engaging in serious academic work and attaining higher standards (Hereford 1999b). Many educators attempt to prevent or mediate disputes through conflict resolution programs. These programs impart problem-solving expectations and skills so that students can resolve their conflicts peacefully.

> Unlike a disciplinary system of social control, the peer mediation approach is based on the belief that properly trained student mediators are capable of guiding student disputants through the problem-solving process. Under the system, disciplinarians are replaced by the expectation that students should work collaboratively to solve their conflicts. A primary goal is not to punish but to prevent repetition of aggression by resolving the conflicts underlying a student's use of aggression in conflict resolution. Another goal is to give students actual experience in using positive social behavior so the student's primary concern becomes the non-aggressive resolution of conflict. The peer mediation approach also creates role models: peer mediators and student disputants who resolve their conflicts via peer mediation. (White 1994, 50)

Furthermore, school-based peer mediation does not require that teachers and staff members spend an inordinate amount of time on student discipline; instead, students take the time to resolve conflicts. At Cleveland Middle School in Albuquerque, New Mexico, with almost a thousand students, it would be easy for individual students to get lost in the crowd. The population of students is a diverse one, composed of Anglo, Hispanic, Native American, African American, and Asian students. It would be easy for cliques and gangs to form along these lines and to create conflicts among the student population. However, the school is organized into heterogeneous "families." Each family includes approximately fifty-five students and two teachers. The families consider themselves a team and this approach helps to create an atmosphere where everyone gets along. The large school seems much smaller and more manageable to students and staff. Everyone is part of a team and has teammates (Hereford 1999b). According to Principal Mary Lou Anderson,

> Children this age need to belong. Many of our students don't have strong family situations. Kids will join a gang to find that sense of family. We offer a more constructive alternative. Because they are with the same group of students and have their core subjects taught by the same two teachers, children in our school become very attached to their family group. We don't have a lot of negative behavior because of our tight-knit families. (Hereford 1999b, 14)

The "anonymity feature" may spark undesirable behaviors in students in large middle schools without supports (Frankfurt 1999). Large schools do not facilitate individual relationships with staff members, making teasing and other problem behaviors a concern. Sometimes, school staff members and administrators ignore the slurs that they hear in the hallways and on the playing fields. This sends a tacit but clear message to students that such language is tolerated. Administrators must take the lead in working to create a climate in which name calling and sexual taunts are not tolerated. If they do not, this verbal harassment may escalate to violent behavior.

> In fact, a study by the American Association of University Women showed that "when students were asked to what degree they would be upset if they were the target of 14 different types of sexual harassment outlined in the survey, 86 percent said they would be "very upset" if they were called gay or lesbian—85 percent of boys and 87 percent of girls. No other type of harassment—including actual physical abuse—provoked a reaction this strong among boys. (Frankfurt 1999, 26)

If staff allow antigay remarks to go unchecked, students will assume that they can continue to make them. Individuals who are the targets of these comments, who may be struggling with their identity and worth, will question them even more.

Cooperative learning strategies can be used to help students get to know others, experience teamwork, and feel that they always have someone on their side. It also may be possible to build more positive attitudes and healthier self-esteem in a school through a program such as the "Power of Positive Students." This program is built upon four research-supported beliefs:

- A strong, positive relationship exists between self-concept and achievement.
- A positive self-concept is learned and, therefore, can be taught.
- Children must experience success in order to develop and sustain a positive self-concept.
- A positive learning climate at school and home and in the community is crucial. (Friedland 1999, 16)

A comprehensive student activities program at the middle school and high school, involving all students, can accomplish many of the same objectives. Only when students feel comfortable and valued will they be successful. School is an opportunity for young people to grow and learn. If they don't feel that they are valued, they can't grow.

Recommendation #1 in chapter eight of the National Association of Secondary School Principals' *Breaking Ranks* is as follows:

> The principal, the school community, and the school board will promote policies, practices, and decisions that recognize diversity in accord with the core values of a democratic and civil society and within the mission of teaching and learning. (NASSP 1996, 69)

High schools should demonstrate that they respect differences among people and work toward preventing those differences from obstructing any student's achievement. In addition to learning tolerance, students should learn to recognize the strengths and advantages of living in a diverse population. High schools must also have clear expectations for all students and a written code of conduct to deal with students who don't respect the expectations. Following the tragedy at Columbine High School, the Elbert (Colorado) High School student council undertook activities that were dedicated to teaching tolerance during National Student Leadership Week. During an all-school assembly, students were encouraged to sign a Columbine Commitment Pledge (Bishop 1999).

The pledge sets a personal goal of increasing tolerance within the school. Individuals signing pledges would try to become more inclusive of other groups different from theirs. They would also try to greet and "pull in" others who seemed alone or isolated. Signed pledge cards were posted as a reminder of individual and school commitment to the program. The pledge states: "I pledge a personal commitment to become more tolerant of others' differences. I will avoid put-downs and bashing of others and instead replace them with a more positive form of communication. I pledge a personal commitment to become a member of the helping majority that becomes a friend to other students being taunted" (Bishop 1999, 42).

In short, "high schools should, if necessary, be islands of tolerance where those whose customs and traditions and ideas might subject them to derision elsewhere can find refuge" (NASSP 1996, 70).

Some of the school reform and school improvement movements that have been given extensive coverage in professional journals include authentic learning, authentic assessment, cooperative learning, inclusion, lesson planning, higher-order thinking/problem solving, service requirements for graduation, constructivist activities, prior knowledge, curricular integration, common core, less is more, transitioning, and the whole child or total learner (Gholson 1996). The student activity program has for decades provided the participants with most of the experiences suggested by the terms in this list. Consider the following definitions of the above terms:

- Authentic learning in the '90s suggests higher-order thinking and problem-solving skills. The term refers to student-to-student dialogue and interaction, "attacking" real-life situations, or a "product" of a student-teacher cooperative venture.
- Authentic assessment means going beyond the traditional pencil-paper test.
- Cooperative learning has received significant media coverage recently. Some have suggested cooperative learning may be the last best hope for the U.S. classroom and academic achievement. Simply put, cooperative learning may be associated with heterogeneous grouping,

assigning roles to learners, attacking authentic issues, and instruction provided by the teacher as a guide or coach rather than as the dispenser of knowledge.

- Inclusion suggests involvement of students with a diverse range of mental, emotional, and physical abilities and/or skills in the same classrooms at the same time.

- Lesson planning or planning for instruction, during the past decade or so, has truly come of age. In many of the state education agencies and school districts around the country, the Madeline Hunter direct instruction model is the standard by which teacher effectiveness is measured. School administrators charged with evaluating faculty members look for objectives and materials, then anticipatory set, instruction, modeling, independent and guided practice, response, and closure phases. Last, of course, is evaluation of the process.

- Higher-order thinking and problem-solving skills are the true buzzwords of instructional challenges in the 1990s.

- Service as an academic requirement for school completion in the '90s is a Johnny-come-lately when one looks to the school and student activities.

- Constructivist activities are basically another way to suggest inquiry and discovery methods of organizing the classroom. Students construct new knowledge from prior knowledge while effectively integrating knowledge from a variety of sources.

- The common core has always been characteristic of student activities. A uniform, a team, a unique subset of the whole has brought members together and created what other real-life organizations have long known: people support what they help to build.

- Unlike a classroom in which thirty-six chapters are covered in as many weeks, student organizations may have half as many activities, but the transition from project to project has a beginning, middle, and end. Closure is always achieved.

- Finally, the whole child or total learner has been a favorite topic for "jargon generators" in education for much of the century. There is no issue here. Everyone agrees that school experience should addresses the cognitive (mental), affective (emotional), and psychomotor (physical) aspects of the learner. (Gholson 1996, 21–22)

It is not hard to think about a particular student activity and how it meets the above themes that are the best practice jargon of the '90s. For many years, student activities participation has allowed students to acquire these skills, attitudes, and knowledge outside the classroom. Changes in classroom instructional practices should allow all students to receive those same benefits. "In developing the well-rounded student, it is important to afford him or her the opportunity to be a participant—academically, ethically and 'actively.' This last area of education is an extension of the classroom and involves learning that builds essential skills used throughout life" (Niestemski 1996, 30).

Consider the following "Checklist for Student Projects" published by NASSP in 1976. Generally speaking, projects should:

- ✔ Contribute to the educational growth of the students.
- ✔ Enable a majority, if not all, of the students to participate or receive benefit.
- ✔ Encourage initiative, originality, creativity, and responsibility.
- ✔ Grow out of and meet students' interests, genuine needs, and concerns.
- ✔ Be practical both as to purpose and outcome in the eyes of the students.
- ✔ Grow out of local school concerns and needs, which are studied objectively.

✔ Satisfy a need in the school or community.

✔ Enlarge students' horizons and widen their interests. Projects never end but lead to further interests.

✔ Be of moderate size so that the organization can complete them within a short period of time or within one school year at the most.

✔ Contribute to the growth of students—emotionally, socially, and educationally.

✔ Help the organization achieve the goals and objectives it wants to attain.

✔ Develop cooperation and better understanding between students, faculty, staff, administrators, and the community.

✔ Be within the ability of the group and willingly undertaken by members.

✔ Be in accordance with local school guidelines and the law. (Niestemski 1996, 31)

Although the jargon is a little dated, the intent is clear. Student activities have always supported student growth and development in ways that many classrooms are now only starting to mimic. They have also always played a key role in the character and leadership development of students.

In NASSP's 1996 publication *Breaking Ranks,* the subject of teaching values in high school was addressed as one of eighty recommendations for the high school of the twenty-first century. The recommendation declares: "The high school community, which cannot be value neutral, will advocate and model a set of core values essential in a democratic and civil society" (Breaking Ranks 1998, 21). America's high schools must have high expectations and standards for all students. They also must enforce their rules and regulations in a fair and consistent manner. High schools must be institutions of learning that impart values on which to build a democratic and free society. In part, schools can accomplish these goals through the infusion of character education in the curriculum. The key character traits of honesty, dependability, trust, responsibility, tolerance, and respect need to be part of classroom lessons and cocurricular learnings. The obligation of preparing students for citizenship clearly falls on the schools. Young people must learn the meaning of life in a democratic and civil society while attending high school. They must prepare to assume the obligations of citizenship (Breaking Ranks 1998). Ideally, the home will serve as the main site for character formation and the high school will try to act in concert with the home.

Throughout its long history, character education has been a part of K–12 public and private character education.

Character education is as old as education itself. Down through history, education has had two great goals: to help people become smart and to help them become good. Acting on that belief, schools in the earliest days of our republic tackled character education head on—through discipline, the teacher's example, and the daily school curriculum. The Bible was the public schools' sourcebook for both moral and religious instruction. When struggles eventually arose over whose Bible to use and which doctrines to teach, William McGuffey stepped onto the stage in 1836 to offer his McGuffey Readers, ultimately to sell more than 100 million copies. McGuffey retained many favorite Biblical stories but added poems, exhortations and heroic tales. While children practiced their reading or arithmetic, they also learned lessons about honesty, love of neighbor, kindness to animals, hard work, thriftiness, patriotism, and courage. (Lickona 1993, 6)

Character education emphasizes instruction in honesty, trust, cooperation, respect, responsibility, hope, determination, and loyalty, and lays the foundation for positive leadership development. These values are important to all students, especially those in leadership capacities. They are needed to be successful and participate fully in society, no matter what a person's race, religion, economic status, or other defining characteristics. Positive student leadership emphasizes all of the character education traits listed above (Fertman and van Linden 1999).

> Character education is a deliberate effort to cultivate virtue. It is not allowing kids to decide for themselves what is right and wrong; rather, the school stands for virtues and promotes them explicitly. It is not an "add-on" or even an elective class, it is a whole-school effort to create a community of virtue, where moral behaviors such as respect, honesty, kindness, hard work, and self-control are modeled, taught, expected, celebrated, and continuously practiced in everyday interactions. (Lickona 1997, 7)

Leaders possess the characteristics of independent thinking, communicating effectively to others, and helping others to understand and act on the beliefs they convey. Their influence is conducted in an ethical and socially responsible way. Leadership, when defined this way, "is a set of skills and attitudes that can be learned and practiced, and all adolescents can develop these skills and attitudes" (Fertman and van Linden 1999, 10). Leadership development and character education help young people answer the questions "Who am I?" and "How do I fit in?" They may also teach civic values and virtue, as well as the moral code to which a community adheres, while steering clear of an overtly religious teaching, although some of these values are held in common with some religious groups. It is not, therefore, unlawful to teach them in school (Vessels and Boyd 1996).

Empathy and self-discipline are two skills that have been identified as prerequisites for character development. "*Empathy* allows the child to appreciate perspectives and feelings of another, to sense violations of justice and care, and to better distinguish right from wrong. *Self-discipline* provides the ability to take action and delay or even forego gratification in order to remain committed to a set of values or goals" (Berreth and Berman 1997, 24). Together, these skills provide the foundation for moral behavior.

To nurture empathy and self-discipline in our young people, we need to help them:

- Learn basic decision-making and perspective-taking skills.
- Delay gratification and persist through obstacles.
- Develop a consistent set of positive values they can translate into action.
- Learn how to act responsibly.
- Have opportunities to successfully test skills. (Berreth and Berman 1997, 24)

One example of a character education program designed to integrate values into a school community is the Community of Caring program. "Through a total school-community approach, the program attempts to create a caring, respectful school environment that supports students as they develop positive values" (Jones and Stoodley 1999, 46). The program is not taught in the classroom.

> When Community of Caring is fully implemented the core values of caring, respect, responsibility, trust, and family permeate the daily life of the school. . . . Teachers use these cornerstones, upon which responsible people base moral decisions, to articulate and demonstrate guideposts for sound decision making for students. The goal is for students to develop an understanding of the five values and how they affect life choices and behavior. (Jones and Stoodley 1999, 46–47)

The school culture itself becomes one of reinforcement and support with the goal that every child feel a personal connection to at least one adult in the school.

The Montclair Kimberly Academy, a pre-K through grade 12 independent school in Montclair, New Jersey, is an example of a school that reached consensus on the character traits it wished to encourage and defined them in terms of observable behaviors.

Students are expected to be:

1. Respectful—civil in their relations to other persons;
2. Friendly—showing good will and compassion in their relations with others;
3. Responsible—doing assigned tasks diligently and volunteering to do things that are worthwhile;
4. Confident—not afraid to decline invitations to join in hurtful behavior;
5. Temperate—intelligent managers of their time and talents and able to deal prudently with both temptations and challenges;
6. Fair—cultivating speech and behavior that can be consistently maintained both in public and private without prejudice or embarrassment;
7. Informed—knowledgeable about the workings of the world around them and reflective about their own experiences. (Lickona 1997, 11–12)

In short, a character education program helps to guide and shape young people's behavior by clearly defining standards. Guiding young people to make positive choices during adolescence is extremely important to their growth and development. The focus is on appropriate behaviors; character education may begin with a single student but it can grow to touch all students in a school community (Harned 1999). School experiences that lead students to value democratic and civil principles are lessons that prepare them for civic life. Of most importance are lessons that involve students in decision making within the classroom and school as well as opportunities for service within and outside the school. "We must provide students with age-appropriate opportunities to participate in the decisions that affect their lives. The *practice* of democracy is vital. Even very young children can participate in class meetings to discuss rules and moral values" (Berreth and Berman 1997, 26).

The young people of today are the leaders of tomorrow. They will be leaders in their workplaces, communities, and families.

> The adolescent years are critical in developing future leaders whose decisions and actions will reflect universal human values. The future of our nation depends on these values, wherein lie the character and leadership of our youth. If schools can integrate these concepts, all students will have a chance to learn more about the benefits of making good choices and creating a world that is rich in opportunities. (Fertman and van Linden 1999, 15)

Change can often occur through the efforts of an individual or small group that recruits others to achieve a goal or objective. Over time, expectations for students change and higher standards for behavior shape the discipline system of the school. Higher standards for student behavior also affect students through the school's mediation program. Students begin to better understand their roles and responsibility to self and others in the school community. A school evolves into a community with shared ideals, common practices, and respect for individual differences through character education

(Harned 1999). "Leadership for character education is often expected to come from teachers, parents, and administrators, but students are pivotal to the process" (Harned 1999, 31). "Student government is fertile ground for examples of justice and fairness, and athletic teams are capable of talking about respect and teamwork. Allow students to become character educators to their peers—character education can breathe life into peer mediation programs" (Harned 1999, 32). The well-planned and well-developed student activities program provides students with a wealth of opportunities to apply academic learnings to practical problems and in real-life situations. The problem-solving, group decision-making, and evaluation skills learned in the classroom are used regularly in the student activity programs. Having applied these skills, students return to the classroom with a better understanding of their studies and a more positive attitude toward the learning process (Sherrill 1997).

Student activities provide more than the opportunities to apply their learning in the classroom situation. They help students develop socialization skills and promote the values of caring and responsibility in the school and in the community. Activity programs provide opportunities for students to participate meaningfully in various organizations and groups. In contrast to the regular classroom setting, students create the agendas, develop and propose projects, and coordinate events when they participate in student activities. "Through student activities, students place responsibilities on each other and work to achieve success for the group rather than seeking individual honors" (Sherrill 1997, 8). A strong, well-balanced activities program can help students gain self-confidence, create meaningful relationships, and develop a sense of responsibility and citizenship. With proper administrative, faculty, and staff support, participants gain both short-term and long-term benefits that extend far beyond achieving better grades (Miley 1998).

In NASSP's 1996 publication *Breaking Ranks*, recommendation seven of chapter twelve, "Relationships—Reaching Out To Form Alliances in Behalf of Students" deals with service program participation. The recommendation states, "the high school will require each student to participate in a service program in the community or in the school itself that has educational value" (NASSP 1996, 89). This section of the report also states, "The health of our democracy depends on students gaining a sense of their connection to the larger community. One of the best ways to create such ties is through service learning, which enables young people to contribute their efforts to activities that are useful to the community and helps them reflect on what they learn from their participation" (NASSP 1996, 94). Through service learning, students are challenged to define themselves vis-à-vis a larger sense of community and the responsibilities they have to it. They have the opportunity to apply judgment and leadership skills to practical problems. "Service learning holds tremendous potential for expanding and enriching a child's education" (Garber and Heet 2000, 677). Through structured community service activities, students improve their academic learning and develop personal skills. Young people working together to contribute to the community develop a sense of pride in their service to others (Jones and Stoodley 1999). The Corporation for National Service reports some of the benefits of participation in service learning:

- Increased understanding of civics and government
- Greater acceptance of cultural diversity
- Higher attendance rates
- Higher likelihood of graduation
- Higher grades
- Decreased referrals for disciplinary action

- Decreased likelihood of engaging in behaviors that lead to arrest or pregnancy
- Improved school climate resulting in greater school connections and decreased teacher turnover
- Improved view of youth as valuable resources (Rourke 2000, 5)

Nearly half of all high schools and one-third of all public schools organize service learning as part of the curriculum, according to the National Center for Education Statistics. Therefore, these programs have a substantial impact nationwide. NASSP, however, acknowledges the critics who require students to perform tasks that society usually considers voluntary (Rourke 2000). These critics find it acceptable that high schools require students to pass certain courses such as English, social studies, math, and science in order to obtain diplomas, but in some school districts, students have sued their schools over "forced volunteerism" (NASSP 1996).

Peace-building programs in schools provide young people with knowledge about alternatives to violence and equip them with important life skill—skills that will be useful to support and maintain peaceful communities in an ever-changing world. "Students who have been affected by violence may be unable to sit still in class because they are either depressed or afraid. Academic work is viewed as secondary to recognizing warning signs of impending trouble. One in four children believe that violence has lessened the quality of their learning" (Harris 2000, 5–6). Schools can respond with peacekeeping strategies. "Peace-keeping strategies can help school administrators deal with physical threats within their schools. Peace-making strategies can help address problems of normative violence within school buildings, but peace-building strategies are necessary to deal with environmental and structural problems of violence" (Harris 2000, 20).

The three strategies of peacekeeping, peacemaking, and peace building are helping to reduce violence in schools (Harris 2000). In peer mediation, the focus is on peacemaking and avoiding violence. Students learn to arbitrate conflict among their peers and negotiate peaceful solutions in order to prevent violence. The peace movement of the 1960s and 1970s popularized this technique and it became more widespread by the late 1980s. "Today, about 10,000 schools and community groups are using peer mediation" (Vail 1998, 22). The goal of mediation is peaceful coexistence in the school environment to allow learning to take place. Empowerment is the philosophical foundation for programs in which peers help each other resolve conflict. The mediators also reap benefits. They become better listeners and are able to resolve their own as well as others' conflicts. "Teachers find that peer mediation helps them improve their classroom management skills" (Brooks 1994, 28).

According to Brooks, the steps to implementing a peer mediation program are as follows:

1. Gather support from students and staff members by exposing them to videos and literature explaining peer mediation.
2. Ask staff members and students to recommend student mediators—students whom their peers respect.
3. Train mediators and those staff members who will oversee the program.
4. After training, stage a mock mediation session at a staff meeting to inform the entire staff about the program and to elicit their support.
5. Orient the entire student body to the process. Ensure that they understand mediation, how it works, and where they should go if they believe a conflict needs mediation.
6. Involve parents in the process. The more involvement they have, the more support they will provide.

7. Keep mediators' schedules on hand for easy access so they can be called upon at a moment's notice.
8. When a conflict has been mediated, the students should sign an agreement that prevents future disputes.
9. Evaluate the program regularly and make necessary changes.
10. Train new students each year to replace those who graduate.
11. Recognize and support mediators. (Brooks 1994, 27–28)

Today, 25 percent of Americans are of African, Asian, Hispanic, or Native American ancestry. In fifty years, that percentage will be 33 percent. This diversity is reflected in our changing K–12 student enrollment. Schools now enroll students from more diverse backgrounds than at any other time in the history of America. Many educators and other leaders are concerned about possible racial, religious, and gender intimidation and violence in our schools and in their hallways. "In Oakland, Calif., for example, 74 languages are represented by the student population" (Duvall 1995, 17). The related issues and concerns help make a strong case for the establishment of a multicultural club as a student cocurricular activity. The club can help educate all students and also provide a bond to the school for those who participate. For maximum effectiveness, the general goals of the club should be:

- To understand diversity
- To take a personal journey into the area of discrimination
- To work toward unity (Egger 1998, 30)

Three similar reasons exist for tolerance in our schools:

- The more you learn, the less you fear.
- Tolerant people are more self-confident.
- Tolerance makes life more interesting. (Duvall 1995, 17)

The goals of these programs are for students to learn to appreciate, value, and respect others as individuals and as representatives of cultural heritages that may differ from their own. Through these programs, society will become more pluralistic, allowing everyone to prosper and benefit from living in a democracy (Promoting Pluralism 1998). This will not be achieved unless there are ongoing efforts on the part of the school and the community. One week of activities will not accomplish the goal. Hopefully, schools will become more relevant and less anonymous for many students.

Reports dating from the 1940s indicate the unsatisfactory state of secondary education in America. The "Eight-Year Study" clearly identified fifteen inadequacies, including these that related to irrelevance and anonymity:

1. Secondary schools do not prepare students adequately for the responsibilities of community life.
2. Schools neither know their students well nor guide them wisely.
3. Schools fail to create conditions necessary for effective learning.
4. The creative energies of students are seldom released and developed.
5. The conventional high school curriculum is far removed from the real concerns of youth.

6. The traditional subjects of the curriculum have lost much of their vitality and significance. (Lounsbury 1996, 18)

One of the recommendations of NASSP's *Breaking Ranks* is that "High schools will create small units in which anonymity is banished" (NASSP 1996, 45). This recommendation is predicated on the belief that when students experience a sense of belonging and bond with the school, they will be better school citizens and achieve more. If they become invisible and disappear into their surroundings, schools lose the opportunity to fully engage them academically and do not benefit from their unique talents and abilities.

> Teachers should know their students and students, in turn, should know their teachers. . . . House plans and cluster programs, for example, group students into smaller, more intimate units. Such approaches seek to reduce the number of teacher and other students with whom a student comes in contact each day. An organizational approach that produces some kind of school-within-a-school moves toward combating the bigness that shrouds so many youngsters in a cloak of anonymity. . . . reducing size guarantees nothing in and of itself. Some schools fail to exploit their smallness in ways that give students a sense of belonging. (NASSP 1996, 46)

Some of the organizational changes needed to make schools "smaller" are the establishment of teacher/student teams, block scheduling, common planning time for teaching teams, creation of schools within a school, and institution of advisory programs. Attempts to change administratively and actual changes always produce resistance on the part of those who are established and have accepted routines. The established routines that are in place, effective or ineffective, appeal to those who follow them. The intended changes, therefore, may never occur. "Change efforts don't break down in the superintendent's office or in the curriculum center, they break down at the level of the individual classroom. . . . The American high school must make some bold moves if it is to avoid a gradual decline and even extinction via vouchers, privatization, and alternate forms of schooling" (Lounsbury 1996, 20–24). Efforts to personalize the high school will require student participation and involvement. Service learning and volunteering in the school and community are two avenues that could help personalize high school and help facilitate change.

We know that younger children look up to older children. They pattern their behaviors, dress, speech, and attitudes after older children who serve as role models. Many school districts develop programs that channel this influence by using older students to teach leadership skills, tutor, mentor, and promote safe behaviors, thereby affecting younger students in positive ways (Fiscus 2000). Many times, younger students are taught by older students in leadership training workshops.

> The benefits are twofold—the younger students learn problem solving, communication, team-building, and other leadership skills and in preparing to teach the workshop the older students solidify their own skills. . . . Another area in which it is fairly common for older students to work with younger students is in improving academic performance." (Fiscus 2000, 14)

Mentoring is also a way for older students to volunteer to help younger students. The interaction between the ages is the key to a mentoring program. The mentor-student interaction depends on the student's need. Some students need academic help while others just need someone to talk to. Older students also can promote positive behaviors in younger persons by helping them make healthful choices regarding the use of drugs and alcohol (Fiscus 2000).

A 1995 report on "The Condition of Education," published by the U.S. Department of Education, National Center for Education Statistics "found that participation in extracurricular activities may affect academic performance, attachment to school and social development" (National Federation 1998, 7). However, the exact nature of the participation and academic relationship remains unclear. (Does participation increase the academic orientation of students or does the academic orientation explain the rate of participation [Buss 1998])? A central finding of "The Condition of Education" was that cocurricular activity programs exist in almost every U.S. high school. Frequently in place were music, academic clubs, and sports programs. "These activities provide opportunities for students to learn the values of teamwork, a channel for reinforcing skills and the opportunity to apply academic skills in other arenas as part of a well-rounded education" (National Federation 1998, 7).

Despite the potential benefits of participation, barriers remain that prevent students from participating in cocurricular activities. Barriers to participation can be concrete issues such as family or work responsibilities, lack of financial resources for equipment, and transportation concerns. They can also be complex issues such as a lack of interest in school and the activities offered. Low-SES students participate less frequently than high-SES students, despite the wide availability of extracurricular activities in most schools. "This particular gap is cause for concern, especially if extracurricular activities can be a means of bringing at-risk students more fully into the school community, thereby increasing their chances of school success" (Extracurricular Participation 1995, 15).

The question is often raised, should American secondary schools be academic or developmental? The proponents of an academic perspective believe that the purpose of schooling is the pursuit of academic excellence and the transmission of formal knowledge. Schools, therefore, should focus on intellectual competence. Accordingly, cocurricular activities provide a means of relaxation and fun, but are not as important to the primary purpose of schools. The proponents of the developmental position believe that school programs provide experiences that help to further individual development. School programs, including student activities, provide experiences that are important to the total development of individual students. The developmental position is more egalitarian in its assertion that the development of all individuals must be considered when planning a school program. Nonacademic programs as well as academic programs facilitate the development of the individual (Holland and Andre 1987).

Most secondary schools serve a diverse population of students. Schools help in the socialization process and provide many of the developmental tasks necessary for individuals to master on the way to becoming an adult. The academic program provides some of these tasks and the cocurricular program is a rich resource for accomplishing others (Holland and Andre 1987).

Holland and Andre (1987) report five areas in which cocurricular activities have shown a positive impact on the development of students. Several key points taken from the twenty-nine-page document are:

1. Personal-social characteristics—participation was more predictive of self-esteem in small schools than in large schools. The highest self-esteem scores were among successful small school participants. Also, cocurricular activities are an important source of cross-racial cooperation with students reporting cocurricular activities as their main source of interracial contact.
2. Academic achievement and athletic participation—in general, reviews of the literature have reported that male high school athletes receive somewhat higher grade point averages than do non-athletes. For female athletes, GPAs do not differ significantly from the GPAs of non-athletes.

3. Educational aspirations and attainment—the results of studies have generally indicated a positive relationship between activity participation and increased aspirations and attainment. The type of activity, however, does seem to moderate this relationship. For example, males who participate in non-athletic, service/leadership-orientated activities are more likely to achieve educational aspirations than males who participate only in athletic activities.

4. Degree of activity involvement—studies in this area, involving both athletic and non-athletic activities, suggest that degree of involvement in cocurricular activities is significantly correlated with positive personality–social characteristics among secondary school students.

5. Factors that mediate participation effects—an inverse relationship between school size and cocurricular participation has been demonstrated in numerous studies. The largest schools had 65 times as many students as the smallest schools but only 2.3 times the number of academic activities and 4 times the number of athletic activities. In small schools, the typical student participated in more than twice as many activities as students in larger schools. Participation rates for lower SES students were much higher in small schools than in large schools. In small schools students at risk of dropping out were more likely to be involved in student activities, felt a greater obligation and pressure to be involved, and were more integrated into the social activities of the school.

In summary, "participation [in student activities] may lead adolescents to acquire new skills (organizational, planning, time management, etc.) to develop or strengthen particular attitudes (discipline, motivation), or to receive social rewards that influence personality characteristics" (Holland and Andre 1987, 447). However, the current literature only provides hints that participation leads to these outcomes and does not establish a causal relationship between participation and the outcomes listed above (Holland and Andre 1987).

Consider the following four points in support of cocurricular activity participation, which one student wrote about in a recent leadership magazine:

- Participation in many different types of activities—cocurricular activities allow young adults an opportunity to try something new and different from what we have done in the past. Others see us and we begin to see ourselves in a new perspective. Personal growth is bound to be the outcome.
- Cultivate your interests and talents—find something of interest to improve your skills or to develop new talents.
- Shore up your weak areas—make yourself a more well-rounded individual by taking a risk. Explore an area in which you would like to improve.
- Create your own opportunities—start a club or activity and get others involved. Look for a need in the school or community to address through service. (Kaplan 2000)

All cocurricular activities sponsored by the high school should fit into a comprehensive program that is designed to meet the developmental needs of all students. This requirement applies to all clubs and activities—academic and athletic. Meeting this objective will keep the program focused on the needs of students. It will also allow a diverse spectrum of students to participate in a wide variety of organizations. No student should miss this important part of his or her education (NASSP 1996).

In closing:

Attendance is the best predictor of graduation and student school performance. Poor attendance is the best predictor of academic credit loss (Schellenberg 1998).

"I am only one person. What would I say? What can I do? Why would people listen or follow me? How can I do something like this?" It only takes a spark to get a fire going. It only takes one person with a vision to get things moving in a positive direction. (Namey 2000, 11)

5

WHAT ARE THE SHORT-TERM AND LONG-TERM BENEFITS OF STUDENT ACTIVITIES FOR COMMUNITIES?

Many students fill a need for a sense of belonging and closeness to others through involvement in extracurricular student activities at school or in the community. The word *extracurricular* often brings school sports to mind. Athletics serve well, but often only serve a few. Let us not de-emphasize athletics, but instead celebrate every other activity in the lives of young people (Koerner 1992, 64).

What goals ought today's high schools embrace? The following nine purposes represent NASSP's vision:

1. High school is, above all else, a learning community and each school must commit itself to expecting demonstrated academic achievement for every student in accord with standards that can stand up to national scrutiny.
2. High school must function as a transitional experience, getting each student ready for the next stage of life, whatever it may be for that individual, with the understanding that, ultimately, each person needs to earn a living.
3. High school must be a gateway to multiple options.
4. High school must prepare each student to be a lifelong learner.
5. High school must provide an underpinning for good citizenship and for full participation in the life of a democracy.
6. High school must play a role in the personal development of young people as social beings who have needs beyond those that are strictly academic.
7. High school must lay a foundation for students to be able to participate comfortably in an increasingly technological society.

8. High school must equip young people for life in a country and a world in which interdependency will link their destiny to that of others, however different those others may be from them.
9. High school must be an institution that unabashedly advocates in behalf of young people. (NASSP 1996, 2)

"High schools will guarantee that students can meet performance standards in entry-level jobs. Recent graduates who fail to meet these basic standards will have the opportunity to return to school for additional studies" is one of the recommendations of NASSP's *Breaking Ranks* (NASSP 1996, 53). A curriculum that combines rigor and relevance is called for. The workplace is being transformed by technology; unskilled and low-skill jobs are disappearing. Employees from entry-level workers to senior management are increasingly required to have a wide base of knowledge, the ability to access information, and the skills to manipulate data. "Like it or not, we compete today in a global economy. And the reality of it is, we either have to compete against high skills or low wages, and we surely aren't able to compete against the low wages found in other nations" (O'Neil 1995, 46). The global economy and the rapid growth in the use of technology in the workplace have changed the necessary skills and competencies young people now need to bring to a job. The work environment has radically changed in the last quarter of the twentieth century. The Secretary's Commission on Achieving Necessary Skills (SCANS) addresses worker know-how to meet the challenge of successful job performance. This know-how has two elements: competencies and foundations.

> This report identifies five competencies and a three-part foundation of skills and personal qualities that lie at the heart of job performance. These eight requirements are essential preparation for all students, both those going directly to work and those planning further education. The five SCANS competencies span the chasm between school and the workplace. Because they are needed in workplaces dedicated to excellence, they are hallmarks of today's expert worker. They lie behind the quality of every product and service on today's market. (U.S. Department of Labor 1991, xv–xvi)

The competencies required are at least as important as technical knowledge required for success in a particular occupation. The competencies represent the characteristics of workers employers need in today's marketplace.

A Three-Part Foundation

1. Basic Skills: Reads, writes, performs arithmetic and mathematical operations, listens, and speaks
   A. *Reading*—locates, understands, and interprets written information in prose and in documents such as manuals, graphs, and schedules
   B. *Writing*—communicates thoughts, ideas, information, and messages in writing; and creates documents such as letters, directions, manuals, reports, graphs, and flow charts
   C. *Arithmetic/Mathematics*—performs basic computations and approaches practical problems by choosing appropriately from a variety of mathematical techniques
   D. *Listening*—receives, attends to, interprets, and responds to verbal messages and other cues
   E. *Speaking*—organizes ideas and communicates orally

2. Thinking Skills: Thinks creatively, makes decisions, solves problems, visualizes, knows how to learn, and reasons
   A. *Creative Thinking*—generates new ideas

    B. *Decision Making*—specifies goals and constraints, generates alternatives, considers risks, and evaluates and chooses best alternative

    C. *Problem Solving*—recognizes problems and devises and implements plan of action

    D. *Seeing Things in the Mind's Eye*—organizes and processes symbols, pictures, graphs, objects, and other information

    E. *Knowing How to Learn*—uses efficient learning techniques to acquire and apply new knowledge and skills

    F. *Reasoning*—discovers a rule or principle underlying the relationship between two or more objects and applies it when solving a problem

3. Personal Qualities: Displays responsibility, self-esteem, sociability, self-management, and integrity and honesty

    A. *Responsibility*—exerts a high level of effort and perseveres toward goal attainment

    B. *Self-esteem*—believes in own self-worth and maintains a positive view of self

    C. *Sociability*—demonstrates understanding, friendliness, adaptability, empathy, and politeness in group settings

    D. *Self-Management*—assesses self accurately, sets personal goals, monitors progress, and exhibits self-control

    E. *Integrity/Honesty*—chooses ethical courses of action

Five Competencies

Resources: Identifies, organizes, plans, and allocates resources

    A. *Time*—selects goal-relevant activities, ranks them, allocates time, and prepares and follows schedules

    B. *Money*—uses or prepares budgets, makes forecasts, keeps records, and makes adjustments to meet objectives

    C. *Material and Facilities*—acquires, stores, allocates, and uses materials or space efficiently

    D. *Human Resources*—assesses skills and distributes work accordingly, evaluates performance and provides feedback

Interpersonal: Works with others

    A. *Participates as Member of a Team*—contributes to group effort

    B. *Teaches Others New Skills*

    C. *Serves Clients/Customers*—works to satisfy customers' expectations

    D. *Exercises Leadership*—communicates ideas to justify position, persuades and convinces others, responsibly challenges existing procedures and policies

    E. *Negotiates*—works toward agreements involving exchange of resources, resolves divergent interests

    F. *Works with Diversity*—works well with men and women from diverse backgrounds

Information: Acquires and uses information

    A. *Acquires and Evaluates Information*

    B. *Organizes and Maintains Information*

    C. *Interprets and Communicates Information*

    D. *Uses Computers to Process Information*

Systems: Understands complex interrelationships

    A. *Understands Systems*—knows how social, organizational, and technological systems work and operates effectively with them

B. *Monitors and Corrects Performance*—distinguishes trends, predicts impacts on system operations, diagnoses deviations in systems' performance, and corrects malfunctions

C. *Improves or Designs Systems*—suggests modifications to existing systems and develops new or alternative systems to improve performance

Technology: Works with a variety of technologies

A. *Selects Technology*—chooses procedures, tools, or equipment, including computers and related technologies

B. *Applies Technology to Task*—understands overall intent and proper procedures for setup and operation of equipment

C. *Maintains and Troubleshoots Equipment*—prevents, identifies, or solves problems with equipment, including computers and other technologies (U.S. Department of Labor 1991, xvi–xvii)

In a related 1995 document, "College Expectations: Recommendations of the SUNY Task Force on College Entry-Level Knowledge and Skills," the State University of New York clearly stated expectation for entering students: "The entry-level knowledge and skills expected of beginning college and university students are obviously closely related to the learning outcomes desired for graduation from high school" (State University of New York 1995, 1–2). Entry-level skills recommended by the task force were:

Academic and Personal Support Skills

Students should be able to:

- Plan, organize, set priorities, and manage time
- Listen, communicate, and take notes effectively in class
- Appreciate and profit from diversity and pluralism
- Study and learn by using different learning styles
- Accept both success and failure and learn from both
- Acknowledge and promote values and ethics
- Develop high levels of self-esteem and self-challenge
- Embrace task-setting and the desire for lifelong learning
- Profit from cooperative as well as independent study

Information Management Skills

Students entering college should be computer and information literate. The task force recommends students have skills that support:

- Effective use of computational tools and terminology appropriate for solving problems with computers
- Familiarity with library organization, library services, and information sources
- Knowledge of the categories into which specific subjects fall and the print or non-print information tools needed to retrieve specific material
- The ability to plan a logical sequence of steps (search strategy) to solve an information problem
- Experience in identifying and analyzing information needs from diverse subject areas

Communication Skills

Alert critical thinking and the ability to convey meaning are essential in all successful communications. This active rather than passive quality entails the development of an interest and a willingness to engage in reading, writing, listening, and speaking.

Reading—to build communications in reading, students should be able to:

- Read the Standard English prose typically found in newspaper editorials and current freshman textbooks
- Read fiction, drama, and poetry reflecting different cultural perspectives, of the kind found in anthologies for freshman English courses
- Summarize and articulate the author's perspective on his or her work, as well as critique and compare that material with other works
- Discuss whether he or she agrees with the author and provide reasons for this position
- Discover the relation of a given graph, chart, or picture to the written text

Writing—students should engage in writing as a form of expression and as a primary method of learning. They should have some experience using computers to support their writing activities. In particular, every English course should regularly require the writing, editing, and rewriting of papers of varying lengths. By the time students enter college, they should be able to:

- Write Standard English prose in papers of between 800 and 1,000 words
- Gather and evaluate information from primary and secondary sources; use this information in an original report or research paper; quote, paraphrase, and summarize accurately; and cite sources properly.
- View their own writing as a process that can be improved by restructuring, correcting errors, and rewriting
- Write Standard English sentences with attention to sentence structure, verb forms, punctuation, capitalization, possessives, plural forms, and other matters of mechanics, word choice, and spelling

Listening and Taking Notes—students should be able to:

- Listen to an oral exposition of scheduled class length in Standard English
- Listen to and participate in class discussion
- Understand and accept different speaking styles and the various accents of English that reflect cultural, regional, or national differences in speech
- Take accurate and detailed notes for effective studying
- Understand orally delivered assignments and questions
- Identify important terms and purposes articulated by the speaker

Speaking—students should be able to:

- Answer and ask questions coherently and concisely in Standard English
- Summarize their own views on a given topic clearly and concisely
- Participate in small-group discussion in a way that contributes to furthering the group's goals
- Refine their ideas through dialogue with others

Analytical Skills

Analytical power requires that students be able to discern relations, reason logically, and use a broad spectrum of mathematical methods to solve a wide variety of problems. Students should be taught to appreciate the logical approach inherent in mathematical and scientific process; to seek solutions, not just memorize procedures, to explore patterns, not just learn formulae; and to formulate conjectures, not just complete exercises.

Entry Level Knowledge

Along with the skills just outlined, entering students must also possess entry-level knowledge. Recommendations about what a student entering the university should know are presented in three broad knowledge categories: (1) Humanities, Arts, and Foreign Language; (2) Natural Sciences, Mathematics, and Technical Studies; and (3) Social Sciences and History. Across these categories, the student should be encouraged to recognize and appreciate relationships between disciplines and between types of knowledge and learning. (State University of New York 1995, 3–7)

High schools effectively serve young people when they help them acquire and develop the skills and abilities needed to be successful when they graduate. Each student brings to the school unique interests and abilities. Students also appear at the steps of the school with ambitions and family support that vary widely. Yet the school must meet each individual's needs and prepare them for what will come next in their lives. "A young person who grows into adulthood unequipped to reach his or her full potential will possess neither the knowledge nor the will to contribute to making this a better society" (NASSP 1996, 4).

As schools struggle to prepare students for the twenty-first century, what role will partnerships play in meeting the needs of students and providing additional resources?

The millennium brings with it increasing demands on schools to do more to prepare students for the world of work and for educational experiences beyond high school. As educators, we must accept that we can no longer work in isolation to help our students meet the challenges they face. . . . The contributions of educators and business and community leaders have evolved from paternalistic "adopt us/help be the parent" attitudes to full working agreements by which principals and business and community organizations have learned new ways of working together, developing a vision and sharing responsibility for student growth and development. (Sammon and Becton 2001, 32)

When business and community partnerships develop with schools, students sense that there are caring adults throughout the community who want to see them succeed. Corporations, unions, professional associations, government agencies, and nonprofit organizations are increasingly incorporating commitment to community service in their mission statements. Specifically, a school-to-careers partnership helps all students:

- Understand the changing world of work that faces them;
- Widen their occupational horizons by investigating many options;
- Attain valuable skills they'll need to survive in a rapidly changing labor market;
- Learn and value academic subjects;
- Relate schooling to the world of work and life;
- Make wise choices;

- See clear paths to their futures;
- Feel good about themselves and achieve success as they define it. (Center for Human Resources 1996, 2)

Another means of building a bridge to the community is through service-learning activities. Increasingly, schools include service learning in their curriculum as citizenship preparation for students. Service learning that supplements traditional instruction by directly involving students in community organization work has enriched many classrooms. This kind of involvement and the subsequent classroom reflection on the meaning of service learning helps students understand the many social interactions required of effective citizens (Van Til 1997).

> In fact, service learning may be our best approach to teach participatory citizenship and give young people the skills to be critical thinkers in a complex social and political environment. . . . A systematic approach to service learning means helping students make the connections between subject material and issues in the larger world. It means engaging students in action and reflection on important community, social, political and environmental issues. Instead of seeing service learning as a series of one-time events that teach children about doing good for others, it must be seen as our integral strategy for the development of social, civic, and academic skills that begins in kindergarten and extends through to graduation. (Berman 2000, 20)

Service-learning activities provide young people with a chance to participate as citizens in the community. It also allows them a chance to grow and develop when they can accomplish something worthwhile.

Since the presidential summit in Philadelphia in 1997, there has been a nationwide emphasis on civic responsibility, including a call to raise the caliber of service to a new level—one that provides further integration of learning, magnifies the service experience, and provides a broad range of objectives to meet students' needs and learning styles. The components that will bring students closer to the meaning of the service performed are preparation, action, reflection, and demonstration. Obviously, when students who are involved in student activities became involved in service learning projects, the curricular links are strengthened. Student activities are an important part of school life for those who participate. They provide a variety of educational experiences to many students. "According to *Breaking Ranks: Changing an American Institution*, they undergird the goal of teaching students to be responsible and fulfilled human beings, providing them with opportunities that develop character, critical thinking, social sociability and specific skills" (Kaye 1997, 1).

When student activity advisors support and encourage service learning, it helps students see their activity program as more central to the mission of school and their educational program. The activity advisor's role also changes to one that is clearly cocurricular—not extracurricular. Student activities have had at least a seventy-five year history of involvement with service learning through the National Honor Society, where community service has always been a criterion for membership. But service learning is more than volunteering and community service. It includes the following four steps:

Preparation

With guidance from their advisor or teacher, students:

- Identify a need
- Draw upon their own and other students' skills and knowledge

- Acquire new information
- Collaborate with community partners
- Develop a plan that encourages responsibility
- Incorporate service and learning as natural extensions of the curriculum

Action

Through direct service, indirect service, or civic action, students take action that:

- Provides meaningful service
- Uses previous and acquired academic skills and knowledge
- Offers unique learning experiences
- Has real consequences
- Is in a safe environment to learn, to make mistakes, and to have successes

Reflection

During systematic reflection, as the advisor guides the process using various methods such as role play, discussion, and journal writing, students:

- Describe what happened
- Record the difference made
- Discuss thoughts and feelings
- Place experience in larger context

Demonstration

Students demonstrate mastery of skills, insights, and outcomes by, for example:

- Reporting to their peers, faculty, and/or community members
- Writing articles or letters to local newspapers regarding issues of public concern
- Extending their experience to develop future projects benefiting the community (Kaye 1997, 8)

When students generate ideas with support from faculty and community partners, excellent service-learning activities are developed. The four-step process can be applied to any service project to transform it into a service-learning project; for example:

- Students meet with a nutritionist before they prepare cookies for a Valentine's Day party with senior citizens.
- Students partner with special needs peers as they plan and carry out a park restoration project.
- Students use role-play to prepare to tutor third graders in reading skills, and continue using role-plays at ongoing skill review sessions.
- Students conduct a survey of former new students to find out what went well and the difficulties encountered in their entry to the school as they plan a welcoming project for incoming and transfer students.
- Students participate in these workshops led by a child development specialist as they prepare to offer child care for back-to-school nights and parent education evenings.

- Once their school recycling program is running smoothly, students demonstrate effective recycling strategies for local government offices, businesses, school district headquarters, and other schools. (Kaye 1997, 7)

What is the impact of service learning on the development of participants?

The Impact of Service Learning on Personal and Social Development:

- Service learning has a positive effect on the personal development of public school youths.
- Students who participate in service learning are less likely to engage in at-risk behaviors.
- Service learning has a positive effect on students' interpersonal development and the ability to relate to culturally diverse groups.

The Impact of Service Learning on Civic Responsibility:

- Service learning helps develop students' sense of civic and social responsibility and their citizenship skills.
- Service learning provides an avenue for students to become active, positive contributors to society.

The Impact of Service Learning on Academic Learning:

- Service learning helps students acquire academic skills and knowledge.
- Students who participate in service learning are more engaged in their studies and more motivated to learn.
- Service learning is associated with increased student attendance.

The Impact of Service Learning on Career Exploration and Aspirations:

- Service learning helps students to become more knowledgeable and realistic about careers.

The Impact of Service Learning on Schools:

- Service learning results in greater mutual respect between teachers and students.
- Service learning improves the overall school climate.
- Engaging in service learning leads to discussions of teaching and learning and the best ways for students to learn.

The Impact of Service Learning on Communities:

- Service learning leads to more positive perceptions of schools and youths on the part of community members. (Billig 2000a, 660–62)

Service learning assumes many forms and employs many strategies. The costs associated with these programs depend on the scope, the types of projects, and how they are integrated into the school or district. But for most schools and districts, service learning is a relatively low-cost way to enhance the educational experience.

> Among the smaller, single-school or single-classroom programs in our study, the average cost per participant was approximately $149. Among the broad, districtwide programs, the average cost was approximately $27 per pupil, and the average cost among all the programs in our study was $52 per student. Of those [schools] with community service or service learning, 84 percent reported they received no outside funding to support their programs. The regular district budget was the sole source of funding. (Melchior 2000, 27)

California and Maryland have standards for service learning. Other states are expected to establish standards as well. These standards address both content and performance. They affirm what students will know and be able to do as a result of their participation (Billig 2000a). Philadelphia School District became the first district in the United States to require all students to become involved in service-learning activities. The service learning is directly tied to the district's academic standards and learning goals: "By June 2002, all students in the district will be required to produce a citizenship project as a condition for promotion to grades 5 and 9 and for graduation from high school" (Hornbeck 2000, 665). Every student must be involved in meaningful community activities at least between kindergarten and grade 4, again between grades 5 and 8, and a third time before graduation. The required citizenship projects will be graded against an assessment rubric that calls for the following components: "an essential question, active research and investigation, academic rigor and reflection, a real-world community connection, and applied problem solving in addressing an authentic school or community issue, need, or problem through direct service or advocacy" (Hornbeck 2000, 665).

The South Carolina General Assembly passed three laws during the 1990s that provided the infrastructure for institutionalizing service learning throughout the state.

The recommendations that follow might assist other states considering the institutionalizing of service learning in their state:

- Analyze local and state policies, plans, and programs to determine how service learning might promote and enhance these efforts.
- Establish a statewide policy council composed of decision makers representing government, business and industry, education, and human services.
- Align service-learning initiatives with policymakers' visions, goals, and programs.
- Develop a well-defined staff development program that will ensure the implementation of high-quality service-learning programs.
- Link service learning to state academic standards.
- Link service learning with teacher education programs and develop prekindergarten through grade 12 teacher education partnerships.
- Create a network of trained advocates, including young people, who can serve as ambassadors and providers of technical assistance. (Tenenbaum 2000, 668–69)

Young people who participate in service learning have the opportunity to be leaders in their schools and communities. Many of these young people would not otherwise have had this opportunity at this point in their lives. Service-learning participation challenges students to use their skills and abilities in a new and possibly different environment. The leadership skills learned will be applied over and over again in high school and as an adult. "And to the learning is added the feeling of being a part of something greater than oneself—the feeling of knowing that one has made a difference; the feeling that one's contribution is important, even critical, to the success of a service-learning project. As a result, students are more engaged in their learning" (DesMarais, Yang, and Farzanehkia 2000, 680).

The National Service Learning Clearinghouse based in St. Paul, Minnesota, reports that from 1984 to 1997 the number of high school students performing service increased nearly sevenfold, when 6.1 million students did some form of community service (Loupe 2000). The scope and quality of service programs that students participate in varies widely and Maryland is the only state that requires every student to perform seventy-five hours of community service to receive a high school diploma. Maryland leaves the details of implementing the program to the local school systems. What are the pluses and minuses of mandatory service? The educational advantages of mandating a minimum number of service hours is summarized by the Commission of the States:

- Trains young people for citizenship by engaging them in active civic participation
- Enables students to explore careers and gain work skills
- Provides learning opportunities for all students
- Looks good on a college applicant's transcript
- Meets community needs and aligns with academic standards
- Can be implemented easily

The arguments against mandatory service are as follows:

- Forces a system of nontheistic religion upon students in violation of their right to freedom of religion and constituting involuntary servitude
- Interferes with extracurricular activities, part-time jobs, and homework
- Places unsupervised students in the community in potential danger
- Offers less than meaningful experiences when students participate in "make work" programs (Loupe 2000, 34)

Service learning is commensurate with the nation's standards movement, especially when it is taught as project-based, problem-based, or inquiry-based learning and is integrated into the academic curriculum. New standards require students to apply basic learning to solve problems. Instead of simply memorizing material, students use knowledge in real-life situations. Students are assessed on what they know and what they can do. Service-learning projects are a perfect means to show what you know and can do. "Within the language of a state's standards, service learning occasionally is referenced directly, as in the case in Indiana. But strong support for the idea can also be found in the underlying principles that accompany a state's academic standards, as in Maine, or in legislation establishing the context for standards, as is the case in South Carolina" (Pickeral and Bray 2000, 9).

Six guiding principles precede Maine's academic standards, known as Learning Results. One of the guiding principles asserts that "every student will leave school a responsible and involved citizen," who:

- Recognizes the power of personal participation to affect the community and demonstrates participation skills;

- Understands the importance of accepting responsibility for personal decisions and actions;
- Knows the means of achieving personal and community health and well-being; and
- Recognizes and understands the diverse nature of society. (Pickeral and Bray 2000, 11)

Teachers can also help students to make the connections between their service and instruction. When students understand the social issues and political trends that contributed to the community need, they understand why there is a need and how it arose. Through reflection, they may also be able to see solutions to the community need through positive citizenship. "Among the strongest finding in the research literature on service learning and youth development was that students who engaged in service learning were more sensitive and showed greater acceptance of cultural diversity (Billig 2000b, 16).

"In 1995, Independent Sector reported that 59% of teenagers volunteered an estimated 3.5 hours per week and a staggering 95% of those who volunteered did so when asked" (Kielsmeier 2000, 653). Although only about one in five schools requires community service for graduation, more students continue to volunteer. The schools that require service learning report that they usually do so to foster active citizenship among young people. These programs help develop important social and personal skills, as well as a feeling of worth in young adolescents, at a difficult time for many young people (McPherson 1997).

However, for the past several decades—and sometimes even today—students are required to perform community service as punishment. A policy that uses community service as a punishment sends the wrong message. The benefits of service learning should be seen as a reward, not a punishment.

"How will I ever use this?" "Why do I need to know this?" When students ask these or similar questions they are searching for meaning, for a connection between their learning in the classroom and application in the real world. Many students need this connection to make sense of classroom lessons and to engage them in the learning process.

It is important to look beyond the box of the insular, self-contained high school to a broader conception of secondary education that takes advantage of the rich variety of learning contexts, teachers, and resources a community has to offer. In this vision of high school reform, the student experience encompasses not only rigor and relevance in school, but also high-quality learning opportunities in the workplace and community settings, where results support and push them to do their best work."(A. Steinberg 2000, 41)

The citizens of the future will be multidimensional and will need the following characteristics:

- Ability to look at and approach problems as a member of a global society
- Ability to work with others in a cooperative way and to take responsibility for one's roles and duties within society
- Ability to understand, appreciate, and tolerate cultural differences
- Capacity to think in a critical and systemic way
- Willingness to solve conflict in a nonviolent manner
- Willingness to change one's lifestyle and consumption habits to protect the environment
- Ability to be sensitive toward and defend human rights

- Willingness and ability to participate in politics at local, national, and international levels (Shumer 2000, 36)

Student involvement with community organizations also introduces them to future possibilities for service and instills a sense of the necessity of community service. In time, some programs will grow beyond the boundaries of any one school or community. Youth Leadership St. Louis is such a program. It brings high school students together in a neutral setting and allows them to investigate and study community issues. The students then become part of the solution to the issues they have identified. The program objectives are:

- To challenge each student to get in touch with his or her own values, think through the issues, and test basic assumptions;
- To motivate at-risk students to rise above their environment to seek their fullest potential;
- To expose students to a wide spectrum of people and ideas;
- To involve student participants in problem-solving activities and seminars that address selected topics and issues that affect the region;
- To enable the student participants to share information gained and the skills acquired within their school so that the impact of their participation in the leadership program has a broad outreach. (Levine and Courier 1996, 21)

Each St. Louis high school agrees to have at least six students participate and must provide a teacher to serve as an adjunct staff person. The program then has the advantage of a school partnership with area high schools. This partnership allows students to participate regardless of financial resources and is linked back to each high school through the teacher liaisons.

A similar joining of forces among young adults, a city council, and citizens can occur in small communities, such as the program in Olton, Texas. In this Texas Panhandle town, the student council has taken on a number of projects that have affected the community. Some of their projects are Veterans Day celebration, teacher appreciation, community day, park beautification, and emergency training (Couch 1996).

Another example of a community school partnership is the Granite City (Illinois) High School/Home Foundation relationship. National Honor Society members assist the Home Ownership Made Easier Foundation to provide renovated, low-income family housing in the community. The foundation purchases a home, completes repairs, and then rents it to a family chosen by a selection committee and the Home Foundation board of directors. The rent is held in an escrow account for two years and then returned to the family. The money is used by the family as a down payment on a house in the school district (Home Ownership Made Easier 1996). In addition to fund-raising and construction labor, three presidents of the local NHS chapter have served on the HOME Foundation board of directors.

According to Shumer (2000), all quality service-learning programs pay attention to two key variables: intensity and duration. Intensity (the amount of time) and duration (the length of engagement) have a great effect on the outcomes. Ideally, program intensity should be thirty-five hours or more and its duration should be the entire school year (Shumer 2000). It is also important for civic achievement to receive recognition at school through such vehicles as morning announcements, a personal acknowledgment from a school leader, the school newspaper, and/or the yearbook.

In the summer of 1995, the "School Improvement: Strategies for Connecting Schools and Communities" conference was held. Their Declaration of Principles from that meeting states:

Principle 1. All children can achieve higher levels of academic success while learning to serve if they are provided challenging standards and given the opportunity to reach them.

Principle 2. By solving real-life problems, students engaged in service-learning are challenged to exercise leadership and responsibility.

Principle 3. Teachers engaged in school improvement and service-learning require continuing professional development and training.

Principle 4. Improving our schools requires parent and community involvement.

Principle 5. Improving our schools requires the participation of the private sector and a full range of resources from every community.

Principle 6. School improvement and service learning build on the realization that ours is a nation of diverse cultures. (Riley and Wofford 2000, 670–72)

The pressures from peers and teen culture greatly increase for children in middle school. An important role for parents during this period is to help their children see how crucial schooling is to their future success. However, "parents are apt to become increasingly disengaged from their teenagers' schooling because of the pressure brought to bear by the teenagers themselves ('you'll embarrass me') or increased pressures at work" (Riley 1995, 19). To counter this perception on the part of teens, schools need to find ways for parents to become actively involved in daily activities during and after school hours. Involving students in apprenticeships with business and nonprofit groups is an excellent means of accomplishing this goal. Students may also complete service learning by cleaning a park or helping at a retirement home. Activities such as these will help students make a positive connection with adults. Indeed, the new National Education Goal on parent involvement states that, "by the year 2000, every school will promote partnerships that will increase parental involvement and participation in promoting the social, emotional, and academic growth of children" (Riley 1995, 20).

An example of increased parental involvement is ASSIST (Adults Supporting Students in School-related Tasks), whose function is to help sponsor cocurricular activities and to provide fundraising opportunities for students and parents. "Both parents and students who work on fund-raising events earn credit based upon the hours worked and the profit realized" (Upton 1995, 23). The credit earned can then be "given" to a specific student. The benefits of this parent program at Burlington (Iowa) High School are:

- Students who could not previously afford to buy class rings or go on class trips are now able to do so.
- The program creates good will and publicity within the community.
- Parents who work closely with students come to realize that the majority of teens are kind and dedicated. This program has increased communication and understanding.

- The program serves as an excellent learning experience for students who are trained to work cooperatively and collaboratively with other students and adults, to accept responsibility, and to complete assigned tasks and obligations.
- The involvement of students with these supportive parents makes significant contributions to the positive perception of our school and the students within the community. (Upton 1995, 23)

The idea of family involvement in education is not new. The research indicates that meaningful family involvement is a powerful predictor of student achievement. Students with involved parents usually earn higher grades, have better attendance, complete more homework, are better motivated, and are less likely to be cited for disciplinary action. The findings are true for all racial and ethnic groups, socioeconomic levels, and parents' education differences (Henderson and Berla 1995).

However, there are many barriers to family involvement, including the following:

- Lack of teacher time and opportunity
- Teacher misperceptions of parents' abilities
- Lack of understanding of parents' communication styles
- Limited family resources
- Parents' lack of comfort
- Difficulties of involvement in upper grades (Caplan 2000, 3)

Collaboration between home and school occurs when parents and educators strive toward common goals, see each other as equals, and both contribute to the process (Christenson n.d.). Collaboration can begin by conducting a needs assessment, possibly surveying parents as to their satisfaction with current school programs and outreach efforts, and asking them to suggest changes in practice or additional programs (Caplan 1998).

Service learning has become an important way for students to connect to their communities, to create a balance between learning and living, and to cement the connections between learning and community. Students learn experientially when they apply newly learned skills to real situations.

For example, the traditional community service activity of collecting cans for a food drive was transformed into service learning when the event was connected to understanding the nutritional value of the foods the students collected, when students used graphing skills to chart the collection of food, learned about the issues of homelessness in the community, read relevant literature, and wrote about their insights. (Kinsley 1997, 3)

Unless some connection is established to the educational goals and objectives of the instructional program of the school, service such as a food drive does not automatically produce learning on the part of the student. In fact, its meaning may be lost.

Service learning is defined as a method during which students learn and develop through participation in organized community service experiences that meet real needs. Research indicates that we remember 10 percent of what we hear, 15 percent of what we see, and 20 percent of what we see and hear. Students retain 60 percent when they learn by doing, when they engage in service-learning activities. Retention increases to as much as 80 percent when a supervised reflection component accompanies the experience (Johnson 1996).

The practical experience of service learning often gets students more engaged in the material they are studying and leads them to a deeper understanding of course content.

How does this work in a school?

Our committee was responsible for informing students about what to bring in. First we called to set up a meeting with the director of a local shelter. She came to the school and we interviewed her to find out what food would be most helpful to the population she served. Before she came we had no idea that the shelter also distributed can openers, and that their stockpile was completely depleted! After that, we staged three informational presentations, sort of skits that we performed for students during lunch time. They were meant to catch everyone's attention, and present facts about people who are hungry or homeless in our community. Then we distributed flyers to the entire school with information we learned, and a pretty specific list about what to bring in. We collected more cans than in previous years, plus 135 can openers! Eight club members took the stuff over to the shelter. They stayed awhile to play with some of the children who were there. Afterwards, during our reflection session, someone mentioned how those little kids had just a few old books and games to keep them busy. So now we have a new project. We've met again with the director and are collecting and repairing books and games. And the shop class is building a bookshelf. (Kaye 1997, 2–3)

Positive changes occur when young people engage in service learning. It improves self-esteem, the cornerstone for ego development, leading to good mental health and a productive future (Krystal 1998–1999). It provides a balance between learning and living.

Nearly 100 Minnesota secondary schools currently offer community service-learning courses. Typically, students spend one or two periods each day, three or four days a week, at service placements. Placements include day care centers, nursing homes, hospitals, Head Start programs, English as a Second Language programs, hospices, schools, and programs for people with disabilities. One or two days a week students participate in class discussions and training on such topics as learning styles, discipline for young children, or Alzheimer's disease.

The power of these programs results from students' face-to-face service. Students serve more than 100 hours and truly get to know people in a variety of life situations. (Cairn and Cairn 1999, 67)

All good projects follow these seven steps:

1. Evaluate the need.
2. Develop goals based on evaluation of problems or activities for each project.
3. Develop a plan of action for each goal.
4. Communicate more.
5. Practice good human relations.
6. Publicize.
7. Evaluate your progress. Have an evaluation meeting and make written records. (Couch 1996, 23)

There are many social and service projects conducted by both middle school and high school students that benefit the community. An example would be the:

statewide service project of the Illinois Association Junior High Student Councils (IAJHSC). Each year, student councils in individual middle level schools throughout the state raise—by various means—and then pool their funds for the year's selected service project. Consequently, substantial contributions, totaling thousands of dollars, have been donated over the years by IAJHSC to children's hospitals, special camps for children with disabilities, childhood disease research, and other worthy causes. (McCracken 1998, 35)

In closing:

When I accompanied 14-year-old Justin Martin and a group of his fellow students to a nearby public school where they tutored 5th graders in reading, I witnessed the spiritual effects of service learning. Justin, a special education youngster, gawky and uncomfortable with his body, was involved in a Learning Helper Model, in which older youth read to young children. He and his peers had prepared diligently for the week's tutoring lesson because, as his teacher explained, "They don't want the 5th graders to know a word that they don't." (Krystal 1998–1999, 60)

"It's better than watching TV all the time or playing cards," Sylvia said, adding that she is very positively impressed by the students who have taken the time to teach her about computers. "I think they're awfully good. They're awfully patient because they're good at teaching us what we don't know. . . . The computer is a foreign language to people my age." (Lundt and Vanderpan 2000, 21)

6

WHAT IS THE DIFFERENCE BETWEEN EXTRACURRICULAR AND COCURRICULAR ACTIVITIES?

Student activities are a vital part of the school curriculum, which makes them "cocurricular." To term them "extra" diminishes their importance and places their continued existence in jeopardy. (Marano 1983)

The term *extracurricular* designates an activity program as distinct and separate from the curriculum and connotes a subordinate or inferior status in relation to the formal curriculum. Some states' legal statutes make reference to some of the activities as extracurricular (Marano 2000a). For those who view student activities as of equal importance to the academic components of the curriculum, the use of cocurricular is preferable. This term suggests that these activities are a legitimate part of the curriculum, with parallel yet separate roles for learning (Buss 1998).

Defining exactly what is meant by student activities in our secondary schools is not easy. However, the following statements have been used to define the student activities program and distinguish it from the formal curriculum:

- Students volunteer to participate.
- Students set the agenda and take responsibility for the activity.
- Teachers, counselors, or administrators act as advisors or guides.
- The activity typically does not bear academic credit.
- The activity occurs under the auspices of the school.
- Students normally meet after school or during open periods in the school schedule.
- The activity serves the social and personal developmental needs of youth. (Buss 1998, 85)

However, this list has limits in its ability to describe the student activity program. There are exceptions to the listing. For example, many activities are not self-directed; an advisor or coach sets rules, determines the agenda, and regulates participation. Are student activities the "third curriculum," along with the required and elective curriculum? Or are they the fourth curriculum, along with:

- General education, where students acquire core academic learnings that prepare them for citizenship in a democratic society;
- Specialized education that prepares students for a career or for higher education; or
- Exploratory, free electives that allow students to pursue an area of interest for personal or career purposes? (Buss 1998)

In 1961, James Coleman argued that extracurricular activities undermined the schools' academic goals. Ten years later, Robert Havighurst argued that schools should develop "self-governing adults"—a goal that lent support to the learnings gained through participation in student activities. He realized that the opportunities needed to accomplish this goal might not be available in the academic program. Holland and Andre (1987) support the use of developmental goals for schooling with participation in extracurricular activities as a means of achieving them (Lewis 1989). However, not all researchers agreed with Holland and Andre; B. Bradford Brown concluded in 1988 that "the strongest conclusion one can draw from existing research is that the effects of extracurricular participation on secondary school students' personal development and academic achievement are probably positive but very modest, and are definitely different among students with different social or intellectual backgrounds" (Lewis 1989, 4–5).

Yet, college admissions decisions often favor students who have participated in service or other worthwhile activities in high school. In fact, Harvard and Radcliffe place great value on students' nonacademic or cocurricular activities. "As it makes its decisions, the Admissions Committee looks carefully to see how each applicant has used time, and how attentively and how well he or she has developed academic and nonacademic talents" (Fitzsimmons and Lewis 1996, 18). Because students learn a great deal from each other, a class with diverse interests, abilities, and backgrounds is important for providing a stimulating environment. Typically, the vast majority of the applicants are academically qualified for Harvard and Radcliffe but only a small percentage can be admitted. While some students are admitted solely on the basis of their academic record, most who are admitted "usually present one or more cocurricular accomplishments that make them stand out as good matches for Harvard and Radcliffe" (Fitzsimmons and Lewis 1996, 18).

Students with serious cocurricular commitments use college resources other than the library, computer center, or other academic resources. This participation also helps define who they are for the admissions committee. "From noting participation in cocurricular activities, the Committee can learn a lot about a person's interests, energy level, drive, self-discipline and generally how well a candidate uses available opportunities" (Fitzsimmons and Lewis 1996, 19).

At the high school level, is participation in student activities viewed as critically as it is at Harvard and Radcliffe? One high school's beliefs are clear:

Broken Arrow High School students believe that quality education incorporated with an activities program is a right, a privilege, and the responsibility of each individual. We believe that in order to grow we must develop skills that enable us to be active in society. To develop those skills, we must have a strong educational foundation and a willing attitude. Life's experiences, along with the development of academic and career skills and identified community values, allow us to advance as individuals and as a school. To achieve these goals we must provide activities and organizations to enhance our talent and to build character. (Lannert 2000, 27)

The school's curriculum determines, to a large degree, the student activities that are offered. Every activity should have a link to at least one academic subject area. Table 6.1 provides an overview.

Restructuring the school day to allow for interdisciplinary teams, career path–related classes, and seminar period for advisement also benefits cocurricular activities. At Farmington High School (Missouri), these included "the development of a leadership course, access to participation in cocurricular activities during the school day, and the aligning of cocurricular organizations with career fields" (Waters and Waters 1997, 21). Students take five seventy-two-minute periods each day. Classes meet on alternate days with each student enrolled in nine classes and an advisement seminar.

> The leadership class which is open to any student has been a catalyst for positive changes in our school. . . . Some of these include Low Risk Involvement, Positive School Ownership, [and] Betterment of Student/Teacher/Administrator Relations. Alternate day 10-block scheduling has also allowed students to have access to participation in cocurricular activities during the school day. This has had an enormous impact on student involvement in career and service related clubs. Clubs that were almost extinct have been revitalized because meetings can now be held during the seminar/advisement period. (Waters and Waters 1997, 21–22)

However, block scheduling by semesters and club memberships that are not yearlong may result in reduced student participation (Mutter, Chase, and Nichols 1997).

If it is not possible to schedule a club/activities period during the school day, it may be possible to coordinate the cocurricular program through an organizational homeroom. At Lacey Township High School in Lanoka Harbor, New Jersey, "the administration and advisers developed a plan to maximize daily adviser/members contact without intruding on academic time by creating a homeroom comprised of the officers and advisers of the school's major organizations" (Van Dyk 1997, 37). The Student Government Association, the National Honor Society, and each of the four sets of class officers are also included in the homeroom and it meets in the school library. It was decided that group enrollment would be limited to thirty students. SGA president John Vircillo stated, "The organizational homeroom allows us to get work done faster and easier than if we worked alone. It allows us to unify our ideas, but divide the work load" (Van Dyk 1997, 38). The merger of different grade levels in the homeroom allows younger members to learn from more experienced officers. Over the last five years, this arrangement has allowed the school to coordinate and expand community service efforts in conjunction with the Rotary Club.

In many schools, the academic program is directly affected by student activities that motivate and recognize students. The following are examples:

- *Influencing Behavior*—a little extra incentive is sometimes needed to elicit desired behaviors from students. In an effort to encourage students to come to class on time, Lassen High School in Jamesville, California, sponsors a "No Tardy Party."
- *Academic Support*—many student groups sponsor tutoring programs for their students or students at a lower level. For example, the Eden Prairie (Minnesota) High School National

Table 6.1 Categories and Examples of Activities and Their Relationship to the Formal Curriculum

Activity Category	Examples	Curriculum Association
Governance	Student council, student senate, student judiciary	Social Studies
Cheerleading/pep club	Cheerleading squad, pep club, pom-pom groups	Physical education, music
Class	Future Business Leaders of America, Future Homemakers of America, Future Farmers of America, science club, math club, language clubs, etc.	Vocational programs and virtually all academic subjects
Hobby/leisure	Photography, chess, skiing, hiking, riding, skating clubs	Physical education, art
Athletic/sport	Interscholastic and intramural sports, basketball, baseball, softball, soccer, tennis, golf, swimming, track and field, letter clubs	Physical education
Music	Band, orchestra, chorus, marching bands, color guards, drum and bugle corps, twirlers, singing groups, etc.	Music
Speech/drama	School plays, class plays, debate teams, National Forensic League, National Thespian Society, production crews	Language arts (speech, theater)
Publications	Newspaper, yearbook, literary magazine, student handbooks	Language arts
Service	Audiovisual, library, student patrol, monitors, ushers, National Junior Red Cross, color guards, teacher/administrative assistants, ecology clubs, model United Nations	Variable
Social	Dances, YMCA, YWCA, HI-Y, Y-Teens	Variable
Honors	National Honor Society, Key Club, Quill and Scroll, foreign language honor societies	Variable (languages, social studies)
Special events days	Assemblies, awards programs, commencement, prom, pageants/festivals, trips, and tours	Variable

Source: Adapted from Gholson and Buser 1981, 44–45; Gholson and Buser 1983, 7–9; quoted in Buss 1998.

Honor Society has a list of tutors available for high school, middle level, and intermediate school students and parents.

- *Food Motivates*—students will often go to great lengths to obtain free food. Using that knowledge, the student council at Washington (Missouri) High School sponsors a Friday doughnut victory. Each first-period class that has had perfect attendance and no tardies for the week is treated to doughnuts on Friday morning. The National Honor Society at Linesville (Pennsylvania) High School organizes an academic luncheon each year in honor of all students who have made the honor roll at least once during the year.
- *Faculty Awards*—activity groups often involve faculty members in programs to recognize student efforts. A "Viking Pride" program at William Fremd High School recognizes students for such things as extra effort, assisting teachers and/or students, grade improvement, and other objectives. Departments are assigned certain months of the year and during that time, teachers in those departments recommend students for the "Viking Pride" award.
- *Borrowing from Athletics*—many ideas traditionally used to recognize athletes can be adapted to support the academic program. At West Bloomfield (Michigan) High School, students can earn an academic activity letter for continued involvement in the activity program and academic excellence. Students accumulate points toward their letter by participating in clubs and class spirit activities. There is also a progressive point structure for semester grade point averages.
- *Public Recognition*—at Fredonia High School, students who are nominated by teachers for things including good effort and grades are recognized through a "Wall of Stars" in the cafeteria commons area. (Fiscus 1999c, 17–21)

In summary, cocurricular activities are the key to any school's climate. To increase student participation, consider the following suggestions:

- Obtain background data. Students fail to participate in curriculum activities for a number of reasons.
- Develop and implement a strategy that is best suited for your individual school community. One strategy that has been most effective is the implementation of an in-school activity period. (Papagiotas 1998, 1)

Student participation in cocurricular activities increases when activity periods become part of the school schedule. As a consequence, students feel a greater affiliation with their school, which enhances student pride and creates a positive ethos for the entire school learning environment (Papagiotas 1998). Student activities groups show their own commitment to excellence by sponsoring activities that support the academic mission of the school. As the NASSP Department of Students Activities' motto suggests: "Activities + Academics = Excellence" (Fiscus 1999c, 21).

In closing:

A variety of terms have been used to identify and describe the more student-orientated positions of the school program. These include extracurricular, extra-school, noncurricular, semicurricular, paracurricular, cocurricular, the supplementary curriculum, the third curriculum, the other curriculum, school activities, and student activities. (Gholson and Buser 1983, v)

Bradley describes himself as "pretty much the standard West Point candidate," meaning he was no stranger to leadership positions even before he came to West Point. In his case that means captain of his high school football and baseball teams, student council president, and member of the National Honor Society. While the admissions office has no checklist of minimum achievements for a candidate, the academy does look for young men and women with "demonstrated leadership potential." Bradley was a good candidate for success on the day he walked in. In his three years at West Point he has worked his way up through positions of increasing responsibility, supervising anywhere from one to a handful of cadets. (Ruggero 2001, 21)

7

HOW CAN STUDENT
ACTIVITIES FULFILL
TODAY'S STANDARDS
FOR LEARNING?

T he current standards movement began in 1983 with the publication of *A Nation at Risk*, which decried the deficiencies in the national educational system. One outcome related directly to that report was the ratification of six national educational goals by the Bush administration in 1989. One of these goals mandated the development of challenging national achievement standards in five core areas (Berger 2000).

The five recommendations from the 1983 *A Nation at Risk* report were:

1. Strengthening high school graduation requirements
2. Raising the standards for academic performance and college admission
3. Increasing the length of the school day and/or school year, or more effective use of the existing day
4. Improving teacher education
5. Providing financial support and leadership to effect the proposed reforms (National Commission on Excellence 1983)

Standards or proficiencies help stakeholders agree on what is important in education, defining the essential learnings or outcomes students should develop. Whatever they are called, the following quote should serve as a guiding principle:

Education means to lead forth, but it is impossible to lead anyone anywhere without knowing where you want to go. If you do not know what you are trying to accomplish, you will not accomplish much. Content standards—what children are expected to learn—are necessary for educational improvement because they are the starting point for education. When educators fail to agree on what children should learn, it means that they have failed to identify their most fundamental goals. In the absence of such agreement by educators, decisions about what should be learned are left to the marketplace—textbook publishers, test makers, and interest groups. (Ravitch 1996, 134)

Efforts to establish essential learnings and corresponding standards for student performance should be guided by four questions:

1. What, specifically, is it that we want students to know and be able to do when they leave our school?
2. How well do we want them to know/do these things?
3. How will we know if students know and can do these things?
4. How will we redesign (restructure) schooling to better ensure that we will get the results we want? (Westerberg 1997, 5)

A school with high and consistent expectations for all students in all courses is considered to have standards. Standards provide a measure against which we can judge performance. In sports, a par of 72 on the golf course is such a standard. Being able to read, write, listen, and speak effectively on state assessments is another.

> Standards are upheld by the daily, local demand for quality and consistency at the tasks deemed important; standards are met by rigorous evaluation of *necessarily varied* student products and performances against those standards. . . . They are *specific* and guiding pictures of worthy goals. Real standards enable all performers to understand their *daily* work in terms of specific exemplars for the work in progress, and thus how to monitor and raise their standards. (Wiggins 1991, 19–20)

A standard is an ideal, a goal toward which everyone can strive and against which progress can be measured.

However, agreement on the use of standards in our schools is far from universal. The positive effects are as follows:

1. Standards serve to improve student achievement by clearly defining what is to be taught and what kind of performance is expected.
2. Standards are necessary to create equality of opportunity.
3. Standards serve to coordinate the functioning of a district.
4. Standards serve to refocus the efforts of an educational system on student learning.
5. Standards help ensure more consistency for students moving from district to district and from state to state.
6. Standards and their related assessments provide consumer protection by supplying more accurate and specific information to students and parents as student achievement progress.
7. Standards serve as a watermark for expectations.
8. Standards can help to create high expectations for students and accountability for those standards.
9. Standards serve to align instruction to curriculum. (Berger 2000, 59–60)

The reasons why others believe that standards-based reform will continue to fall short of its desired outcomes are as follows:

1. Student achievement is strong in some districts where standards-based reform is not present.
2. Top-down mandates are a poor way to effect real change.
3. Few educators truly understand how to undertake standards-based reform.
4. There is no clear consensus regarding the terms *standards* and *standards-based reform*.
5. Standards-based reform is unfair to minority populations and special needs learners.
6. There are differing ideas on "who decides" which standards are THE standards.
7. How do you effectively measure "student achievement"?
8. The process of developing standards, particularly state standards, is too politicized to be functional.
9. There is a lack of ability to hold schools truly accountable for engaging in this type of reform.
10. A focus on the enforcement of state standards from a regulatory perspective puts the focus on minimum levels of acceptable performance (looking down) versus a mode of implementing best practices (looking up) and does nothing to reinforce schools that want to better themselves.
11. Federal, state, and regional education agencies cannot meet the local school's demands for technical assistance on how to implement this type of reform. (Berger 2000, 60–62)

The standards question is ultimately twofold: What are the essential tasks worth mastering? And how good is good *enough* at those tasks? The former question concerns the quality of the *input*—the work that is given to students to do. The second question concerns *output*—what are the criteria student work must meet, and how demanding should the standards be? (Wiggins 1991, 23)

The best school has the smallest gap between the achievement of the strongest students and the weakest students.

The issue of excellence in U.S. schools has generated a great deal of discussion in public and private circles. Is the U.S. system ineffective, especially in comparison to international competitors? The critics argue:

- SAT scores have declined.
- The broad selection of courses available to students only serves to confuse them rather than to focus on rigorous academics.
- American students consistently rank poorly on tests administered to certain age groups when compared to students in other countries.
- Even comparison scores that show no change or only moderate improvement over the years are not sufficient to keep up with the demands of the twenty-first century.
- The business world frequently complains that students are not prepared to enter the workforce.
- Those who choose to ignore or reinterpret the data that support these findings are singing a song of complacency. (Wallinger 1999, 82)

Those who defend the U.S. school system do so based upon the following:

- The accepted SAT standard was set in 1941 by an elite group of test takers composed primarily of Northeastern white males destined for Ivy League colleges

- With regard to international assessments, the differences among scores is very small, but this leads to great differences among ranks.
- The discrepancy in performance of U.S. students as compared to their international counterparts reflects differences in the curricula and teaching strategies across countries.
- In some countries, a student is commended for being selected to take a test for the "honor" of his country.
- Since U.S. analysts have performed most of the sampling of international comparisons, they are able to regulate the U.S. control group to reflect a true distribution of the country's population (race, income level, and parent background).
- Rather than focusing on the school performance of our children, particularly in the areas of mathematics and science, we should be focusing on the output of our professionals who are the products of this system.
- We are a nation of immigrants whose public schools try to serve the entire population. (Wallinger 1999, 82–83)

"The standards movement in education strives to provide a national consensus on what students should know in content subjects. *Knowing* is not sufficient in itself—rather, students must apply knowledge to construct new understandings, to solve problems, to make decisions, to develop products, and to communicate" (Thomas and Knezek 1999, 27). The International Society for Technology (www.ISTE.org) developed the following technology foundation standards for all students:

1. Basic operations and concepts
   - Students demonstrate a sound understanding of the nature and operation of technology systems.
   - Students are proficient in the use of technology.

2. Social, ethical, and human issues
   - Students understand the ethical, cultural, and societal issues related to technology.
   - Students practice responsible use of technology systems, information, and software.
   - Students develop positive attitudes toward technology uses that support lifelong learning, collaboration, personal pursuits, and productivity.

3. Technology productivity tools
   - Students use technology tools to enhance learning, increase productivity, and promote creativity.
   - Students use productivity tools to collaborate in constructing technology-enhanced models, preparing publications, and producing other creative works.

4. Technology communications tools
   - Students use telecommunications to collaborate, publish, and interact with peers, experts, and other audiences.
   - Students use a variety of media and formats to communicate information and ideas effectively to multiple audiences.

5. Technology research tools
   - Students use technology to locate, evaluate, and collect information from a variety of sources.
   - Students use technology tools to process data and report results.
   - Students evaluate and select new information resources and technological innovations base on the appropriateness to specific tasks.

6. Technology problem-solving and decision-making tools
   - Students use technology resources for solving problems and making informed decisions.
   - Students employ technology in the development of strategies for solving problems in the real world (International Society for Technology 2000, 14–15)

In conjunction with these ISTE NETS standards, the National Educational Technology Standards Project developed profiles describing the technology competencies that students should exhibit upon the completion of four grade ranges (pre-K–grade 2, grades 3–5, grades 6–8, and grades 9–12). These technology competencies are divided into six categories:

1. Basic operations and concepts
2. Social, ethical, and human issues
3. Technology productivity tools
4. Technology communications tools
5. Technology research tools
6. Technology problem-solving and decision-making tools (International Society for Technology 2000, 15)

By the time a student completes high school, the standards for a technology-literate student indicate that he or she will:

1. Identify capabilities and limitations of contemporary and emerging technology resources and assess the potential of these systems and services to address personal, lifelong learning and workplace needs. (2)*
2. Make informed choices among technology systems, resources, and services. (1, 2)
3. Analyze advantages and disadvantages of widespread use and reliance on technology in the workplace and in society as a whole. (2)
4. Demonstrate and advocate for legal and ethical behaviors among peers, family, and community regarding the use of technology and information. (2)
5. Use technology tools and resources for managing and communicating personal/professional information (e.g., finances, schedules, addresses, purchases, correspondence). (3, 4)
6. Evaluate technology-based options, including distance and distributed education, for lifelong learning. (5)

---

* Numbers in parentheses following each performance indicator refer to the standards category to which the performance is linked.

7. Routinely and efficiently use online information resources to meet needs for collaboration, research, publications, communications, and productivity. (4, 5, 6)
8. Select and apply technology tools for research, information analysis, problem solving, and decision making in content learning. (4, 5)
9. Investigate and apply expert systems, intelligent agents, and simulations in real-world situations. (3, 5, 6)
10. Collaborate with peers, experts, and others to contribute to a content-related knowledge base by using technology to compile, synthesize, produce, and disseminate information, models, and other creative works. (4, 5, 6)

In order to reach higher standards, many school districts have restructured their school programs and school day. In 1984, Lubbock High School (Texas) instituted a four-day academic week with a half-day "Activity Friday" program (Cates 2000). Whenever possible, field trips and music, dance, and other performances are scheduled for Fridays so that students will not miss their academic classes. "Activity Friday" classes provide excellent experiential learning opportunities for all students and appeal to a wide range of student needs and interests, although they do not count as credit toward graduation. Friday homeroom is one of the most constructive aspects of this schedule. Activities such as class meetings, student course scheduling, all school assemblies, pep rallies, student elections, school projects, fine arts performances, guest speakers, as well as all noninstructional student activities and assemblies are scheduled during homeroom period. Academic classes are not interrupted for student council and cheerleader elections, counselor information assemblies, talent shows, pep rallies, dance recitals, and other assemblies. Many Lubbock High School students volunteer with community agencies on Fridays and they report directly to their respective agencies rather than the school to fulfill their four-hour attendance requirement (Cates 2000). Many other schools have also implemented various forms of block or alternative schedules to assist in the scheduling of student activities so academic classes are not interrupted.

When learner outcomes are defined, three questions need to be answered:

1. Upon completion of high school, what should students know?
2. What should students be able to do? and
3. What should students feel or believe? (Fitzpatrick 1991, 18)

The exit outcomes for students in Township High School District 214 in Arlington Heights, Illinois, are:

- ability to communicate (in reading, writing, speaking, listening, and numeracy skills);
- facility in social interaction;
- analytic capabilities;
- problem-solving skills;
- skill in making value judgments and decisions;
- skill in creative expression and responding to the creative work of others;
- civic responsibility;
- responsible participation in a global environment;
- skill in developing and maintaining wellness;

- skill in using technology as a tool for learning;
- skill in life and career planning. (Fitzpatrick 1991, 18–19)

The key question is, have students achieved the exit outcomes as defined by the school district? There is no mention of when and at what level those exist outcomes have been achieved. All fifty states now have some form of statewide testing program in addition to individual school district requirements for graduation. New York State currently employs a combination of multiple choice, short answer, and essay questions at the elementary, middle, and high school levels. New York State has adopted specific standards for elementary, middle, and secondary students in four core academic subjects—English, math, science, and social studies (Heiser 2001). However, there is some concern that lower-achieving students won't be able to meet the standards and will not receive a high school diploma. By 2004, New York will require all high school students to complete twenty-two high school credits and pass five Regents exams in order to receive a high school diploma (Wilson 2001). New York, as well as a few other states, have set timelines for the implementation of these new graduation requirements.

Passing a Regents exam was first required of the graduating class of 2000 in order to receive a diploma. The results, however, were cause for concern.

> While 97 percent passed the English Regents, they did so in a year when the passing grade for the test was set at 55. About 15 percent of those who passed the test scored between 55 and 64, which in years to come, will be a failing grade. Students who entered ninth grade for the first time in the fall of 2000 must score 65 on their Regents exam to graduate. (Wilson 2001, 29)

In order to be useful, standardized tests must be authentic. Multiple-choice standardized tests are suspect as to their usefulness, validity, and authenticity. Authentic achievement is optimally represented through projects, reports, and portfolios that demonstrate mastery, engage students' imaginations, and help them meet course standards. According to Bonstingl (2001), "It is sensible that tests and other assessment instruments are used to gather information about how well our students are learning, so educators can use this information to more effectively teach for understanding and real world application. But most standardized tests do not give teachers and their students this essential feedback" (Bonstingl 2001, 13).

Traditional tests ask, "What do you know?" John Dewey advocated for experiential learning through conducting field studies, community involvement, and projects. The legacy of that tradition can be seen in community service and civic projects, such as reading to the blind and cleaning up neighborhood graffiti (Fogarty 1999). Howard Gardner views intelligence as multidimensional. According to this framework, the ability to solve problems involves using eight realms: verbal, logical, spatial, musical, kinesthetic, interpersonal, intrapersonal, and naturalist (Fogarty 1999). Therefore, there are many ways of knowing about the world and making personal meaning, but also in recognizing that there are many ways of expressing what students know and are able to do. Life in school is not just preparation for life, it *is* life. Students must learn to effectively use their intelligence in school because they spend much time there (Sternberg, Okagaki, and Jackson 1990).

In younger children,

> research conducted in the last 10 years suggests that one source of the differences between the highest- and lowest-achieving children is the degree to which they become self-regulators of their

own learning. High-achieving students engage in a number of strategic skills, including goal setting, planning, self-interrogating, self-monitoring (checking answers), asking for help, using aids, and using memory strategies. (Biemiller and Meichenbaum 1992, 75)

Teachers can help individual students attain mastery and expertise by observing how they approach tasks and giving them tasks appropriate to their abilities, while refraining from the urge to "think for" less self-directed learners. However, all students need to prepare for the transition from school to workplace. In the workplace, they must be prepared to learn using the strategies developed during their school years.

New York State has defined student learning and standards in seven disciplines. They are:

English Language Arts

Standard 1: *Language for Information and Understanding*. Students will listen, speak, read, and write for information and understanding. As listeners and readers, students will collect data, facts, and ideas; discover relationships, concepts, and generalizations; and use knowledge generated from oral, written, and electronically produced texts. As speakers and writers, they will use oral and written language that follows the accepted conventions of the English language to acquire, interpret, apply, and transmit information.

Standard 2: *Language for Literary Response and Expression*. Students will read and listen to oral, written, and electronically produced texts and performances from American and world literature; relate texts and performances to their own lives; and develop an understanding of the diverse social, historical, and cultural dimensions the texts and performances represent. As speakers and writers, students will use oral and written language that follows the accepted conventions of the English language for self-expression and artistic creation.

Standard 3: *Language for Critical Analysis and Evaluation*. Students will listen, speak, read, and write for critical analysis and evaluation. As listeners and readers, students will analyze experiences, ideas, information, and issues presented by others using a variety of established criteria. As speakers and writers, they will use oral and written language that follows the accepted conventions of the English language to present, from a variety of perspectives, their opinions and judgments on experiences, ideas, information, and issues.

Standard 4: *Language for Social Interaction*. Students will listen, speak, read, and write for social interaction. Students will use oral and written language that follows the accepted conventions of the English language for effective social communication with a wide variety of people. As readers and listeners, they will use the social communications of others to enrich their views.

Mathematics, Science and Technology

Standard 1: *Analysis, Inquiry, and Design*. Students will use mathematical analysis, scientific inquiry, and engineering design, as appropriate, to pose questions, seek answers, and develop solutions.

Standard 2: *Information Systems*. Students will access, generate, process, and transfer information using appropriate technologies.

Standard 3: *Mathematics*. Students will understand mathematics and become mathematically confident by communicating and reasoning mathematically, by applying mathematics in real-world settings, and by solving problems through the integrated study of number systems, geometry, algebra, data analysis, probability, and trigonometry.

Standard 4: *Science*. Students will understand and apply scientific concepts, principles, and theories pertaining to the physical setting and living environment and recognize the historical development of ideas in science.

Standard 5: *Technology*. Students will apply technological knowledge and skills to design, construct, use, and evaluate products and systems to satisfy human and environmental needs.

Standard 6: *Interconnectedness: Common Themes*. Students will understand the relationships and common themes that connect mathematics, science, and technology and apply the themes to these and other areas of learning.

Standard 7: *Interdisciplinary Problem Solving*. Students will apply the knowledge and thinking skills of mathematics, science, and technology to address real-life problems and make informed decisions.

Social Studies

Standard 1: *History of the United States and New York*. Students will use a variety of intellectual skills to demonstrate their understanding of major ideas, eras, themes, developments, and turning points in the history of the United States and New York.

Standard 2: *World History*. Students will use a variety of intellectual skills to demonstrate their understanding of major ideas, eras, themes, developments, and turning points in world history and examine the broad sweep of history from a variety of perspectives.

Standard 3: *Geography*. Students will use a variety of intellectual skills to demonstrate their understanding of the geography of the interdependent world in which we live—local, national, and global—including the distribution of people, places, and environments over the Earth's surface.

Standard 4: *Economics*. Students will use a variety of intellectual skills to demonstrate their understanding of how the United States and other societies develop economic systems and associated institutions to allocate scarce resources, how major decision-making units function in the United States and other national economies, and how an economy solves the scarcity problem through market and nonmarket mechanisms.

Standard 5: *Civics, Citizenship, and Government*. Students will use a variety of intellectual skills to demonstrate their understanding of the necessity for establishing governments; the governmental system of the United States and other nations; the United States Constitution; the basic civic values of American constitutional democracy; and the roles, rights, and responsibilities of citizenship, including avenues of participation.

The Arts

Standard 1: *Creating, Performing, and Participating in the Arts*. Students will actively engage in the processes that constitute creating and performing in the arts (dance, music, theater, and visual arts) and participate in various roles in the arts.

Standard 2: *Knowing and Using Arts Materials and Resources*. Students will be knowledgeable about and make use of the materials and resources available for participation in the arts in various roles.

Standard 3: *Responding to and Analyzing Works of Art*. Students will respond critically to a variety of works in the arts, connecting the individual work to other works and to other aspects of human endeavor and thought.

Standard 4: *Understanding the Cultural Contributions of the Arts*. Students will develop an understanding of the personal and cultural forces that shape artistic communication and how the arts, in turn, shape the diverse cultures of past and present society.

Health, Physical Education, and Home Economics

Standard 1: *Personal Health and Fitness*. Students will have the necessary knowledge and skills to establish and maintain physical fitness, participate in physical activity, and maintain personal health.

Standard 2: *A Safe and Healthy Environment*. Students will acquire the knowledge and ability necessary to create and maintain a safe and healthy environment.

Standard 3: *Resource Management*. Students will understand and be able to manage their personal and community resources.

Languages Other Than English

Standard 1: *Communication Skills*. Students will be able to use a language other than English for communication.

Standard 2: *Cultural Understanding*. Students will develop cross-cultural skills and understandings.

Career Development and Occupational Studies

Standard 1: *Career Development*. Students will be knowledgeable about the world of work; explore career options; and relate personal skills, aptitudes, and abilities to future career decisions.

Standard 2: *Integrated Learning*. Students will demonstrate how academic knowledge and skills are applied in the workplace and other settings.

Standard 3a: *Universal Foundation Skills*. Students will demonstrate mastery of the foundation skills and competencies essential for success in the workplace.

Standard 3b: *Career Majors*. Students who choose a career major will acquire the career-specific technical knowledge/skills necessary to progress toward gainful employment, career advancement, and success in postsecondary programs. (New York State Education Department n.d.)

New York's revised learning standards place a clear emphasis on helping students develop problem-solving abilities and independent thinking skills. When these skills and abilities are combined with content knowledge, students should be able to identify and solve real problems. The strategy for raising standards includes three elements:

1. Setting clear, high expectations/standards for *all* students and developing an effective means of assessing student progress in meeting the standards;
2. Building the local capacity of schools/districts to enable *all* students to meet standards; and
3. Making public the results of the assessment of student progress through school reports (New York State Education Department n.d., 4).

The Career Development and Occupational Studies Learning Standard 3a is "demonstrate mastery of the foundation skills and competencies essential for success in the workplace" (State University of New York and the State Education Department 1996). This workplace goal is defined as follows:

Basic Skills—Basic skills include the ability to read, write, listen, and speak as well as perform arithmetical and mathematical functions.

Thinking Skills—Thinking skills lead to problem solving, experimenting, and focused observation and allow the application of knowledge to new and unfamiliar situations.

Personal Qualities—Personal qualities generally include competence in self management and the ability to plan, organize, and take independent action.

Interpersonal Skills—Positive interpersonal qualities lead to teamwork and cooperation in large and small groups in family, social, and work situations.

Technology—Technology is the process and product of human skill and ingenuity in designing and creating things from available resources to satisfy personal and societal needs and wants.

Managing Information—Information management focuses on the ability to access and use information obtained from other people, community resources, and computer networks.

Managing Resources—Using resources includes the application of financial and human factors, and the elements of time and materials to successfully carry out a planned activity.

Systems—System skills include the understanding of and ability to work within natural and constricted systems. (State University of New York and the State Education Department 1996, 6–9)

Students who have acquired the foundation skills and competencies listed above will become workers able to perform at higher levels. These workplace competencies and skills are also important for improving student performance. Technology will continue to bring rapid change in the workplace and students and workers will be required to regularly learn new skills and develop new competencies. These skills are not occupation specific but are broader and more general, mainly involving interpersonal and problem-solving capabilities, as well as the need for teamwork, among project-based groups. Table 7.1 itemizes the characteristics of the modern workplace.

Recently, the New York Association of Training and Employment Professionals (NYATEP) conducted a survey of over 2,500 employers throughout New York State. They wished to identify the skills and competencies that employees must already possess or acquire prior to employment. Table 7.2 ranks the top ten responses from the New York State Employer Survey.

In 1956, Benjamin Bloom and a group of educational psychologists developed a taxonomy of learning. It classified levels of intellectual behavior that are important in learning. This classification includes three overlapping domains: the cognitive, psychomotor, and affective.

Cognitive learning involves recall of knowledge and intellectual skills, such as comprehending information, organizing ideas, analyzing and synthesizing data, applying knowledge, choosing among alternatives in problem-solving, and evaluating ideas or actions. Bloom identified six levels (Table 7.3) within the cognitive domain, which are arranged in a hierarchy and range from recall or recognition of facts to evaluation (Bloom 1956).

The Illinois Learning Standards contain a section for each standard, called "Applications of Learning." Five cross-disciplinary abilities are discussed as they apply to the learning area.

Through Applications of Learning, students demonstrate and deepen their understanding of basic knowledge and skills. These applied learning skills cross academic disciplines and reinforce the important learning of the disciplines. The ability to use these skills will greatly influence students' success in school, in the workplace and in the community. (Illinois State Board of Education 1997, 2)

The five cross-disciplinary abilities are as follows:

Solving Problems: Recognize and investigate problems; formulate and propose solutions supported by reason and evidence.

Communicating: Express and interpret information and ideas.

Using Technology: Use appropriate instruments, electronic equipment, computers, and networks to access information, process ideas, and communicate results.

Table 7.1   The Characteristics of Today's and Tomorrow's Workplace

Traditional Model	*High Performance Model*
STRATEGY	
• Mass production	• Flexible production
• Long production runs	• Customized production
• Centralized control	• Decentralized control
PRODUCTION	
• Fixed automation	• Flexible automation
• End-of-line quality control	• Online quality control
• Fragmentation of tasks	• Work teams, multiskilled workers
• Authority vested in supervisor	• Authority delegated to workers
HIRING AND HUMAN RESOURCES	
• Labor-management confrontation	• Labor-management cooperation
• Minimal qualifications accepted	• Screening for basic skills abilities
• Workers as a cost	• Workforce as an investment
JOB LADDERS	
• Internal labor market	• Limited internal labor market
• Advancement by seniority	• Advancement by certified skills
TRAINING	
• Minimal for production workers	• Training sessions for everyone
• Specialized for craft workers	• Broader skills sought
CONTENT	
• Teacher assigns topics	• Ill-defined problems are worked through
• Text reveals everything discovered	• Text tells what the reader needs to know
LOGIC	
• Theoretical; "academic."	• Problem-solving, pragmatic, goal-oriented
CORRECTNESS	
• Usage, handwriting, spelling and punctuation are a focus for evaluation, accounting for 50–100 percent of a document's value.	• Same factors are a given, not a focus for evaluation

Source: Competing in the New International Economy, Washington D.C.: Office of Technology Assessment, 1990, developed by Fort Worth Public Schools, Fort Worth, Texas, as published in New York State Education Department n.d., 3.

Table 7.2   Results from the New York State Employer Survey

ANALYSIS OF DATA *Must Know to Begin/Must Know to Advance*	Percent Responses Statewide
1. Foundation Skills: Personal Qualities Can be trusted; recognizes when faced with making honest/dishonest decisions based on values; understands the impact of violating organizational beliefs and chooses an ethical course of action.	97.4
2. Competencies: Interpersonal Skills Works cooperatively with others.	94.4
3. Foundation Skills: Personal Qualities Demonstrates understanding of personal appearance (i.e., clean clothing/uniform) and hygiene (e.g., washed and styled hair, clean teeth) appropriate for industry/company policy; wears appropriate clothing/uniform and maintains personal hygiene regularly.	93.7
4. Foundation Skills: Basic Skills Receives, interprets, and responds appropriately to verbal messages and other clues such as body language: (e.g., to comprehend, to learn, to critically evaluate, to appreciate, or to support the speaker).	88.3
5. Foundation Skills: Personal Qualities Demonstrates understanding, friendliness, adaptability, empathy, and politeness in new and ongoing group settings; asserts self in familiar and unfamiliar social situations	87.6
6. Foundation Skills: Personal Qualities Exerts a high level of effort and perseverance toward goal attainment; works to become excellent at doing tasks even when assigned an unpleasant task.	85.7
7. Foundation Skills: Personal Qualities Believes in own self-worth and maintains a positive view of self; demonstrates knowledge of own skills and abilities	83.5
8. Foundation Skills: Basic Skills Communicates thoughts and key information in writing; records information completely and accurately.	82.0
9. Foundation Skills: Basic Skills Organizes ideas and speaks clearly; communicates appropriately to listeners and situations; participates in conversations, discussion, and group presentations; asks questions when needed.	81.1
10. Competencies: Interpersonal Skills Exhibits appropriate behavior when dealing with clients.	80.6

Source: New York State Education Department n.d., 4.

Working on Teams: Learn and contribute productively as individuals and as members of groups.
Making Connections: Recognize and apply connections of important information and ideas within and among learning areas. (Illinois State Board of Education 1997, 2–3)

However, it is not enough to have strong standards alone. Standards must have assessments that measure what the schools expect in order for the success of standards-based school improvement.

Schools that demand more from students agree that raising standards cannot be the only strategy for improving student achievement. It must be part of a wide-ranging program of educational

Table 7.3   The Taxonomy of Learning

Learning Level	The Student Is Expected to:	Descriptive Words Often Used
#1: Knowledge Knowledge of: • Specifics • Ways or means of dealing with specifics • The universals and abstractions in a field	√ Remember an idea phenomenon, or a fact in somewhat the same form in which he/she learned it.	List Choose Find Label Select Match Name Show Identify Define
#2: Comprehension Comprehension through: • Translation • Interpretation • Extrapolation	√ Communicate an idea or thing (event) in a new or different form (translation) √ See relationship among things. It may also mean qualifying ideas in relation to one's own experiences (interpretation) √ Project the effect of things (extrapolation)	Reword Describe Explain Outline Propose Calculate Change
#3: Application Application through: • The use of abstract forms in concrete situations • Abstractions in the form of general ideas, rules, or procedures	√ Use what he/she knows (data) from a variety of areas to find solutions to problems √ Relate or apply ideas to new or unusual situations	Relate Utilize Solve Operate Demonstrate Manipulate Apply Illustrate Investigate
#4: Analysis Analysis focuses on: • Elements • Relationships • Organizational principles	√ Break "things" down into their component parts. √ Uncover the unique characteristics of a "thing"	Examine Analyze Compare Differentiate Assess Contrast
#5: Synthesis Synthesis through: • Communication in a unique way • The development of a plan or proposition of a set of operations • The development of a set of abstract relations (to hypothesize)	√ Think creatively (divergently) √ Make or create new or original "things" √ Take "things" and pattern them in a new way	Create Reorganize Develop Construct Generate Predict

#6: Evaluation Evaluation in terms of: • Internal standards • External criteria	√ Make judgments about "things" based on either external or internal conditions or criteria √ Rate ideas, conditions, objects, etc. √ Accept or reject "things" based on standards	Rate Prioritize Determine Classify Evaluate Critique

Source: From table of contents, Part 2: *The Taxonomy and Illustrative Methods*, Benjamin S. Bloom Taxonomy of Educational Objectives, Book 1: Cognitive Domain (New York: Allyn and Bacon), as published in New York State Education Department n.d., 9–10.

approaches that include comprehensive support services for students. Educators are renewing their efforts to attract parents into the school community. Schools are promoting parental involvement in several ways, including school visits, developing programs designed for parents, encouraging communication with teachers, helping students with career and college plans, promoting parental volunteer programs, helping parents establish discipline or homework guidelines, and allowing participation in school decision-making committees. Schools receive many benefits from parental involvement; most important, parental involvement in their children's education appears to improve academic achievement (Visher and Hudis 1999).

Even if there were agreement as to standards and even if the assessments were good ones, there is still doubt that what schools teach is applicable in the wider world. Are students able to solve genuine math problems that relate to real-world situations? Isn't it more important for schools to teach what adults need to know? Students should be taught how to gather and manipulate information, how to cooperate, and how to communicate, because these are skills that all adults need (Merrow 2001).

The skills emphasized in leadership classes (and student activities) are also part of some states' standards. For example,

> New Jersey's standards ask that students "use critical thinking, decision-making, and problem-solving skills." Alaska's Department of Education says, "Students need skills in working on teams, in problem solving about their work, in recognizing quality work." Performance goals in Missouri state that "students in Missouri public schools will acquire the knowledge and skills to recognize and solve problems" and "students in Missouri public schools will acquire the knowledge and skills to make decisions and act as responsible members of society." (Bloomstran 2001b, 5)

Maryland became the first state to require students to perform service in order to graduate from high school. Over the past fifteen years, Maryland developed a strong support system for service learning. As defined by the Maryland Student Service Alliance, service learning implies that there will be a substantial increase in the percentage of students who demonstrate the ability to reason, solve problems, apply knowledge, and communicate effectively. Students will be involved in activities that promote and express good citizenship as well as community service and service learning. In addition, students will become knowledgeable about the cultural heritages of the world. Maryland's service learning requirement reads:

> Students shall complete one of the following: (1) 75 hours of student service that includes preparation, action, and reflection components, and that, at the discretion of the local school system, may

begin during middle grades; and (2) a locally designed program in student service that has been approved by the state superintendent of schools." (Finney 1997, 37)

Students' learning is heightened when they realize that their actions have value to the people they serve or the organization they assist. For example, assuming responsibility for improving the nutritional status of senior citizens is more educational than merely serving them lunch. The key is responsibility. The more responsibility students are given for activities that have real consequences, the greater the likelihood that they will take the tasks seriously and learn effectively (Shumer 1997). Florida students who participated in service learning showed improvements in attendance, conduct, and academic performance (Follman and Muldoon 1997).

How can student activities fulfill today's standards for learning? Consider the following responses:

The benefits of participating in student activities reach far beyond the social benefits one generally associates with involvement in an activity. Skills that are typically developed and used through student activity participation include *time management, organization, problem solving, communication*, and others. These are the very skills that students need to draw upon to successfully meet increased standards for completion of high school. Let's look at these one by one:

Time Management: In order to be a group member or leader in one or more student activities, students need to be aware of how much time is involved in addition to the basic logistics of keeping a schedule. Students learn quickly when an activity meets and generally for how long. The fact that they are now a part of a group, having chosen to operate out of isolation in an activity, makes them more conscious that their presence or absence will be noted by other members and the advisor. Therefore, they will be more likely to show up for a meeting or activity. This ability to be aware of "time" in the form of scheduling and the amount needed for an activity transfers to every aspect of a student's life. Today's educational standards are higher than ever and require more than just mastering an increased level of difficulty in a subject area; they require more material being mastered. In New York State, students must be successful in additional content material in math, science, and foreign language. Not only has the content become more difficult but there is more to master. The ability to manage time is a learned skill, accomplished by practice. Therefore, being involved in student activities and practicing that skill enables one to gain useful practice.

Organization: Organization is also a skill that is developed through student activity participation. To be a member of a group or a leader, students have certain responsibilities. Not only are students expected to participate but in varying degrees will be required to fulfill a purpose in that group. If a student is expected to call a local business to rent a room for the prom and forgets to do so in a timely manner, the whole prom may be jeopardized. Knowing this task has to be done in a certain time frame forces the student to be organized in his or her thinking and actions, remembering to place the call, and then placing it. This skill also transfers to the academic arena. To be successful in mastering today's standards, which are more in number and in complexity of material, the student needs to be increasingly aware of the requirements in each of his subjects and organize even more within each subject area. Teachers and students are under increased pressure to master more in the same amount of time. Being organized is an essential skill.

Problem solving: Within the framework of a student activity, there are many issues that require attention. Some of these issues are: Who does what? When are these activities accomplished? How much will these activities cost? What supplies are needed? These are only some of the many "problems" to be solved. In order to solve these problems, students need to know how to look at a situation positively, know how to break down a problem into manageable pieces, and know how to work with others in solving a problem. These skills are essential in meeting higher standards. As material in each subject becomes more complex and if a student is now required to show mastery in a subject that is extremely difficult, the ability to solve problems is essential. A good example is the New York State requirement of a year of study in foreign language. Many students have been able to avoid this requirement by substituting other subjects. However, this is now a graduation requirement that will present a challenge for many students. This will definitely require a positive approach; the breakdown of the subject in manageable pieces and accepting help from others—all problem-solving approaches.

Communication: This is an essential skill necessary not only for success in student activities but in the classroom. If good communication skills are lacking, the road to success will be very difficult. A student can possess intellect, athletic ability, excellent technical skills, and any number of other positive attributes, but without strong communication skills, success will be elusive. The reason for this is that our society has become a global community—one that not only requires a command of the English language but the ability to communicate with those of a different culture and viewpoint. This not only means the command of a second language but the willingness to reach out and share ideas, express problems, and work well with those of opposing views. Being a part of a student activity program greatly enhances a student's ability to develop this important skill.

There are many other skills that are developed in student activity programs that translate into an increased ability to meet the higher educational standards of today's schools. Research shows that participation in student activities also develops lifelong abilities that help individuals become contributing members of the community and the world. Today, where the world is now our backyard for better or for worse, individuals need to be able to contribute to a complex, multicultural, highly technological society, in ways that will solve problems of great magnitude. We need to prepare students of today for the highly complex world that needs thoughtful, problem solving, collaborative individuals to keep our world safe and at peace. Student activities provide the forum in which these skills can be developed.

—Jan D'Onofrio
New Hartford High School

How can student activities fulfill today's standard for learning? Just as at one time student activities were referred to as "extra" curricular, because they indeed seemed "extra"—an addition to the school's program—today the term "cocurricular" best describes the vast activity offerings at schools because they complement school programs. It is not a coincidence that the name change corresponds to the changing face of student activities and the direct connection to student learning.

Let's look at athletic programs. When I first entered the field of education, being a member of a sports team was just that—the athlete was on a team and hoped for as much playing time as possible. Today, as the public cries for schools to offer a strong character education, athletic leadership programs are offered as an adjunct to athletic skill development.

The vast array of club offerings are more closely tied to a school's curriculum than ever before. Writing for the newspaper and working on the school's yearbook used to be natural extensions of the English curriculum. Opportunities for "reporting" and captioning pictures allowed for student expression. Today, creative writing clubs and book clubs help fulfill standards for learning. They provide a solid academic venue for writing, critiquing, creativity and group expression.

Students interested in math join math clubs that spend the vast majority of the time preparing for competitions. Students interested in science join science groups such as Science Olympiad, where they build bridges out of Popsicle sticks and enter their bridges in competitions. Foreign language clubs help prepare students for national competitions. Student governments prepare students to participate in state-level leadership programs.

When did this evolution begin? And why? Is it necessary? When did clubs cease being "fun" and become directly tied to curriculum and competitions? Is this a positive trend? Are schools focusing too much on "standards" and not enough on children?

Are there easy answers to these questions? Not really. The reality is that there is more to learn today—and new ways of learning. The fact is, if we don't offer activities that supplement and enhance what we teach during the day, we may not be getting the job done. As an example, the instruction and practice available during a routine computer club meeting enables students to better use the technology in core subjects.

In my opinion, student government and community service clubs are other examples of student activities that support standards for learning. Understanding the role of compassion, honesty, goal setting, responsibility, integrity, and risk taking are but a few of the elements that are integral to successful classroom performance. In addition, the importance of teaching the skills necessary to work in teams and cooperative groups are addressed in government and community service clubs.

Perhaps an overlooked component of an activity that supports standards for learning is the "relationship"—that is, the relationship between students and their teachers, advisors, deans, counselors, and administrators. Are not those conversations sprinkled with support for what the students are doing in the classroom?

The little red schoolhouse is gone. The intact family is in crisis. Even the most ardent supporters of the "basics" realize the new responsibilities facing schools today. No longer seen as "fluff," student activities are a vital part of the educational process. That's simply the way it is today.

—Marsha Hirsch
Pembroke Hill School

One of the constant debates and issues of contention within my school is the participation of students in cocurricular activities. As is the case in many school districts, there are a number of teachers who believe their courses are sacred and any interruption or instance in which students miss their class is an abomination. The mere suggestion of absence from chemistry class to attend a student council conference of all things is practically criminal. They protest "I cannot afford to give up even one minute of my class if I am to prepare them for the state exam. Don't you know there is a new test? There are new state standards, you know, and it's my duty to prepare these students. We already have too many interruptions as it is. Isn't this supposed to be a place that focuses on academics?" I sometimes think these teachers get together and develop a script! My answer is simple. Yes, I do know there are new state standards and I am attempting to assist students in meeting these standards in my cocurricular organizations which are absolutely academically focused.

The first dispute I often have with these valued colleagues—who, by the way, are outstanding teachers—is that student activities are not extracurricular clubs. They should not be regarded as something that is an extra part of the student's day. They should not be something that is considered outside of the curriculum. Rather, they are cocurricular activities that richly supplement and reinforce classroom instruction. If properly implemented and utilized, student activities are not extra at all. They are as important to the educational process as any chemistry lecture or experiment. And, the student activities will assist the chemistry teacher in producing highly effective lessons. I believe classroom instruction and student activities must be designed to be symbiotic rather than mutually exclusive of one another.

Educators have undoubtedly been inundated with the standards movement. In my own school, we are expected to address New York State Learning Standards, Standards of Excellence, SCANS skills, Goals 2000, and our own district goals. As new federal standards are implemented, even more learning standards will be part of our educational planning. At first glance, it certainly seems over-whelming for teachers. Classroom teachers are justifiably concerned with interruptions to their instruction. What they fail to understand, however, is that student activities play a major role in fulfilling standards for learning. It is not classroom instruction alone that meets these standards. In fact, when carefully analyzing learning standards, one will find that cocurricular activities satisfy a host of standards. What better experience to meet a standard of citizenship and responsibility than involvement in an active student leadership organization such as student council or National Honor Society? These activities teach skills such as effective public speaking and other English language arts proficiencies, a multitude of social studies skills, as well as opportunities for cultural exchanges and other experiences directly related to learning standards. In addition, student activities address activities closely related to character education and service learning that are an imperative component of the various learning standards. Student activities are critical to educating the whole student. Standards of learning are intended to produce students with certain skills and proficiencies. Student activities are some of the most effective tools educators can utilize to meet standards and produce outstanding, productive graduates. Now all we need to do is convince the chemistry teacher!

—Jason Andrews
Windsor Central High School

In closing:

Students are more likely to acquire the habits of responsibility when staff members build into the academic program, the extracurricular program, and the various mechanisms of institutional support an abundance of opportunities for youngsters to learn, through practice, what it means to be an ethical person and to be a member of an ethical community. (Starratt 1994, 60)

In leadership class, students learn from actually planning student activities. (Lenz 1997a, 21)

The Board of Education recognizes that the fundamental task of schools is to prepare young people for life. In order for this preparation to be done properly, the educational program of the schools must be as wide as life itself. (New York State Education Department 1999, 34)

8

HOW DO SPORTS AND ATHLETICS FIT?

Before the match, one newspaper wrote that Karelin was a 2,000-to-1 favorite to beat Rulon Gardner. Few argued. Karelin was the three-time defending Olympic gold medal winner in the super heavyweight division (286 pounds) of Greco-Roman wrestling. He was unbeaten in the previous 13 years and had not been scored upon in over 10 years. (Berkow 2001)

Rulon Gardner is a graduate of the University of Nebraska and teaches school in Wyoming.

"I had a learning disability," Gardner said. "People were always telling me that I wasn't good enough: "You're not going to make it in junior college, then four year college." Then, "You're not going to get your degree." People were always putting restrictions on me, or trying to. I don't think they were being mean. They were just being honest, as they saw it. But I never listened to those people. I might have. Coming from a small town, the rest of the world looked very big. It was a big event if we were able to get to Salt Lake City once a year. But I was very competitive. I just kept giving myself opportunities in difficult situations. (Berkow 2001)

Gardner's path to Olympic gold started with milking cows and hauling hay on the family farm. After attending Rick's Junior College in Rexburg, Idaho, he attended the University of Nebraska where he majored in physical education. He was not an All-American in wrestling but made the Olympic wrestling team and upset the heavily favored Karelin. His ticker-tape parade in Afton, Wyoming, traveled through the two blocks of downtown twice. Everyone attended to cheer for their Olympic champion (Berkow 2001).

In the *Palm Beach Post* of December 18, 1990, there was a short story about another athlete who—at age thirteen, only five feet tall, and 100 pounds—was abandoned at a Greyhound bus station. In junior high school, Ronald Jean was small and shy, but contentious. "I fought with other kids in the foster homes," he said. "At school, kids would tease me that nobody wanted me and I'd fight there, too" (Drape 1999). During one of his foster home placements, he became friends with an older boy who played football for Pahokee High School as a running back. They worked out together and Nathaniel introduced Ronald to football. "It was something I could do for myself, away from the people who were smoking and drinking and getting in trouble," Ronald said. In junior high, he learned how much he loved the game when he was ruled ineligible for poor grades. Never again. "I decided then I would do what it takes, study as long as I needed, to play," said Ronald (Drape 1999). After high school, Ronald attended Lehigh University where he sat out his freshman year to concentrate on academics. However, as a sophomore, he began playing sporadically and in 1998, as a junior, he won a starting position and scored fourteen touchdowns during the season. Returning to Florida in the summer, he worked out with current NFL players to stay in shape and practice for his senior year. Ronald realizes that playing in the NFL is a long shot, but anyone who knows him believes that they will be watching him on television someday. But if he does not make the NFL, Ronald plans to go to graduate school (Drape 1999). Athletes who do make it to the professional level earn a small fortune in their brief careers. They can earn millions of dollars in careers that average only four to seven years (Holson 2001). Because of the long odds of "making it" to the professional level and the generally short career of an athlete who does, academic success while in school is important.

Combining schoolwork and athletics is not easy; determination and persistence are key to achieving success as a student athlete.

> The "no pass, no play" enactments were designed to increase the academic requirements for participation. Depending on the state or district, the requirements took many forms: Arizona adopted a policy that required a passing grade in every class; California imposed a 2.0 or "C" average requirement with the provision that local districts could increase the restrictions; Texas adopted a 70 in every class with a no failing grades requirement for participation; Hawaii adopted a standard that established a minimum 2.0 grade point average and passing grades in all courses required for graduation. (Buss 1998, 107–8)

Consider also the following:

- There are nearly 1 million high school football players and about 550,000 basketball players. Of that number, about 250 make it to the NFL and about 50 make an NBA team.
- Less than 3 percent of college seniors will play one year in professional basketball.
- The odds of a high school football player making it to the pros at all—let alone having a career—are about 6,000 to 1; the odds for a high school basketball player—10,000 to 1. (Dempsey 2001, 1–2)

In one study of the effects of the Arizona "no pass, no play" rules on students, data were gathered in the Mesa School District. Students records for the first two years of "no pass, no play" (1989–1990 and 1990–1991) were studied. The following hypotheses were tested:

1. Student GPAs will increase owing to the rule.
2. The rule will result in fewer students becoming ineligible (i.e., failing classes and/or making unsatisfactory progress).
3. Teachers will change their grading patterns to minimize the effects of the NPNP rule.
4. Students will take less-challenging courses to avoid the possibility of getting a failing grade.

5. The NPNP rule will increase dropout rates, especially for participants.
6. Students will be less likely to take six or more classes and risk failing them.
7. The NPNP rule will have a disparate effect on different racial groups. (Buss 1998, 108)

The study was conducted by O'Reilly (1992) and Buss (1998) summarizes his results:

O'Reilly's data indicated that grades increased somewhat; the percent of ineligible students fell after the first year but increased slightly after the second year; teachers did not inflate grades; students did not take easier or fewer classes; and, the dropout rate was low and within the ranges experienced in previous years. Looking at minority groups, he found no clear disparate effect except that there were differences in ineligibility rates among African Americans, Hispanics, and Native Americans, for whom the rates were much higher. O'Reilly concluded that the policy had a short-term modest success; however, this was at the cost of a potential long-term negative effect for some minority students. (108)

However, the O'Reilly study and a similar one conducted in Texas made no attempt to control for the effect of other variables when studying "no pass, no play." The Sabatino (1994) study in Austin, Texas, had similar findings to O'Reilly's study in Arizona. Results indicated that the "no pass, no play" strategy has not met the hopes of legislators who enacted the laws; on the other hand, it has not proved the fears of coaches correct, either (Buss 1998).

Is athletic eligibility a right or a privilege? Should athletics and academics in the same school day be an "either-or" proposition? As Joel Kirsch, executive director of the American Sports Institute in San Francisco, said "To shut kids off from sports is absurd" (Reeves 1998, 11). Shouldn't we allow kids the opportunity to use what they know and can do well as a catalyst for learning? What good will taking away something that they love and to which they are dedicated do? "The real issue is not no pass, no play. It's using whatever we can to get our children to pass" (Reeves 1998, 11). However, students and parents are pushing what they see as the absolute right of the student to compete on their school teams. Many studies have been conducted regarding the relationship between high school athletics and academic achievement. The results are inconclusive. Some show a positive correlation between athletics and academic achievement and others report a negative correlation. Most of the published reports on the relationship between sports and academic achievement, however, pertain only to male students (Stegman and Stephens 2000).

In a study at Westside High School in Omaha, questionnaires were given to a sample of juniors and seniors. Students' grade point averages (GPA), class rank (determined by a mark point system that factors in course difficulty as well as GPA), and math GPA data were collected. Students were grouped by gender and participation.

High participants included any students who were consistently in at least one sport in each year of school. With that in mind, a high participant junior was defined as any junior whose number of seasons of participation was greater than or equal to three and a high participant senior was any senior whose number of seasons of participation was greater than or equal to four. Any student who tried a sport or two their freshman year and did not participate further fell into the low participant group along with those who participated in no sports. The low participants and high participant groups were compared with respect to GPA, class rank, and math GPA. In all four subgroups, the high participant group outperformed the low participant group for all three measures of academic achievement (class rank, GPA, and math GPA). (Stegman and Stephens 2000, 38)

It is clear from the results of this study that academic success was not harmed by participation in athletics.

Roger Whitley conducted a larger study in 1998. He analyzed the records of 243,000 students in 133 North Carolina schools over three years. Student athletes had higher grades, better attendance, fewer behavior problems, and lower dropout rates compared to nonathletes in the same schools. He concluded that, "if you really want to do something to improve student grades, you need to get students more involved in the school, in extracurricular activities, not less" (Reeves 1998, 11). The results of a study by W. J. Jordan show that participating in high school sports is associated with higher grades, better self-concept, greater academic self-confidence, and higher academic achievement. "Across each racial/ethnic group analyzed in the study, the effects of participation were positive" (Jordan 1999, 68).

Sports and schooling are highly linked, yet data indicate that most high school students do not participate in school-sponsored sports.

About 21% of all 10th grade students were found to participate in team sports of some kind while only 15% were involved in individual sports. For African American students, 18% reported having participated in team sports by 10th grade, with nearly 10% having participated in individual sports. This suggests that whatever positive outcomes might have accrued from sports participation, few students realize those benefits. (Jordan 1999, 67)

Which is the causal factor? Do students perform better academically because of their participation in sports or do they participate in sports because they are better students (Stegman and Stephens 2000)?

One benefit of participating in sports is the development of leadership skills. "In a sample of 60 suburban high school students, athletes demonstrated significantly greater leadership ability than nonathletes (according to their mean scores on the Leadership Ability Evaluation)" (Dobosz and Beaty 1999). Although the difference between scores was not statistically significant, female athletes showed greater leadership ability than male athletes. Leadership was defined as the ability to guide others toward achieving a common goal. Attributes of effective leaders include decisiveness, determination, interpersonal and organizational aptitude, loyalty, self-efficacy, and self-discipline. The authors concluded that athletics provides an opportunity to develop and demonstrate leadership qualities (Dobosz and Beaty 1999).

The National Collegiate Athletic Association (NCAA), which was founded in 1906, has always required students to meet initial eligibility requirements in order to participate as a freshman in athletics. The NCAA "is made up of 977 schools classified in three divisions (Division I has 318 schools; Division II has 264 schools; and Division III has 395). Schools in Division I, which are divided into two subdivisions for football, (Divisions IA and I-AA), compete at the major college level" (National Collegiate Athletic Association 2001a, 2). Although eligibility requirements changed several times over the years, the chief goal of these requirements remains the same: to ensure that student athletes are prepared for college coursework and athletic competition during the freshman year. High school principals are currently responsible for identifying courses that meet the NCAA's core curriculum requirements previously decided by a college academic committee. Beginning in academic year 2000–2001, incoming student athletes may apply Internet courses, independent study, correspondence, distance learning, and similar alternative courses to establish their initial eligibility status (Dickman and Lammel 2000).

The NCAA established the Initial-Eligibility Clearinghouse in 1993 to determine if high school student athletes met NCAA academic standards for freshman eligibility. Students not meeting these standards are unable to compete in athletics in their freshman year. The clearinghouse is the center for receiving, processing, and evaluating freshman eligibility information, and for providing impartial decisions based on a student's high school academic record. It evaluates courses based on course descriptions provided by the high schools and is run by American College Testing (Reith 1996). Students who wish to compete in Division I or II sports must complete thirteen core academic courses and achieve a minimum grade point average. Student athletes cannot compete in college athletics until they are determined to be eligible by the clearinghouse. The core courses must include:

- Four Carnegie units of English
- Two units in math (one year of algebra and one of geometry or a higher-level course that requires geometry as a prerequisite)
- Two units in natural or physical science (including one lab course, if offered by the high school)
- One additional unit of English, math, or natural or physical sciences
- Two units of social science
- Two additional units in academic courses. Those two additional units may be in any of the already mentioned categories or in a foreign language, computer science, philosophy, or nondoctrinal religion. (Reith 1996, 16)

A student athlete is required to have at least a 2.0 grade point average in the core courses and an SAT score of 1010, or an 86 sum score on the ACT. "There is a sliding scale so the higher the grade point average (up to 2.5), the lower the test score that is required. If the student-athlete has a 2.5 GPA or higher in the core courses, he or she can score as low as an 820 on the SAT or 68 sum score on the ACT" (Reith 1996, 16).

A partial qualifier status allows the student athlete to get an athletic scholarship and practice but not compete during the freshman year. The student must achieve a core course grade point average above 2.5 and a standardized test score between a 720 and an 810 on the SAT and 67 sum score on the ACT. Table 8.1 lists the indexes.

Aid based in any degree on athletics cannot be awarded for more than one academic year. Decisions about awarding institutional financial aid to student athletes are made on a year-by-year basis, depending on the specific regulations of the institution.

If a student-athlete is receiving institutional financial aid based in any degree on athletic ability, that financial aid **MAY** be reduced or canceled during the period of award (e.g., during that year or term) only if the student-athlete:

1. Renders himself or herself ineligible for intercollegiate competition; or
2. Misrepresents any information on an application, letter of intent or financial aid agreement; or
3. Commits serious misconduct which warrants a substantial disciplinary penalty (the misconduct determination must be made by the university's regular student disciplinary authority); or
4. Voluntarily quits the sport for personal reasons. In this case, the student-athlete's financial aid may not be given to another student-athlete during the term in which the aid was reduced or canceled.

Table 8.1 Qualifier Indexes

Core GPA	ACT* sum of scores	SAT** on or after 4/1/95
Division I Qualifier Index		
2.500 and above	68	820
2.475	69	830
2.450	70	840–850
2.425	70	860
2.400	71	860
2.375	72	870
2.350	73	880
2.325	74	890
2.300	75	900
2.275	76	910
2.250	77	920
2.225	78	930
2.200	79	940
2.175	80	950
2.150	80	960
2.125	81	960
2.100	82	970
2.075	83	980
2.050	84	990
2.025	85	1000
2.000	86	1010
Partial Qualifier Index		
2.750 and above	59	720
2.725	59	730
2.700	60	730
2.675	61	740–750
2.650	62	760
2.625	63	770
2.600	64	780
2.575	65	790
2.550	66	800
2.525	67	810

* Previously, ACT score was calculated by averaging four scores. New standards are based on sum of scores.
** For SAT tests taken on or after April 1, 1995.
Source: NCAA 2001a, 2.

Institutional financial aid based in any degree on athletics ability *may not* be reduced, canceled, or increased during the period of award:

1. Based on a student-athlete's ability, performance, or contribution to a team's success; or
2. Because an injury prevents the student-athlete from participating; or
3. For any other athletics reason. (NCAA 2001b, 2)

High school athletic participation can have a positive impact on students. Becoming physically fit, focused, and disciplined; being a team member; and being able to cope with the ups and downs of winning and losing are important skills. High school athletes also make outstanding mentors for elementary and middle school students. Younger students who are first encountering pressure and problems related to being successful athletes can learn useful skills and benefit from having older star athletes as mentors (Fibkins 1999). In 1991, the National Federation of State High School Associations reported that in the average high school, 50 percent of the student body participates in at least one cocurricular activity. The cost for this participation is only 1–3 percent of the total school budget (Pressley and Whitley 1996). Cocurricular activities in general and interscholastic athletics in particular may be the least expensive way to improve academic performance or instill socially acceptable values and norms of conduct.

Participants in sports and other cocurricular activities generally have higher GPAs than students who do not participate. This is especially true when comparing athletes to nonathletes. Spreitzer and Paugh suggest the following five factors that might explain the higher academic performance of athletes:

1. The athlete might receive special academic encouragement and assistance from teachers, coaches, and counselors.
2. The physical conditioning and discipline required for participation in athletics might transfer to educational endeavors.
3. Eligibility requirements and the hope of qualifying for college scholarships might motivate athletes to achieve higher grades.
4. The prestige resulting from athletic participation may produce a more positive self-concept and higher aspirations in other activities, including academics.
5. Athletic participation often facilitates membership in the "leading crowd" in high school, which is disproportionately middle class in origin and typically college oriented. (Pressley and Whitley 1996, 77)

As a group, student athletes also have fewer discipline problems and lower dropout rates than nonathletes. Athletic participation seems to have a holding influence over some students who perhaps might have dropped out of school. It gives some students a way to achieve recognition and status, leading to a higher level of scholarship and higher academic aspirations (Pressley and Whitley 1996).

Not long ago, most high school athletes were boys. Approximately 3.6 million boys participated in high school sports in the 1971–1972 school year, more than twelve times the number of girls. Title IX of the Education Amendments of 1972 states that no individual "shall, on the basis of sex, be excluded from participation in, be denied the benefits of, or be subjected to discrimination under any educational program or activity receiving federal financial assistance" (Sommerfeld 1998, 34). After passage of Title IX, girls' involvement in school-based sports skyrocketed. "By 1978, more than two million girls were active in high school sports, a sevenfold increase" (Sommerfeld 1998, 33). For John Jordan, superintendent in Oxford, Mississippi, instituting a girls' sports program was both an equity and wellness issue. Jordan initiated expansion of the number of varsity sports for girls as part of a broader strategy to promote good health among teenage girls and to discourage teen pregnancy (Sommerfeld 1998).

The rights of students with disabilities to participate in interscholastic sports remains unclear. Despite a large body of case law, the courts have been split on this issue. The majority upholds the rules of athletic associations. However, the courts have tended to hold school district policies and actions affecting students with disabilities to a stricter standard. Three federal statutes offer protection to students with disabilities against discrimination. "The Individuals with Disabilities Education Act mandates and provides funding for certain special education services. Section 504 and the ADA are civil rights statutes that offer protection from discrimination and accommodations to individuals with disabilities" (Sullivan, Lantz, and Zirkel 2000, 258).

Individuals with Disabilities Education Act (IDEA) regulations require that school districts "shall take steps to provide nonacademic and extracurricular services in such manner as necessary to afford children with disabilities an equal opportunity for participation in those services and activities" (Sullivan, Lantz, and Zirkel 2000, 258–59). Section 504 applies to all agencies that receive federal funding, which includes almost all public schools. The regulations concerning IDEA's extracurricular directive add supporting language specific to athletes.

The Americans with Disabilities Act (ADA), passed in 1990, contains three sections that apply to different types of organizations. Title II applies to public school districts, and uses language similar to Section 504's discrimination prohibition: "[N]o qualified individual with a disability shall, by reason of such disability, be excluded from participation in or be denied the benefits of the services, programs, or activities of a public entity, or be subjected to discrimination by any such entity" (Sullivan, Lantz, and Zirkel 2000, 259).

Congress has barred discrimination against students with disabilities in the way schools administer sports through section 504 and the ADA. In addition, participation in school athletics is part of the "free, appropriate, public education" that every student with disabilities is entitled to under IDEA. Section 504 and the ADA apply even in cases where participation in sports is not considered necessary to ensure an appropriate education (Goedert 1995).

In football, as well as soccer, baseball, or other cocurricular activities, the following traits have been observed, which makes them "better than school":

1. In football, teenagers are considered important contributors rather than passive recipients. A football team is framed around the abilities and preferences of the players.
2. In football, teenagers are encouraged to excel. We congratulate players on their accomplishments, but we don't give them much time to be complacent—we ask them to do even more.
3. In football, teenagers are honored. Football players get extraordinary amounts of approval: award banquets, letter jackets, banners around the campus, school festivals, team photos, whole sections of the yearbook, newspaper coverage, trophies, and regional and even state recognition for being the best.
4. In football, a player can let the team down. Personal effort is linked to more than personal achievement: A single player can make his peers better than they would have been without him.
5. In football, repetition is honorable. In football, students do the same drills over and over all season long—and, in fact, get better at them. The skills get easier, and players start to use those skills to do things that are more complex.
6. In football, the unexpected happens all the time. There's no opportunity to coast, to tune out, to sit back and watch others work. Every player is required to be involved and absorbed in his work.
7. In football, practices run a lot longer than fifty minutes. And when they end, there's a reason to stop: the players work until they get it right or until they're too tired to move anymore.
8. In football, the homework is of a different type from what's done at practice. Players work at

home to find and build their strengths and then bring those strengths to practice to work together with their teammates on specific skills.

9. In football, emotions and human contact are expected parts of the work. When players do well, they get to be happy. When they do poorly, they get to be angry. Players are supposed to talk to one another while things are going on.

10. In football, players get to choose their own roles. They choose their sport, but they also choose their favorite position within that sport.

11. In football, the better players teach the less-skilled players. Sometimes this teaching is on purpose, but mostly it is by example.

12. In football, there is a lot of individual instruction and encouragement from adults. A coach who has only the nine defensive linemen to deal with for an hour is going to get a pretty good sense of who these youngsters are, what drives them, what they can and can't do.

13. In football, the adults who participate are genuinely interested. The adults involved in football are more willing to tell you that they love to play, that they love to coach.

14. In football, volunteers from the community are sought after. No sports program in a high school could ever operate without assistant coaches, trainers, and other local people who aren't paid to help out.

15. In football, ability isn't age linked. Freshman who excel can play varsity.

16. Football is more than the sum of its parts. Players practice moves over and over in isolation, but they know that their job at the end is going to mean putting all those moves together.

17. In football, public performance is expected. The incentive to perform in front of family and friends was a great motivating force for athletes I knew. (Childress 1998, 617–19)

Tennis superstar Arthur Ashe raised public awareness about the many ways that participation in sports promotes the healthful development of young people. Believing that lessons learned on playing fields, courts, and in swimming pools transfer to educational settings and to the wider world, Ashe realized that sports could make a difference for at-risk youngsters and give them a positive direction in life. He cofounded the National Junior Tennis League to help at-risk youth by getting them involved in tennis (Poinsett 1996). In order for all young adolescents to become effective adults, ideally they must:

- Find a valued place in a constructive group.
- Learn how to form close, durable human relationships.
- Feel a sense of worth as a person.
- Achieve a reliable basis for making informed, deliberate decisions especially on matters that have large consequences, such as educational futures.
- Know how to use available support systems.
- Find ways of being useful to others beyond the self.
- Believe in a promising future with real opportunities.
- Cultivate the inquiring and problem-solving habits of mind for lifelong learning and adaptability.
- Learn respect for democratic values and understand responsible citizenship.
- Build a healthy lifestyle. (Poinsett 1996, 3)

This list summarizes the meaning of youth development, but no single institution by itself—not even the family—can produce it. It requires cooperation among several institutions, including schools and youth sports organizations. Participation of boys and girls in interscholastic athletics is summarized in table 8.2.

Participation in sports offers promise for promoting responsible social behavior and increasing academic success, building confidence in one's physical abilities, developing an appreciation for personal health and fitness, and creating strong social bonds between individuals and with institutions. Although it seems apparent, it is difficult to find supporting evidence for the contribution of sports to the socialization process. The evidence that does support this contention may actually be due to the selection process that attracts and retains students in sports activities. These students may already possess the values and behavioral traits that coaches demand and that lead to athletic success (Spreitzer 1994). "In other words, youths are not randomly assigned to athletic and nonathletic groupings on an experimental basis (see also Snyder and Spreitzer 1992). Rather, they arrive in these channels as a result of a filtering and screening process begun in the little leagues and certainly by junior high school" (Spreitzer 1994, 373). Students who participate in sports are also more likely to participate in nonathletic cocurricular activities between the sophomore and senior years.

A 1998 study of 134 high school students (52 athletes and 82 nonathletes) in a rural Canadian high school found that participation in athletics doesn't harm grades and may actually improve them, that athletes have fewer behavioral problems than other students, and that the time committed to athletics per week equals the time spent in class and doing homework for one academic course (Zaugg 1998).

Table 8.2   Participation of Boys and Girls in Interscholastic Athletics

Sport	Boys		Girls	
	Number of Schools	Number of Participants	Number of Schools	Number of Participants
Baseball	14,174	444,476	75	**1,340
Basketball	16,574	545,596	16,198	445,869
Cross Country	11,360	168,203	10,744	140,187
Field Hockey	—	—	1,460	56,142
Football (11 man)	13,004	957,573	79	**791
Golf	11,394	140,011	5,469	**39,634
Gymnastics	177	2,635	*1,522	19,398
Ice Hockey	*985	**24,281	165	**1,471
Lacrosse	539	24,114	375	14,704
Soccer	*8,182	**283,728	6,526	209,287
Softball–Fast Pitch	83	1,932	11,452	305,217
Softball–Slow Pitch	8	161	1,523	34,195
Swimming and Diving	*4,852	**81,000	4,948	**111,360
Tennis	9,214	136,534	9,165	146,573
Track and Field (outdoor)	14,505	454,645	14,410	379,060
Volleyball	1,381	**31,553	12,669	357,576
Wrestling	8,677	221,162	225	1,164

* Includes some coeducational teams
** Includes girls playing on boys' teams and boys playing on girls' teams.
Source: Table reproduced is a partial listing of the original table, from Poinsett 1996, 7–8. Survey conducted by the National Federation of State High School Associations, based on competition at the High School Level in the 1995–96 school year.

Participation in sports can help young people appreciate health, exercise, and fitness. It can help them learn about themselves and sportsmanship, how to work with others cooperatively, and how to handle adversity. Sports programs enhance the educational, social, emotional, and physical development of all students. While participating in sports students learn honesty, self-esteem, respect for authority, and skills improvement. In emphasizing character, discipline, goal setting, and respect, sports programs contribute to a student's self-concept and self-esteem (Rasmussen 1999–2000). Because of its central position in shaping the identity of schools and small communities, athletics is important, and athletes are often the dominant social category in schools. The big social event of the week is the football game, which everyone attends. Sports programs contain the following elements that help students develop their potential:

- A firm belief that athletes can perform at a high level if their motivation and encouragement remain focused
- A collective agreement and sustained effort by teachers, leaders, community members, and families
- Instruction that is intensive, explicit, and future-oriented
- Emphasis on progress and demonstrable outcomes
- Clear rules and rationale for participation
- Assessment of performance
- Tangible and intangible reinforcement for outstanding performance (Taylor 1999, 77)

Central to athletics and education is the process of growth and development. Students who succeed in both carry their hopes, dreams, and skills with them when they leave high school.

Participating in sports does not on its own provide the skills and resources necessary for future success in college but it stimulates aspirations due to its high visibility, status, and rewards (Spady 1970). Students without service and leadership experiences in high school tend to lack the attitudes, abilities, and motivations necessary to sustain them in college (Buss 1998). This is especially true of "low-resource" students. While sports develop physical skills, service activities develop interpersonal, leadership, and intellectual skills that appear to have a significant and enduring impact. A combination of athletics and service activities usually results in higher attainment than service alone.

Some schools develop programs that stress and reinforce good sportsmanship for athletics in all school and nonschool activities. In Illinois, Hoffman Estates High School sends a strong message that participating in athletics is a privilege with concomitant responsibilities (George 2001). School policy stipulates that students or coaches ejected from a game for unsportsmanlike behavior are ineligible for the next scheduled game. If ejected a second time, the student or coach faces suspension for the remainder of the season. Unacceptable behavior that does not lead to ejection is reviewed by the principal and the athletic director with the student or coach to determine disciplinary action. The sportsmanship program also pertains to cheerleaders, the pom-pom squad, and the band. Positive pep rallies that focus on school pride and spirit are the norm. All spirit signs and cheers must support the team in a positive way. Derogatory cheers or comments directed at opponents are forbidden. Finally, "spectators and athletes are reminded to demonstrate an attitude of good sportsmanship throughout the contest no matter what personal feelings of loyalty he or she may have toward one team or the other" (George 2001, 21).

Many schools also have developed rules governing participation on athletic teams, which address the behaviors that athletes must exhibit during the season to be allowed to participate in practices and in competitions. Statements of the rules are usually signed by athletes and their parents prior to the start of a season. Student athletes also can be governed by a "Code of Conduct," such as the following adopted from the North Carolina High School Athletic Association:

- The student athlete shall keep academics as his or her number one priority.
- The student athlete shall play for the joy of the sport, the success of the team, and to win.
- The student athlete shall play hard, but fairly, always mindful of the rules and the spirit or intent of the rules.
- The student athlete shall treat opponents with respect, shaking hands before and after contests.
- The student athlete shall be modest in victory and humble in defeat.
- The student athlete shall respect the judgment of contest officials and accept their decisions.
- The student athlete shall exhibit exemplary behavior, thus serving as a positive role model for teammates, opponents, and spectators.
- The student athlete shall accept the privileges and responsibilities of representing self, school, and community. (Kessie 2001, 9)

The Texas "no pass, no play" policy of 1984 is considered by some to be the watershed case on secondary school athletic eligibility. These policies were not new to Texas or the nation, but the "no pass, no play" policy was probably one of the strictest standards ever set for high school athletics. Reforms to the Texas "no pass, no play" legislation have cut the suspension period of athletes from six weeks to three weeks and students were allowed to practice during suspension, although they were prohibited from playing in games (Reeves 1998). In some districts, the "no pass, no play" policy is expanded to encompass all cocurricular participation.

The competition for varsity-caliber athletes at the college level is so great that even academically demanding colleges are more likely to admit sports stars than minority-background students and children of alumni. Contrary to the belief that high-profile sports events enrich school coffers, the truth is that "almost all athletic programs lose money," according to the Shulman-Bowen study (Honan 2001a, 20). A series of remedies for ameliorating the growing problems associated with college sports was proposed by a panel of fourteen present and former college presidents. Their report, entitled "A Call to Action: Reconnecting College Sports and Higher Education," proposes reforms such as:

- Requiring athletes to go through the same academic processes as other students
- Improving athlete graduation rates
- Reducing playing times, practices, and postseasons to afford athletes a realistic opportunity to complete their degrees
- Creating minor leagues so that athletes not interested in undergraduate study would have an alternative route to careers in professional sports
- Giving universities greater control of game schedules, how events are broadcast, and which companies are permitted to use the university's athletics contests as advertising vehicles, instead of bowing to television and other commercial interests (Honan 2001b)

Other items under review include redefining the coach's job to be that of an educator of young people and requiring teams to graduate at least half of their players in order to participate in playoffs and championships. "While that sounds like a modest goal, it's one that more than half of the 321 colleges with top-tier basketball teams failed to meet last year" (Jurgensen 2001). Finally, the Knight Commission has recommended that scholarships be "tied" to the individual athletes and not be reawarded if athletes flunk out. Under the current system, the scholarship is awarded to another player (Jurgensen 2001).

At the middle school, there have been few studies of the effects of activity participation. One study of peer status and popularity effects of participation "found that boys showed consistent gains in status and popularity over the three years of middle school if they participated in high-status interscholastic sports. For female students, cheerleading conferred the highest status and popularity and, to a lesser extent, involvement in some sports also enhanced popularity" (Buss 1998, 96).

Perhaps more than any other area of middle school, current practices in interscholastic sports programs reflect the difficulty of changing traditional practices in a society where there is widespread lack of knowledge about the ramifications of placing students in highly competitive sports programs. In this age group, the injury rate has increased significantly in the last few years (McEwin and Dickinson 1997).

Young adolescents cut from sports teams lose the benefits of developing their physical skills, playing team sports, spending time with peers, and building confidence in their athletic abilities. About 35 percent of youths drop out of competitive sports programs annually, with about 50 percent dropping out by the age of twelve. "Reasons for dropping out include: (a) emergence of new interests, (b) lack of playing time, (c) the way practices are conducted, (d) interactions with teammates, (e) dislike of coaches, (f) a feeling of unworthiness, (g) not having fun, and (h) needing time to study" (Swain, McEwin, and Irvin 1998, 73).

Intramural programs can be an important aspect of successful middle level schools. They provide young adolescents with opportunities to benefit from participation in sports without some of the negative aspects. "The hierarchy of programs serving young adolescents should begin with physical education, which serves all students, move to intramural programs that involve all who are interested, and last to interscholastic sports programs for the relatively small number of those wishing higher levels of participation" (McEwin and Dickinson 1997, 21).

In 1990, Gardiner Middle School in Oregon had an excellent sports program involving students at three different ability levels. Students could choose from a variety of sports that included basketball, football, volleyball, wrestling, cross-country running, and track. All interested students had an opportunity to represent Gardiner in interscholastic competition because the school fielded teams at three different ability levels. One year later, however, everything had changed (Hereford 1999a). In November 1990, a state ballot passed that reduced funding to education. Cocurricular programs, including athletics, were the first to be affected. Eight years later in the 1998 school year, the state increased funding to the Oregon city schools and Gardiner Middle School was able to restart some cocurricular activities. The school was also able to form some sports teams at the intramural level. "School spirit really took a dive" after the cutbacks, said Principal Chris Mills. "Students didn't feel as connected to the school anymore. They had no teams to play on or to cheer. There was no reason for students to be on campus after 3 P.M." (Hereford 1999a, 25).

Lacking the incentive to participate in sports, many students lost interest in school and their grades suffered. Discipline problems and vandalism in the surrounding neighborhoods increased. "There were a lot of kids just hanging out, with no place to go after school," recalled student manager Denise Andersen. "We worry about young adolescents making bad choices and engaging in risky behavior. Organized activities after school help many students make better choices. They have a safe, supervised place to be, rather than on a street corner or in an empty house" (Hereford 1999a, 25).

Sports programs allow many students the chance to excel in an area other than academics. For some, it is the only way to gain recognition. Through their participation, they learn valuable life skills and how to interact with positive adult role models. They learn to cooperate with teammates and build self-confidence. Through their participation, many students find an alternative to delinquency—especially middle school students (Hereford 1999a). However, if the programs are limited to a few, the benefits accrue to only a few.

The number of families in the United States that homeschool their children increased at least eightfold between the early 1970s and 1987. As many as one million children in the United States are educated at home. According to the Home School Legal Defense Association, about 50,000 of the 200,000 high school-age, homeschooled students participated in public school activities (Webb 1997). Whether or not an athlete is eligible to participate in public school athletics is determined by regulations of the governing state board or state athletic associations. An athletic organization's eligibility rule must be reviewed for purposes of due process and equal protection to determine its constitutionality (Webb 1997).

In California, participation in public school athletics by homeschooled students is permissible if the school district has a system for monitoring the quality of the homeschoolers' education. The state athletic association in Kansas actively opposed a legislative proposal that would have permitted homeschooled students to play sports at their nearest public school. The New York State Board of Regents has clear rules that prohibit sports participation by homeschooled students—they do not meet eligibility rules. "Sports is a privilege and as such, it's something that can only be earned by students who attend a public school in a member district," says Lloyd L. Mott, assistant director of the New York State Public High School Athletic Association. "Plus, athletics is all about teamwork, training, being part of a school atmosphere. A student who is not enrolled in school misses much of that" (Lafee 1998, 20).

Finally, potential student athletes who have been homeschooled during their high school years do not have to register with the NCAA Initial-Eligibility Clearinghouse. Their certification status will be determined through an initial eligibility waiver (NCAA 2001a).

In closing:

West Point tells prospective cadets that the academy is a physical place. The admissions website specifies that candidates must have "above average strength, endurance and agility." A commercially published handbook for candidates shows a photograph of cadets playing a game of pick-up basketball. The caption reads, "If you don't like athletic competition, you will be a misfit at West Point." The beginnings of this emphasis on athletics came from Douglas MacArthur's observation that young soldiers in World War I respected officers with athletic ability. When he became Superintendent after the war, in 1919, MacArthur decreed "every cadet an athlete." Participation in sports, either varsity, club, or intramural, has been mandatory for most of the twentieth century (Ruggero 2001, 233).

Participating in cocurricular activities is a privilege not a right. It is qualified first by eligibility requirements and secondly by performance requirements. (Hogan and Sarzynski 1998, 37)

9

HOW ARE STUDENT
ACTIVITIES EVALUATED?

When schools integrate their essential ideas and vision into every aspect of the organization—into the goals, strategies, tactics, policies, processes, cultural practices, management behaviors, accountability systems, and role design—they set a clear course toward effective teaching and learning. According to Tewel (1996), three benchmarks are critical to successful high schools:

1. Identify the school's fundamental beliefs about students, learning, teaching, organization, governance, and relations with parents and community.
2. Align components of the school community to support and sustain the basic vision and beliefs and to stimulate improvement.
3. Guideposts for principals:
   a. Take a comprehensive view—schools that are driven by their belief systems do not rely on any one program, strategy, tactic, mechanism, cultural norm, symbolic gesture, or principal's speech to stimulate progress.
   b. Focus on the details of day-to-day working lives—workers must deal with the nitty-gritty details. They are important and the little things add up.
   c. Strive for coherence—schools guided by a stable vision and set of beliefs do not enact random processes or mechanisms unless they pertain to the whole.
   d. Be steadfast—don't be taken in by fads. Remaining consistent and true to one's vision means being guided by one's true beliefs, not the forces, trends, fads, fashions, and buzzwords of the educational world.
   e. Seek out and remove inconsistencies—inconsistent practices prevent the school from achieving its learning goals. (Tewel 1996)

Student activities join the mainstream of school activities when schools recognize that they must concentrate their efforts to create a fully integrated curriculum that goes beyond the boundaries of traditional academic disciplines. In this way, all students will achieve common goals (Sherrill 1998). Student activities in secondary schools are an important part of student preparation for adult life. Effective methods for evaluation should determine whether the goals of the activities program, as well as those of the school, are being met. Evaluation serves many purposes and can be accomplished in a variety of ways (checklist, rating scale, etc.). Some criteria to be considered in assessing a student activities program are:

- ✔ Are activities in keeping with the school's philosophy?
- ✔ What percentage of the student body participates?
- ✔ Are activities varied enough to meet all student needs?
- ✔ Are students new to the school encouraged to participate?
- ✔ Are activities designed to develop skills that will be useful after graduation?
- ✔ Are services to the school and community provided?
- ✔ Are students exploited in any way?
- ✔ Are provisions made to prevent a small group of students from monopolizing the leadership positions? (Is there a point system?)
- ✔ Are supervision and security adequate for all activities?
- ✔ Are accounting procedures adequate to account for activity funds?
- ✔ Are activities adapted for handicapped students? (Grady 1981, 7–8)

A comprehensive system for the evaluation of student activities is Management-by-Objectives/Results (MBO/R). This process allows for the following:

- A means of setting goals that are relevant to purposes or intentions
- A tool for planning a course of action and for planning experiences to accomplish the goals that are set
- A tool for measuring progress toward a goal
- A tool for use in evaluating the results of the planned course of action (Christensen 1978, 1–2)

The MBO/R evaluation focuses on the results, comparing the real (what was accomplished) to the ideal (what was intended to be accomplished). Evaluation is a judgment about the extent to which or degree that something is accomplished or the quality of the outcome produced. It indicates the degree of progress toward a goal by comparing the results of the action plan to the goal. Evaluation that provides information about the success of the action plan focuses on the results attained. The central question is, were the intended results achieved? MBO/R is a continuous improvement cycle. It seeks to move the individual or organization toward the realization of its purpose and potential (Christensen 1978). MBO/R can be adapted to task or event planning. This occurs in a six-step process as follows:

1. The *task* is defined.
2. The *strategy* or plan for accomplishing the task is outlined.
3. *Responsibilities* are delegated.
4. Necessary *resources* are defined.
5. *Deadlines* are established.
6. *Results* are evaluated. (Christensen 1978, 7)

Whatever the system, evaluation should be continuous and ongoing to help organizations understand their strengths and weaknesses in order to improve. Why evaluate student activity projects? Consider the following reasons:

- To determine whether the objectives of the group have been reached
- To bring about improvements in projects and programs
- To redirect or emphasize the movement of the program
- To measure and record progress
- To encourage self-appraisal and improvement by looking for the good as well as the bad in a project
- To promote leadership growth with continual feedback of information to assist the leaders in making decisions
- To increase participation and improved public relations by seeking the opinions and support of students and faculty
- To serve as a record for subsequent groups and to give direction to planning for the next year (Fiscus 1995, 208)

What should be evaluated?

- The organization as a whole should be evaluated in terms of attaining its stated goals and objectives.
- Individual activities should be evaluated continuously in terms of achievement of established goals.
- Each individual should evaluate himself or herself in terms of his or her own performance.
- Meetings and procedures should be evaluated in terms of effectiveness and involvement.
- The group's members should be evaluated in terms of responsibilities and effectiveness in carrying out their duties with the organization.
- The leaders of the group (including the advisor) should be evaluated in terms of their job descriptions and effectiveness. (Fiscus 1995, 208)

School counselors, teachers, and school administrators may be able to help design the evaluation. Obviously, it is important to "cast a wide net" in order to capture information from everyone involved in the project or activity. Involve the following groups or individuals in the process (Fiscus 1995, 209):

- Members of the organization
- School administrators
- Members of the student body
- Community members
- Parents
- Advisers or sponsors
- School faculty members
- Leaders of the organization

When gathering information or data, the methods chosen should be simple and easy to manage. The following (Fiscus 1995, 209–10) are some techniques or instruments useful for completing an evaluation:

- Questionnaires
- Interviews

- Response checklists
- Progress reports
- Observation forms and reports
- Descriptive reports
- Worksheets
- Group discussions
- School newspaper surveys
- Suggestion boxes
- Interviews
- Random telephone surveys
- Comments from the community
- Open meetings
- Process reports
- Records of participation
- Inventories (how much of something was used, requested, etc.)

And finally, decide how to evaluate by asking the following questions:

- Decide what you want to evaluate (achievement of goals, how good the program is, how smoothly the program operated, program outcomes).
- Decide how the evaluation results will be used (to refine or improve the program, to prepare a report, to develop a new program, to gain broader support for the program).
- Decide when the evaluation should take place (at different times throughout the program, at the end).
- Decide who will be involved in the evaluation (teachers, students, administrators, parents, members of the community).
- Decide what kinds of information need to be collected (what methods will be used to collect the information, and how the information will be analyzed).
- Decide how the findings of the evaluation will be reported and to whom.
- Decide what to do with the feedback from reviewers of the evaluation. (Fiscus 1995, 210)

Developmental appropriateness helps students reach educational goals. Active learning occurs when students are assessed on what they know, not when they take a test to show what they do not know (Anticoli 1996). More often than not, this means producing an actual product that can be assessed—a performance. Hundreds of leadership classes meet regularly in high schools across the United States. In these classes, students enjoin their peers to participate in a variety of activities such as planning a pep rally, discussing national issues, getting involved in local political campaigns, discussing efforts to implement a new philanthropy project, or student governance. With the increased demand for authentic assessment and practical activities, leadership classes are burgeoning (Bloomstran 2001b). Teachers and administrators recognize the benefits of providing students with opportunities to exercise leadership through the classroom settings. Teachers emphasize the connection between their classroom and the world of work as validation for leadership classes. They believe these classes help students develop skills indispensable to adult life, such as time management, problem solving, conflict resolution, and network building. Teachers easily make connections between the curriculum that requires students to plan, implement, and evaluate large-scale projects, and the demands an employer might place on a young employee (Bloomstran 2001b).

Leadership classes involve students in projects and activities that help prepare them for real-world challenges. Students must use problem-solving and other leadership skills when, for example, coordinating a canned food drive or arranging for a guest speaker. Teachers and students themselves can immediately see the results of their work. The grade received by students for their participation in a leadership class might be based on a grading chart or rubric, such as the example of the Student Council Grading Chart found in table 9.1.

When examining a middle school's activities program, questions to be asked are:

1. Are activities "age appropriate"? Are they designed to be sensitive to the physical, social, academic, and emotional characteristics of young adolescents, thereby creating opportunities for high levels of student success, thus raising student self-worth? Do they reflect a responsiveness to the fact that middle-grade students mature at varying rates of speed? Do they reflect a wide range of individual differences?

2. Are activities inclusive? Do they possess inherent universal qualities that allow for the flexibility of the rules/parameters and adaptable features so that:
   a. all students are capable of participating;
   b. students with mental and/or physical impairments may participate without feeling as though major modifications were made on their behalf;
   c. the fundamental characteristics of the activities remain in place; and
   d. excitement levels and/or challenge levels of the activities remain consistent and high for all participants.

3. Is the program "balanced"? Are activities (academics, athletics, music, citizenship, etc.) relatively equivalent in scope and importance? Is there a wide variety of areas (leadership, achievement, performance, cooperation, service) represented, with a primary focus on academic achievement?

4. Are activities legitimate? Are they perceived by students to be fair, positive, and worthy? Do they contain elements of being creative, exploratory, active, and meaningful? (Galletti 1996, 34–35)

Successful middle-level activity programs ensure that students are involved in the planning and monitoring of the cocurricular program. The most effective middle-level activity programs result from undertaking a comprehensive understanding of the physical, academic, social, and emotional characteristics and needs of eleven- to fourteen-year-old adolescents (Galletti 1996). Therefore, evaluation of the program should focus on implementation. Consideration to good evaluation can bring about the following positive outcomes:

- Better planning of future programs is ensured.
- Improved public relations occur.
- Objectives are met.
- Needs of students are met.
- Activities are coordinated.
- The program is enriched.

Table 9.1

Student Council Grading Chart
Loveland High School, Loveland, Colorado

Name: _____ Date: _____

Chair: _____

	High Quality	*Proficient*	*Needs Improvement*
Section 1 Punctuality	A) I have regular attendance (95% of time on job) A) I am on time or will arrive early or stay late A) I promote a team atmosphere A) I am prepared at all times with my materials	B) I am punctual and ready to work (usually on time) B) I am a willing and cooperative team member B) I bring my materials most of the time	C) I have 90% or lower attendance C) I am not punctual (rarely on time) C) I am unwilling to work as a team member C) I don't bring materials more than 50% of the time
Section 2 Behavior	A) I am courteous, considerate, and tolerant of others A) I can be trusted by my employer, coworkers, teachers, and/or customers/peers A) I respect and respond toward authority A) I am enthusiastic and energetic A) I accept leadership responsibilities on a team A) I often use problem-solving skills to make the team productive A) I value team members and encourage their input	B) I understand others but get impatient at times B) I need follow-up B) I respect authority and do the work asked of me B) I exhibit energy in work B) I willingly accept varied responsibilities on a team. B) I sometimes use problem solving skills to make the team productive B) I value team members and their opinions	C) I am insensitive, impatient, or rude to others C) I have demonstrated untrustworthy behaviors C) I do not respond appropriately toward authority C) I have a poor attitude and have no interest C) I am unable to accept responsibilities on a team C) I am unwilling to use problem-solving skills to make the team productive C) I do not value team members and their opinions
Section 3 Communication	A) I have excellent oral communication skills and use them consistently A) I consistently utilize excellent skills in the workplace/school A) I complete quality work ahead of schedule A) I am able to independently identify and complete tasks A) I consistently evaluate situations and respond appropriately (chairs and officers only)	B) My oral communication skills are effective in the workplace/school B) I recognize the importance of listening and demonstrate it in the workplace/school B) I am productive and meet program/industry/school standards B) I am able to complete tasks with minimum supervision	C) I have adequate oral communication skills C) I do not recognize or demonstrate the importance of listening C) I have poor production and rarely meet deadlines C) I need encouragement or frequent supervision.
Section 4 Motivation	A) I anticipate and respond to student needs A) I create quality posters A) I persevere when assigned even a difficult or unpleasant task A) I anticipate and am open to changes in work schedules and assignments A) I am able to identify and solve problems A) I consistently demonstrate appropriate behavior A) I always put away supplies	B) I am aware of and respond to student needs B) I occasionally work hard even when assigned a difficult or unpleasant task B) I am willing to meet program requirements but don't like change. B) I am able to identify but can't solve problems B) I demonstrate appropriate behavior B) I sometimes put away supplies	C) I ignore or am not aware of student needs C) I don't care about the quality of my posters C) I do not follow through on assigned tasks C) I am unwilling to adjust to changes in work schedules and assignments C) I am unable to identify or solve problems C) I seldom demonstrate appropriate behavior C) I rarely put away supplies

Comments:

_____

_____

Source: Olson 2001, 52.

- Worthwhile activities are recognized.
- Unsound programs are rejected.
- Growth of the organization is noted.
- Unacceptable and ineffective approaches are modified. (Fiscus 1995, 213)

Students finishing school today and in the future enter a very different world and labor market from the labor market of even the recent past. Permanent jobs and "career positions" are being phased out in favor of temporary or project-based positions in many fields. Therefore, when a project is completed, the employee's position with the company might also terminate. Many fields will require prospective employees to engage in a regular project hunt rather than a very occasional "job hunt" (Kingsley 1995). In order to meet the challenges of a rapidly changing world of work, students need to leave high school with the following career skills:

- Self-directed worker
- Responsible worker
- Effective communicator
- Skilled worker
- Adaptable worker (Tompkins-Seneca-Tioga 1995, 1–5)

Student activities participation helps many students develop these skills. Evaluation of the programs and outcomes of participation provides an opportunity to improve and measure student activities contribution to meeting school, state, and national standards.

In closing:

The connection between learning in the school and learning outside the school needs to be clear. (Dewey 1964)

Reward those who involve more people. If group members know the goal is to involve more people and they see that behavior being rewarded, more of them will pursue it. (Smith 2001, 11)

10

HOW ARE STUDENTS INVOLVED, ESPECIALLY THOSE WHO ARE NOT MOTIVATED?

Less than 17 percent of seventeen-year-olds had a high school diploma at the turn of the century. Today, nearly 70 percent of students graduate from high school and continue with postsecondary studies. However, almost half of high school graduates do not have the skills or abilities to be successful in postsecondary education or in a career. Although 70 percent of students enroll in college after high school, the percentage that actually attains a baccalaureate degree is about the same percentage as in 1950. "The percentage of students graduating from high school has been dropping slightly since at least 1993" (Viadero 2001a, 18). The decrease in graduation rates is sometimes concealed by rising rates of high school completion. One reason for this discrepancy is that more students are earning high school credentials through alternative programs (Viadero 2001a).

To achieve economic success and to function as a responsible citizen in a democracy, students need to acquire math, problem-solving, and reading skills at a level not usually attained by most high school graduates. "Many [experts] also add to that list such 'soft' skills as an ability to work in groups, to speak well in public, and to write effectively" (Viadero 2001a, 20). Many of these "soft" skills are learned through participation in student activities. Whether students participate depends, in part, on the extent of the activities offered. Neither school size, location, (rural, urban, suburban), nor percentages of minority student population made a difference in the availability of activities (Buss 1998). Even with widespread availability of activities, many students still do not participate in them. Students most frequently cited five reasons for not participating. They are: "not relevant to needs or interests (76.6 percent), took up time from school work (47.0 percent), scheduled during work (38.1 percent), not elected or selected (27.3 percent), and controlled by social groups (26.1 percent)" (Buss 1998, 99).

Most high schools in the United States offer cocurricular activities, such as music, academic clubs, and sports. Such activities provide opportunities to learn the values of teamwork, individual and group responsibility, physical strength and endurance, competition, diversity, and a sense of culture and community. Cocurricular activities provide a means of reinforcing classroom lessons and the opportunity to apply academic skills to real-world situations, and thus can be considered part of a well-rounded education. "Recent research suggests that participating in extracurricular activities may increase students' sense of engagement or attachment to their school, and thereby decrease the likelihood of school failure and dropping out" (O'Brien and Rollefson 1995, 1). If participation in cocurricular activities can lead to academic success, then the availability of these activities to all students becomes an important equity issue.

Almost all public school students report the availability of a core of cocurricular activities, including sports, performing arts, publications, and honor societies, and most had access to academic clubs and student government. Follow-up data from a 1992 National Education Longitudinal study are presented in table 10.1.

The data by grade level are presented in tables 10.2. and 10.3. Regardless of grade level, the highest percentage of students is attracted to varsity and intramural sports. After athletic pursuits, the performing arts (music, school plays) and academic clubs attract the interest of high school seniors. The next most appealing activities are school publications, vocational clubs, student government, and service clubs. Students participating in cocurricular activities have better attendance and are three times as likely as nonparticipants to have a grade point average of 3.0 or higher. They were also more likely to aspire to higher education—two-thirds of participants are expected to complete at least a bachelor's degree, compared to about half of nonparticipants (Extracurricular Participation 1995).

Table 10.1   Students Reporting Availability of Activity (percent)

	All public schools	Less-affluent schools	More-affluent schools
Any extracurricular activity	99.8	99.8	99.9
Publications	99.4	99.3	99.6
Performing arts	98.8	98.7	99.1
Sports (individual and team)	98.7	98.6	99.1
Honor societies	98.1	97.4	98.8
Student government	96.5	94.9	97.6
Academic clubs	95.9	94.6	97.0
Vocational/professional clubs	93.3	93.4	93.7
Service clubs	89.2	87.2	90.7
Hobby clubs	87.5	85.4	89.2

Source: O'Brien and Rollefson 1995, 13.

Table 10.2   Percentage of Eighth Graders and Tenth Graders Participating in Extracurricular Activities by Type: 1988 and 1990

	Extracurricular Activity							
Grade, Year	Any Activity	Varsity Sports	Intramural Sports	School Music Group	School Play or Musical	Yearbook or Newspaper	Academic Clubs	Hobby Clubs
Eighth, 1988	84.3	47.9	42.4	40.1	8.8	21.8	25.0	15.5
Tenth, 1990	83.4	53.9	19.8	20.9	11.0	8.8	30.1	7.2

Source: Buss 1998, 101; adapted from USDE, NCES 1995a, 351–52.

Table 10.3   Percentage of Twelfth Graders Participating in Extracurricular Activities by Type: 1992

					Extracurricular Activity				
Any Activity	*Varsity Sports*	*Intramural Sports*	*School Music Group*	*School Play or Musical*	*Yearbook or Newspaper*	*Academic Clubs*	*Student Government*	*School Service Club*	*School Vocational Club*
82.8	35.8	29.2	19.8	15.4	18.8	25.1	15.4	13.9	17.7

Source: Buss 1998, 101; adapted from USDE, NCES 1995a, 350.

In a small Texas study, high-achieving students list the following benefits from their participation in cocurricular activities:

(1) meeting other people; (2) increasing responsibility; (3) making school more enjoyable; (4) developing leadership abilities; (5) broadening interests; (6) developing self-confidence; (7) preparing for a career; (8) enhancing time management; and (9) maintaining physical condition or health. For low-achieving students the benefits listed were similar: (1) meeting other people; (2) having a learning experience; (3) preparing for a career; (4) making school more enjoyable; (5) increasing responsibility; (6) developing a greater involvement in school; (7) becoming more outgoing; (8) developing leadership abilities; (9) increasing self-discipline. (Haensly, Lupkowski, and Edlind 1985–1986, 117)

Research indicates that regardless of socioeconomic background, students' participation in activities was not related to the social context of the school. Low-SES students participated at the same rate as high-SES students, whether they attended less-affluent or more-affluent schools (Extracurricular Participation 1995). Yet, low-SES students tend to participate less frequently in cocurricular activities than high-SES students. This gap is cause for concern, especially if cocurricular activities are a possible way of incorporating at-risk students more fully into the school community, leading to greater chances for school success. However, in some vocational clubs, participation rates for low-SES students were not lower. For example, participation in clubs such as Future Farmers or Future Teachers of America is twice as likely for low-SES students (Buss 1998).

In 1992, almost three out of ten of sixteen-year-olds worked; more than one in ten of those students worked more than twenty hours per week. Work obligations are frequently cited as a reason nonparticipating students are not involved in cocurricular activities. Clearly, many working students appropriate time from potentially more beneficial cocurricular activities in order to be available for the environment of work. Students who participate in activities have a higher commitment to school. Students who spend several hours working after school have a lower commitment to school (Buss 1998). Students from small schools have higher participation rates than students from larger schools, and students from large schools are less likely to participate in any cocurricular activities at all. Students from small schools participate in a wider variety of activities compared to students from larger schools, holding more positions of leadership and responsibility in a broader variety of activities than do students in large schools. The environment in a small school places more social pressure on students to participate, and they are pressed in more varied directions (Buss 1998).

Dropping out and not completing a high school diploma has always been a concern in a nation where high skills are needed for success and school attendance is compulsory. Rising academic standards put additional pressures on at-risk students and may further alienate them, causing some to leave school prior to graduation.

"In 1992, the estimated dropout rate for Mexican Americans was 35.3% versus 8.9% for White non-Hispanics and 13.6% for African Americans" (Davalos, Chavez, and Guardiola 1999, 61). According to Census Bureau projections, the Latino population will continue to rapidly grow and they will become the largest U.S. minority group in the twenty-first century, surpassing African Americans. Determining how to reduce the number of dropouts among the entire student population would be beneficial not only for individual students but for society as a whole.

Involvement in cocurricular activities "is linked to decreasing rates of early school dropout in both boys and girls" (Mahoney and Cairns 1997, 248). This is especially true for students who were at the highest risk of dropping out. "For students whose prior commitment to the school and its values has been marginal, such participation provides an opportunity to create a positive and voluntary connection to the educational institution" (Mahoney and Cairns 1997, 248). A single cocurricular activity can provide a pathway for students to gain social acceptance and to achieve personal goals. However, appropriate activities must be available and accessible. Thus, the potential for dropping out may be reduced by the support and positive reinforcement the student receives, which strengthens his or her ties to the school and all its programs (Mahoney and Cairns 1997).

Cocurricular involvement may also assist students to develop their interests and abilities, providing them with a better sense of self. The student's role in high school and the recognition for accomplishments of all kinds are significant sources of success for young people. Students also establish a peer group through their involvement in cocurricular activities, all the while developing a broad range of skills that strengthens their bonds to the school. Athletic activities especially are associated with increased motivation, positive effects, and greater interest compared to other activities (Davalos, Chavez, and Guardiola 1999). Participating in sports may be the primary vehicle for socializing disadvantaged youth. Generally, athletes follow the rules of the school and seek to be successful academically as well as athletically. This success may also be incorporated into their beliefs about themselves. Involvement with sports may provide minority students with a sense of support and acceptance that might be difficult to find by other means (Davalos, Chavez, and Guardiola 1999).

The availability of extracurricular activities and their accessibility are sometimes not the same for many students. The question remains, why the differential involvement? Some possible reasons include:

> (a) Many activities highlighted in yearbooks require expertise in particular domains (e.g., music, sports, languages, mathematics, science); (b) certain school activities require nomination, selection, or election and participation, and status may be maintained by exclusion and gatekeeping (possibly mediated by school personnel, peers, or both); (c) some school activities require minimal academic performance (e.g., a "C" average) to be eligible for participation; (d) socioeconomic status, although not a general barrier to participation, may influence the types of activities students choose (or are allowed) to participate in as well as the attainment of status within those activities. (Mahoney and Cairns 1997, 250)

Dropping out of school is a complex decision dependent on multiple properties of both the individual and the social contexts. When a student drops out, it is very likely that more than a single pathway is involved in the decision—yet cocurricular participation helps prevent school dropout for some students (Mahoney and Cairns 1997).

Although upper SES students and those of higher ability are more likely to participate in high school extracurricular activities, there does not appear to be any immediate detriment for racial minorities and girls. Girls are more likely to participate in extracurricular activities than are comparable boys for every type of activity, with the exception of athletics. . . . Racial and ethnic minorities appear to have likelihoods of participation that are either equal to or higher than their White counterparts. (McNeal 1998, 189)

However, a minority student's lower social class and achievement level is a strong mitigating factor, negating any advantage. And when school districts eliminate some activities and place others on a pay-to-play basis, the potential effect is to eliminate a key alternative pathway for specific subgroups within the school (McNeal 1998).

Cocurricular activities are important because they help students bond with their school and create a sense of belonging. A lack of participation in student cocurricular activities is an additional "loosening" factor that results in a sense of alienation which could lead to the students' disengagement from school. By bonding to the school through participation in student activities, students experience significant positive outcomes. (Klesse and D'Onofrio 1993, 12)

The student experiences the "community model"—an extended family atmosphere where success is recognized and rewarded and students develop a sense of belonging (Klesse and D'Onofrio 1993). In this model, students are known by their first names and understand that others know them and care about what happens to them. Most students at risk of dropping out see school as a threatening place and try to avoid it. They are also intimidated by and distrustful of adults. School experiences contribute to low self-esteem, and school is seen as a fragmented and impersonal organization that is geared toward the successful students yet presented under the guise of benefiting all students. Defeated learners want to learn. Their hostility that gets in the way of learning is directed at the organization and delivery of educational activities (Conrath 1986). For marginally at-risk students, one negative experience reinforces the next and becomes a self-fulfilling prophecy. They come to believe that school is not for them. Dropping out results from several factors in combination, including the students' self-perceptions and their lack of potential for school success—real or perceived.

Some young people will find the period of adolescence difficult under current conditions. Many will be unable to reach their full potential. Their basic human needs—such as caring relationships with adults, guidance and support as they experience biological and physiological changes, and a sense of peer-group belonging—are unmet at this critical stage of life. Glasser emphasizes that at-risk students do not have a positive image of school or learning, and until they do, they will feel disconnected from school. Therefore, the school environment must be structured so that students' basic needs are met: survival, belonging, power, freedom, and fun (Greene and Uroff 1989).

Student activities can decrease the sense of alienation that at-risk students feel. Calabrese (1989) offers solutions to the problem of alienation of the at-risk student. One of his solutions is bonding—the process of uniting one person or group with another. If at-risk students do not engage in healthful, meaningful activities with other adolescents, they may bond with music, drugs, alcohol, and other activities outside the realm of legitimate student activities.

Janice May Udry's story, *How I Faded Away*, describes a student who felt invisible to his school (Udry 1986). The main character, Robbie, is traced from the beginning of elementary school where his process of invisibility begins. All that is noticed is the way Robbie differs from others instead of recognizing his unique talents. He never wanted to go to the blackboard or be a helper or play games because others only noticed his mistakes.

He only becomes visible in school when he cries; when the tears stop, he disappears again. One day, he discovers that he has a talent for playing the recorder. He played at school and everyone noticed. Suddenly Robbie was visible. He was finally recognized for doing something positive.

The lesson to be applied to at-risk students is this: Crying brought Robbie attention. Negative behaviors bring attention to the at-risk student.

> Research has shown that it is most likely the academically talented, the athlete, and the popular student who make up the membership of many clubs. There must be an effort, however, to have a more diverse population involved in student activities. Clubs such as drama/theater and school publications historically have involved many "nontraditional" students due to a need for individual talent in many diverse areas. (Klesse and D'Onofrio 1994, 25)

Student leaders tend to be involved in a variety of cocurricular activities. Students attending a leadership class or a summer leadership camp will understand that leadership is more than the acquisition of personal skills. Leadership requires problem solving, risk taking, and a willingness to address problems larger than oneself. Student leaders can have a crucial and unique role in student activities as a solution to the at-risk problem.

Some clubs such as athletics, student council, and cheerleading have criteria that exclude participation for many students. The formula for participation often seems to be: good grades = activity participation. Why not change the formula to: Activity participation = good or improving grades. This idea is supported by a study done by Slotz (1984) that looked at athletic participation and student grades (Biernat and Klesse 1989). Slotz found that students failed proportionately fewer times when actively competing than during the off-season (Slotz 1984). Why not allow participation and determine continued participation by grade improvement rather than a set GPA? Can we also offer a wider variety of student activities?

Is it possible to make student activities accessible to at-risk students? Advisors must take greater responsibility for including at-risk students in their clubs or organizations. Research confirms the notion that one adult can make a difference. Having even one positive connection to the school can keep a student "hanging in there." One relationship can open the door for better relationships with other students and adults in the school. "Training, formally reserved for counselors and other student support staff, should be made accessible for the student activity adviser. Such training should focus on communication skills, problem-solving skills, group process, cooperative learning, and individual learning styles" (Klesse and D'Onofrio 1994, 26). Hopefully, activity advisors will feel more comfortable reaching out and "building a bridge" to at-risk students. Not only is a bridge needed between the at-risk student and the school but a bridge is needed between the at-risk student and the successful student (Klesse and D'Onofrio 1994).

Nontraditional leaders do not take intentional steps to be recognized as leaders in school. They are active in activities such as volunteering, tutoring, being a student assistant, or working outside school; they participate in clubs without holding a position; or are informal leaders among their friends. Among the nontraditional leaders are those viewed as at risk—delinquents, special needs students, nonattenders, teen parents, and others. These teens are often overlooked and undervalued for their leadership potential (MacGregor 2001). Ironically, because they struggle to survive in a complex environment, they develop extraordinary leadership skills. At-risk youth become resilient youth able to take care of their own destinies when equipped with leadership skills. Inviting nontraditional leaders to participate gives them a sense that someone believes in them (MacGregor 2001).

If a select group of kids always participates in all the activities, there is a good possibility that a large group of uninvolved kids will feel excluded from participating. These invisible kids are another kind of at-risk student—at risk of not reaching their full potential, and of becoming alienated from school and community (Fiscus 1999b). "Being denied the opportunity to participate in an academic or cocurricular activity can also result in students feeling unwanted or rejected. [Sometimes] . . . it is simpler to withdraw socially than to face the daily reminders that they are unwanted or denied an opportunity to participate in or out of class" (Manning 2000, 20). Consequently, they may make fewer friendships and do not have an important opportunity to learn about their individual strengths and interests (Manning 2000).

Student activities should be accessible and inclusive to all secondary school students. The film *Remember the Titans* portrays the struggle T.C. Williams High School in Alexandria, Virginia, went through in 1971. In the film, two coaches, one white and one black, empowered a racially mixed team to overcome racial separation and become champions. Many high schools across the nation employ unity-building activities. One such program is Student/Community Enrichment Activity Program (SCEAP) of the Pocono Mountain School District (Swiftwater, Pennsylvania).

[SCEAP] involves students in both after-school and cocurricular activities—activities and programs designed to fill the gap between the classroom and the school community with multicultural programs that continue the educational process. Programs such as Profiles in American History, An American Landscape, Motown Night, and Poetry Night have been carefully developed and planned by SCEAP students and their adviser. One of the most popular SCEAP activities—Neckties Against Drugs—motivated more than 3,500 students to wear neckties in support of the campaign. (L. Thomas 1999, 44)

The program entertains students and educates them about different cultures. It also provides them an opportunity to view history through a different lens.

Gay, lesbian, bisexual, and transgender (GLBT) youth often must endure an extremely hostile school climate. These students are four times as likely to report having been threatened with a weapon at school. Their dropout rate is estimated to be 26 percent annually (Frankfurt 2000). The factor that made the difference in whether gay students felt their schools were safe and affirming environments was the support of their peers. Student leaders can play an important role by helping all students become integral to the larger school community. They can use their positions and access to their peers and administrators to address these challenging issues. Optimally, young people from diverse groups should be represented in leadership positions. It takes a concentrated effort to end entrenched harassment, prejudice, and fear in schools but they can be safe and respectful places for all. This is extremely important because an estimated 30 percent of youth suicides are committed by lesbian and gay people (Edwards 1997). Cocurricular activities need to be accessible and enjoyable for all students.

A student's transition from eighth grade to high school is much more difficult than most of us remember. Two important goals of many transition programs are to reduce the number of students retained in eighth grade and keep students from dropping out in high school. According to Morgan and Hertzog (2001), quality programs should focus on areas of student concerns, such as curriculum, facilities, safety and discipline, teachers, counselors and administrators, and general questions—but should not end when students start high school. Big Brother/Big Sister programs answer these needs in some high schools, keeping the transitions program active all year. According to Morgan and Hertzog (2001), indicators of successful programs also include student and parent participation in school-sponsored activities and programs, and help to eliminate or reduce student failures in various subject areas (math, science, social studies, and English).

The middle school transition is a complex and difficult one for many young people due to rapid physical, emotional, and cognitive changes. Students worry about many of the following:

Logistics of New Building and Routine
- Getting lost in school
- Forgetting your locker combination
- Buying new notebooks
- Eating in a larger cafeteria
- Leaving the wrong books and supplies in your locker or forgetting to bring the right books and supplies to class

Increased Academic Demands
- Having a tough teacher
- Having to do harder school work
- Having too much homework
- Having teachers expect too much

Dealing with Conflict, Authority Figures, Older Students
- Arguing with a teacher
- Being sent to the principal or vice principal
- Getting into fights
- Being talked into doing things you don't want to do
- Having things stolen from you
- Being bothered by the older kids
- Not getting along with all your teachers

Peer Relationships
- Not seeing your friends from elementary school enough
- Having trouble making new friends
- Wishing you were in a better reading group
- Being teased by other kids
- Not being in the "in" group
- Being made fun of in the locker room
- Dating
- Being pressured to take drugs or alcohol
- Drinking beer, wine, or liquor
- Taking drugs
- Smoking cigarettes (Elias 2001, 22)

School performance and peers have more influence than race or family income level on a propensity to drink alcohol, smoke cigarettes, or carry weapons. "Students who spent a lot of time after school with their friends tended to be more likely to drink, smoke, have sex, and carry weapons than young people who spent their after-school hours in supervised settings" (Portner 2000, 5). Community-based programs and organizations as well as school-sponsored activities may make a significant contribution to a young person's learning and development. When compared to many typical young people in the United States, students with significant participation in community organizations were:

- 26 percent more likely to have received recognition for good grades;
- 20 percent more likely to rate their chances of going to college as very high;
- Nearly twice as likely to view themselves as worthy persons;
- 13 percent more likely to believe that they would have a job that they enjoyed;
- More than twice as likely to feel they had control over their lives; and
- More than two and one-half times more likely to express a sense of civic responsibility and a desire to give back to their communities. (McLaughlin 2001, 14)

Participation in community organizations provides support and direction to many young people, allowing them also to experience success. Many times this success carries over to the school, helping students find a positive path to graduation. Schools can support these organizations when they:

- Share space and facilities
- Set up institutional collaborations
- Connect mutual goals
- Integrate school and community resources for teaching and learning by codeveloping curriculums
- Support teacher involvement in community-based organizations
- Develop meaningful measures of youth development (McLaughlin 2001, 16–17)

Despite the benefits and recent focus on after-school programs, most students do not attend such programs. The programs have yet to become universal and many times are operated outside the school facility with little or no school involvement.

By spending their after-school hours involved in cocurricular activities, community activities, or service learning, students have the chance to interact with peers who have similar interests and aspirations. They also interact with positive adult role models. Students so involved generally improve their school achievement and attendance. They also make easier transitions between buildings because their student activity involvement provides a familiar peer group.

Motivating students who are at risk of failing is a growing concern for everyone involved in the education of young people. According to Weiner (1979), the motivation theory of attribution helps explain a pattern of failure. Attributions are the reasons one assigns for having achieved success or failure (Weiner 1979). Students' attributions affect their future expectations and actions. Students use the following four attributions most frequently:

1. Not having the ability—"I'm just not a writer"
2. Not expending enough effort—"I could do it if I really tried"

133

3. Task difficulty—"The test was too hard"
4. Luck—"I guessed right" (Alderman 1990, 27)

"Teachers who are successful in reaching low-achieving students combine a high sense of their own efficacy with high, realistic expectations for student achievement. *Teacher efficacy* refers to teachers' confidence in their ability to influence student learning and motivation. This sense of efficacy, in turn, affects teachers' expectations concerning student abilities" (Alderman 1990, 28).

Four "links" are as follows:

Link One: *Proximal goals*—Goals play an important role in the cultivation of self-motivation by establishing a target or personal standards by which to evaluate or monitor performances (Bandura 1986).

Link Two: *Learning strategies*—Students identify the learning strategies that will help them accomplish their goals.

Link Three: *Successful experience*—The focus in a learning goal is on "how much progress I made," not on "how smart I am," a performance goal.

Link Four: *Attribution for success*—Students are encouraged to attribute success to their personal efforts or abilities. (Alderman 1990, 28–29)

Character education may be most appropriately addressed during the middle school years due to students' rapid growth and development at this time. "It is developmentally appropriate that middle schools provide instructional environments that help students better understand themselves through examining critical personal issues. . . . Thrown, typically, into much larger schools than they attended during their elementary years, young adolescents are likely to encounter a much more culturally diverse population of students" (Brown and Varady 1997, 29–30). Students need to be encouraged to be actively involved in their education through the following instructional practices:

- *Cooperative learning.* Teach students to work with each other and encourage them to develop communication values.
- *Teaching for thinking and reflection.* Develop students' ability to reason and distinguish between shades of meaning, and to apply what they learn in school to the rest of their lives.
- *Reading for character.* Literature such as poetry, nonfiction, parables, and historic documents are invaluable tools for moral lessons.
- *Caring through service to others.* Service learning and volunteerism help students practice virtue in school and in the community. (Bennett 2001, 17)

The outcome of our efforts should be that students develop guiding principles—positive rules to govern individual and interpersonal behaviors, actions, and relationships. According to the International Center for Leadership in Education, the "Twelve Guiding Principles of Exceptional Character" upon which to build a character education program are:

- Adaptability—The ability and willingness to change. To put oneself in harmony with changed circumstances. Be ready and willing to adjust as necessary to the changes in people and circumstances that arise in every day life.
- Compassion—Kindness. The desire to help others in distress. Show kindness and concern for others in distress by offering help whenever possible.
- Contemplation—Giving serious consideration to something. To think things through with proper care before taking action.
- Courage—Bravery. The willingness to put one's beliefs into practice, the capacity to meet danger without giving way to fear. Face difficulty or danger and express your beliefs even if you are afraid.
- Honesty—Truthfulness, sincerity. The act or condition of never deceiving, stealing, or taking advantage of the trust of others. Be truthful in all that you do and never deceive, steal, or take advantage of the trust of others.
- Initiative—Eagerness to do something. Take responsible action on your own, without prompting from others.
- Loyalty—Faithfulness, dependability. The quality of being faithful to another person in the performance of duty, adhering to a contract with another person. Show others that you are dependable when you have a commitment to them.
- Optimism—Positive beliefs. The inclination to take a hopeful view or think that all will work out for the best. Strive to be positive in your beliefs about yourself, others, and the future.
- Perseverance—Hard work. The quality of trying hard and continuously in spite of obstacles and difficulties.
- Respect—Regard, value, admire, appreciate. Special esteem or consideration in which one holds another person or thing. Show regard for yourself, others, and the world around you.
- Responsibility—Accountability. To consider oneself answerable for something. Demonstrate that you consider yourself to be accountable for your actions and that you follow through on your commitments.
- Trustworthiness—Reliability. Dependable, deserving of trust and confidence. (Daggett 2001, 1)

Unless students experience a positive and supportive school climate, built upon guiding principles such as these, some students will never achieve minimal levels of success or involvement in school.

How do we help all students become involved and hopefully succeed in school? Because some students do not know how to connect with the school, they fail to participate in activities within the school community. Many students lack the skills and confidence to attempt to become a member or participant in cocurricular activities. After attempting to involve students in the existing cocurricular activities, the New Hartford Central School District (New York) initiated a cocurricular activity for students who are "disconnected" and, for some, on the edge of dropping out. The district created a "Breakfast Club" that "provides leadership training and dropout prevention. This program is designed to meet the needs of those disconnected students who are ready for the kind of help that we can offer. Not every student is ready. The defining factor for students who become members of this group is readiness for growth that will form a connection between the student and the school" (D'Onofrio 1999, 24). Participating students have the following characteristics in common:

- Attendance difficulties
- Discipline problems
- Poor academic performance
- Little or no student activity involvement

- Most important, despite the above qualities, the student still shows small signs that he or she is connectable. This evidence might be a teacher comment or how a student sporadically takes interest in schoolwork or leadership qualities noticed when with friends. (D'Onofrio 1999, 24)

As part of the Breakfast Club's program, each student is involved in leadership training, has a mentor, completes career exploration activities, and attends weekly or biweekly meetings. Students also complete community service projects and work toward an end-of-the-year group activity (trip). The Breakfast Club helps disconnected students "connect" to the school district (D'Onofrio 1999).

Student activities can be more accessible to all students in three basic areas: activities, advisors, and participants. Student activities can encompass a "wider variety" of students. Advisors must take on greater responsibility to include at-risk students. The "bridge" between at-risk students and the successful students is also very important. Some tips for involving at-risk students include:

1. Request in-service training in areas such as problem solving, decision making, group process, and learning styles. Workshops are available outside the school or, in some cases, may be brought to the school.
2. Gain support from the top. Present goals to the administration for including at-risk students. Develop mission statements to be passed out to students and parents. (Top-down support for bottom-up planning.)
3. Be willing to get more involved on a personal level. You may be just the adult with whom an at-risk student connects.
4. Publicize your group. Openly address the changes that you are trying to institute. At-risk students need to be aware of the changes being made
5. Recruit members. Find a student or students you feel have the talent or ability to contribute to your group. Go after that student and sell your activity. Use anticipation statements such as "Hope to see you next Tuesday" or "Next Tuesday you can be in charge of printing the signs."
6. Don't take rejection personally. The at-risk student is impersonally rejecting the school, not you. Remembering this will help you be less defensive. Try again.
7. Select role models in your group who are willing to "buddy up" with an at-risk student and provide peer support.
8. Be in close contact with a school counselor. Consult with the counselor, go over problems, and keep informal track of attendance and academic progress.
9. Use community resources to the fullest. Bring people to school, take students on field trips, help make school-to-life connections. Have a guest for lunch. Sponsor a community open forum to discuss problems and to determine how students can help.
10. Get student input. Students usually have the most creative ideas to solve problems.
11. Survey all students. Discover their needs and learn what it would take to get them involved.
12. Take your responsibility as adviser beyond the realm of the activity or club you are advising. Look at all students as potential members. Take time out to talk with students in the hall. Eat lunch with a group of students; show you care.
13. Attend an adviser conference or leadership program at the state or national level.
14. Advocate for having student activities be a part of the student's four-year academic plan. This idea could be expanded as far as requiring activity involvement at each grade level.
15. Show students the value of service. At-risk students need role models who are involved. Adults who are active in serving others have a positive influence. Volunteer and serve others. Invite the at-risk student to join you. (Klesse and D'Onofrio 1993, 13–15)

Consider also the following ten ways to break down barriers through student council:

1. Plan low-risk activities. Most students are not the outspoken risk takers that fill our student councils. Students want to be part of activities but could never allow themselves to dress up in a Mickey Mouse outfit or perform in a suitcase relay race. Those activities are too high risk. Draw students into participation with activities that take little to no risk.

2. Pay attention to people. Watch for the nonverbal signals that people send (facial expressions, posture, tone of voice, frequency of eye contact or lack of it). Be responsive to what you hear people saying. Most people are unable to tell you they've been hurt or left out, but their nonverbal expressions may deliver the message. You just have to look and listen for them.

3. Diversify your committees. Standing committees and those set up for special projects should be diverse in their leadership and membership. Ask students who have varied interests and backgrounds to serve on and chair committees. Every student council committee should include nonelected members.

4. Get involved in the lives of others. Spend time informally with students outside your organization. Enlarge your circle by sitting down with someone you hardly know or with someone who always seems to eat alone. Ask about personal interests and look for strengths and ideas about the student activities program. Listen intently to the answer of every question.

5. Develop a sense of family. Promote the sense that the people in your school are a team or a family, rather than a bunch of people who happen to be in the same building every day. Encourage the appreciation of differences instead of promoting cliques.

6. Structure activities to be inclusive. If your group feels it must sponsor an expensive event, such as a formal dance, give students time to save for it. Hold a "worn only once" formal dress sale.

7. Keep track of students who have participated in events like relay race teams in pep rallies. Insist that those students can't participate again until everyone else in the class has been a part of an activity. Put the vice president of each class in charge of asking new people to participate each time.

8. Recognize special events and accomplishments. Write a congratulatory note to students who have won special honors, send a birthday card, decorate a student's locker for a special occasion, or send an e-vite to an event (check out www.evite.com). Personalizing communication with students in this way lets them know that you care about them and encourages them to get involved in your activities.

9. Ask people for help. The power of a personal plea for assistance should not be overlooked. Think about how difficult it is for you to refuse to help someone when they ask you. If members of your organization decided to personally ask students who are good at graphic design, for example, to help with publicity for an upcoming event, these students would be apt to get involved. They would probably also come to the event, because people tend to support what they create.

10. Each one reach one. If each member of your organization brought one new person to the next event or meeting, your numbers would double! (Summarized from Lori Kiblinger, *Total Participation—Is It Possible?* as quoted in Fiscus 1999b, 19)

Students who participate in cocurricular activities during their high school years have a higher than expected academic achievement and lower than expected involvement in risky behaviors. Eccles and Barber (1999) found that participation in five types of activities—prosocial (church and volunteer activities), team sports, school involvement (student government, pep club, and/or cheerleading), performing arts, and academic clubs—predicted better than expected high school GPAs. However, sports participation also increased the use of alcohol.

Knowing an adolescent's activities often reveals the companions an adolescent chooses to be with. Coparticipants become one's peer group. Involvement in cocurricular activities helps fulfill developmental needs in adolescents. They also help one become a member of the school community (Eccles and Barber 1999).

In closing:

> Glasser's studies have shown that when students experience success and identify with significant others, they make healthier choices about their behavior (Glasser 1993). Under current conditions however, far too many young people will not make the passage through early adolescence successfully. Their basic human needs—caring relationships with adults, guidance in facing sometimes overwhelming biological and psychological changes, the security of belonging to constructive peer groups, and the perception of future opportunity—go unmet at this critical stage of life. Millions of these young adolescents will never reach their full potential. . . . Early adolescence for these youth is a turning point towards a diminished future. (Jackson, Davis, Abeel, and Bordonaro 2000, 8)

> One form of diversity that affects every teacher is *transiency*. Although about 3 million children are born each year, up to 40 million Americans move in that same time period, making mobility far more important than births in explaining population changes. (Hodgkinson 2000–2001, 8)

11

HOW DOES THE SCHOOL FINANCE A STUDENT ACTIVITY PROGRAM FAIRLY AND EQUITABLY?

S chools raise money for student activities through direct support by the school system and through fund-raising campaigns, dues, fees, and activity tickets (Williams 1971). "Given the voluntary nature of student activities, it is quite common to see a variety of funding strategies operating to support such programs. The strategies used depend on the regulations and laws established by the separate state and local school boards" (Buss 1998, 112–13).

Many districts and states, believing it would unfairly penalize less-advantaged students and discourage their involvement, have been reluctant to charge student activity fees to participate (Buss 1998). However, hundreds of school districts nationwide must now consider implementing user fees to sustain programs because state legislatures have cut their support for public education. A survey conducted at Ohio Northern University found that "34 states now permit the assessment of fees against students, although the legality of these practices has been adjudicated in less than a quarter of the 50 states" (Goldman 1991, 30). According to the 1991 survey, fifteen states and the District of Columbia prohibited fees; one state, Nebraska, did not have a statute addressing the issue.

When a community first considers implementing fees for activities or participation in classes, it raises questions of equity. "In part that concern stems from the education clauses in state constitutions establishing a system of 'free public education'—a guarantee interpreted in widely different ways by courts, state policy-makers, and local boards" (Goldman 1991, 32).

By 1997, "pay to play" had become common in thousands of school districts across the country because of increasingly dwindling resources.

> Nobody seems to like it—not parents, some of whom pay and then wonder why their children sit on the bench; not administrators, who hate to alienate many of their district's biggest supporters, not coaches, who see parents complain and—in some cases—sports participation decline once fees are instituted. . . . The practice also raises questions about the American promise of a free public

education. Do fees for sports and other extracurricular activities undermine that ideal? (Hardy 1997, 25)

A 1994 survey of its members by the National Federation of State High School Associations (NFHS) found that almost 25 percent of them charged athletic fees. Of the ones that didn't, 17 percent said they were considering them in the future. The median fee charged per sport was $30, but this rate varied widely by individual district. The National Federation of State High School Associations also found that almost 80 percent of participating schools waived fees if parents couldn't afford them—yet fees may discourage some potential athletes from participating (Hardy 1997).

Consider the following example.

During the 1990–91 school year—the year before Rochester [Michigan] instituted pay-to-play—3,295 team slots were filled on middle school and high school rosters. By 1993–94, when fees had reached their highest—$200 for high school sports, $175 for middle school—the number had dropped to 2,715. That year, the program brought in $514,000, just .7 percent of the district's operating budget. During the following two years, the fees were phased out—and sports enrollment increased. For the school year just ended (1996–97), 3,360 slots were filled. (Hardy 1997, 26)

In 1990–1991, the first year of implementing fees, the Tucson (Arizona) Unified School District had 2,000 fewer students participating in interscholastic sports and arts organizations. The district's governing board charged $105 for every athlete and pep squad member and $60 for each performing arts participant in order to make up a $12 million budget shortfall. The district lowered the fee to $50 and $30 respectively, and created a cap on the amount an individual or family could be assessed in the fall of 1991 when the deficit was smaller. Anticipating a loss of students because of the fees, the district worked with a community educational foundation to establish financial aid for students (Goldman 1991).

Some schools are making deals with corporations to obtain revenue. These corporate deals involve, for example, the school selling exclusive marketing rights to companies that sell products like soft drinks, snacks, and athletic goods. Other schools have sold naming rights to their facilities, such as stadiums and auditoriums. Many schools have sold advertising space on buses, rooftops, equipment, and publications. "Another opportunity exists in bundling services to make an attractive package. Consider, for instance, a telecommunications package, which might include long distance services, local phone services, cell phone services, and Internet access" (Morrison 1998, 24).

Coke's agreement with the North Syracuse, New York, Central School District, signed in July, promises $1.53 million over the next 10 years, including an immediate $900,000 payout that will help the district build a new high school athletic complex. . . . The contract, providing $70,000 annual payments to the district for the next nine years in addition to the $900,000 installment, governs aspects large and small of the relationship, including:

- the exclusive beverage distribution rights,
- the pricing of each product,
- location of vending machines,
- nutritional restrictions,

- a bottle recycling rebate and
- sexual harassment and smoking by vendors when on campus.* (Morrison 1998, 25)

The Albuquerque Public Schools district used external fund-raising to reconstruct its athletic program. Albuquerque, the twenty-sixth-largest school district in the country, has 87,000 students and runs eleven varsity and junior varsity sports for boys and girls. Each of the district's eleven high schools gets an equal share of the funding.

> During the late 1980s, the administration was forced to cut the district's athletic budgets by $600,000 over a three-year period, sending shock waves through the community and eliminating competitive sports opportunities for hundreds of students. . . . The school district responded by inviting a local group of leaders to serve on an athletic study committee, which was asked to suggest how Albuquerque might restore a full-fledged interscholastic athletic program. The committee recommended hiring someone to serve as a fund-raiser to bring in supplemental resources targeted specifically for the support of athletics and to reverse the trend of annual budget cuts. (Montano 1998, 30)

The goal for 1998–1999 was to generate more than $400,000 in cash pledges and exceed $300,000 in in-kind contributions and gifts for an ongoing campaign that began in 1989 as "Support Our Sports." Here is how it works:

- Foundations: Local community and business leaders formed two foundations to assist the district in generating support for interscholastic athletics.
- Scoreboard Sponsors: Sponsorship involves a business, corporate, or retail donor and recipient. The donor typically pays for a scoreboard for use at a school gymnasium or football field.
- Award Recognition Programs: Student- and staff-sponsored athletic awards are given weekly, monthly, and annually to recognize individual achievements. These programs are underwritten fully by local businesses or corporations.
- Broadcast Rights: The athletic department sells broadcast opportunities to local radio and TV stations for football, basketball, baseball, and softball games during each sport's season. Specific programs are a source of revenue for teams, cheerleading and drill squads, and booster clubs.
- Special Events and Promotions: Special events vary from a T-shirt giveaway promotion to a celebrity golf tournament each spring.
- Sport Publications: The athletic department publishes weekly, monthly, or seasonal sport-specific programs as a source of revenue for teams, cheerleading and drill squads, and booster clubs. Programs are twenty-four to thirty-six-page booklets, consisting of team photos, rosters, advertising, weekly updates, and statistics on teams and players. Advertising revenue supports the cost of publication, distribution, and editorial work. (Montano 1998, 30–31)

Generally, student activities are funded by many means, some of which are as follows:

- Athletics—gate receipts, fund-raising, community support, and athletic boosters
- Band, chorus, and NJROTC—student fund-raising and booster groups

---

* Copies of the model contract are available from the New York State Education Department, Office of Legal Affairs, 89 Washington St., Albany, NY 12234.

- Individual clubs—fund-raising sales and events
- Student council—beg, borrow, steal! You name it!
- Honor Societies—dues, generally
- Service clubs—work community events for donations
- Classes—buy-out assemblies, car washes, sales, and dances. (Dick and Thomas 2000, 40)

Sales of household and holiday items are a common means of raising money. These sales may include food, candy, and magazines. Fund-raising includes sponsoring events (donkey basketball), can and bottle drives, talent shows, and social activities. Fund-raising through sales, raffles, concessions and dances, and other means will always be a part of student activities. Some general guidelines to follow for success are:

- Establish a fund-raising committee.
- Have a clear goal in mind. Goal setting is one of the first steps in fund-raising. Your group should discuss why they want to raise money and how much they need. Will the fund-raiser be a required activity by each individual in the group?
- Brainstorm Ideas. Brainstorming with the committee is a great way to start getting ideas for how to raise the money and gives everyone a chance to contribute ideas.
- Develop an action plan. The committee should select the best fund-raiser idea and develop a plan of action to present to the entire group. At a meeting, present the idea and involve group members in a discussion of the proposal, then vote on it.
- Post the group's objective in a highly visible spot and regularly update your progress.
- Get students excited about the project. The more you publicize your fund-raiser, the more people will participate.
- Celebrate your success. After the sales period or event is over, have some fun with the students. Plan a social to end the event or have a pizza party at the next meeting.
- Remember the details. The committee should report the success of the fund-raising effort at the organization's next meeting. (Curry 2000, 19–20)

Sometimes, fund-raising for student activities can be quite innovative. In Bayonne, New Jersey, the high school became linked with the New Jersey Film Commission. Films shot on the campus provide funds for student programs (Wanko 1996).

If a professional fund-raising company is to be used, Curry (2000, 20) suggests obtaining the answers to the following questions:

$ How long has the company (and the company's representative) been in the product fund-raising business? The size of the company and the mechanics of the program are less important than the company's financial stability, experience, and reputation.

$ What value-added services does the company offer and how much do these services cost (e.g., assistance to volunteers, communicating with parents)?

$ How will the company tailor the program to fit your organization's particular needs or requirements?

$ Is volunteer safety a key element of the program? Does the company discourage unsupervised door-to-door sales? Will children be encouraged to focus their efforts on family and friends? Will adult supervision be stressed? How will these points be communicated to children? Parents?

$ Are teachers encouraged to take advantage of the educational elements (e.g., oral presentation, math, and marketing skills) of the fund-raising program? If so, how?

$ Does the company understand and comply with your state sales and use tax laws and how these laws affect your program?

$ What is the company's order turn-around time? How are products shipped and how will it affect delivery logistics?

$ How responsive will the company/representative be should problems arise?

$ What is the company's policy if your group receives damaged products? Are returns accepted?

$ How does the company handle back orders?*

The school district also needs to be certain of the following to ensure a successful fund-raiser:

- Make sure the product chosen is marketable. Some schools can have success with one product while other schools have difficulty. Candy is a high-in-demand product and results in profit at most schools.
- Make sure the selling price allows for a profit and is reasonable to the customer. Candy usually has a high mark-up, as much as 100 percent, and still remains at an affordable price.
- Properly order, with approvals, and maintain the right to return unused product. This is a critical control, especially with perishable products. Ordering too much inventory and not returning unsold product reduces the profitability of the sale.
- Safeguard the product from spoilage or theft. Keeping the product in a locked area that protects the product, if perishable, adds to the chance for a successful fund-raiser.
- Issue the product to students in an organized and accountable manner. Many vendors provide student check-out and sign-in forms that track how much product is outstanding and how much has been returned.
- Use numerically controlled receipts to help to document the receipt, transfer, and deposit of funds.
- Promote and schedule activities. Student council involvement in notifying the student body of the sale event and scheduling the activity so it does not compete with other fund-raising activities provides for a greater chance of profitability.
- Review of financial results by the student council. An ongoing and final end-of-event financial analysis presented to the student council allows them to make decisions about the types of fund-raisers that are successful in their environment. (Cuzzetto 1999, 42)

Usually, the activity's treasurer, under the supervision of the advisor, manages the bookkeeping and related paperwork. Duties of the treasurer typically include:

- Maintain an accurate and detailed financial record.
- Chair the finance/budget committee.
- Prepare a financial statement for meetings of the club or organization.

---

* Source: *Fundraising Fundamentals: Elements for Raising Money through Product Sales by the Association of Fundraisers and Direct Sellers [AFRDS]*. Used with permission. To obtain a copy of the brochure, contact AFRDS, 5775 Peachtree-Dunwoody Road, Suite 500-G, Atlanta, GA 30342 or visit www.afrds.org.

- Assist in preparing the budget, present proposed budget to the executive committee for approval, and help explain budgetary items to the membership.
- Prepare and sign all purchase orders and requisitions.
- Coordinate and carry out fund-raising projects with the finance/budget committee.
- Check that all contracts are signed by the appropriate school officials, club president, adviser, and principal.
- Give final approval before invoices are paid.
- Work with the school bookkeeper. (Fortin 2000, 15)

Record keeping requirements for student activity funds are controlled by local policies, state laws and regulations, and the state auditor's office. The ledger must keep an accurate record of all transactions—money received and money spent. A numbered receipt book is also essential. All money received should generate a receipt. Consider using a rubric such as the one shown in table 11.1 to assess money management success.

In the final analysis, the advisor or sponsor is the person responsible for all financial matters of the class or club. The school holds all accounts. The district's internal rules and regulations must be followed, especially those regarding purchases and fund deposits. School purchase orders are usually required for all purchases and verbal quotes. Multiple bids (usually three) are required if supplies, materials, equipment, or contractual costs are expensive, over a certain dollar amount. Funds are usually deposited daily but are required to be deposited when funds received exceed a specified dollar amount. Cash, no matter how little, should always be kept in a safe and secure location. It is good practice to follow the following guidelines:

- A teacher-sponsor shall be responsible for the funds related to each voluntary student activity for which a fee is collected.
- All monies received by teachers and organizations within the school shall be duly receipted and deposited in the appropriate school account.
- All purchases or expenditures of funds shall have supporting evidence in the form of receipts or invoices, or cancelled checks.
- Student activity funds are intended to finance programs within the school and must be expended in a manner to benefit the student body as a whole.
- School activity funds are audited annually. (Henrico County Public School n.d., 77)

School business officials should establish and implement internal controls over student activity funds using standard business practices to oversee student activity or organization account access, deposits, payments, purchases, collecting receipts, bookkeeping, and auditing. Financial record-keeping software can make these tasks easier (Johnson and Steigerwald 1997).

Students often earn their own student activity funds. State or local rules and regulations restrict how the monies designated for student purposes are used. Each fund is covered by the rules and regulations established by its governing body—in many cases, the board of education. Student activities, and their corresponding revenues and expenditures, are usually separated into four categories:

1. *General Student Activities*—affects all students—yearbook, store, etc.
2. *Classes*—class of 2006, sophomore, etc.

Table 11.1   Fund-Raising Rubric

Score	Record Keeping	Educational Experience	Compliance Expectations	Internal Controls
4	Record keeping and monitoring above and beyond what is required.	Capitalizing on the opportunity to teach general accepted accounting practices and state law to students and adults.	Exceeding the expectations of the state auditor's office and other regulatory agencies.	Evidence of strong internal controls.
3	Meeting the requirements of local board policy, your state laws and regulations, and your state accounting manual.	Teaching state ASB law* to students and adults in leadership positions.	Meeting the expectations of the state auditor's office and other regulatory agencies.	Evidence of good internal controls.
2	Failing to meet the requirements of local board policy, your state laws and regulations, and your state accounting manual.	Failing to teach state ASB law to students in leadership positions, but teaching advisors and coaches.	Not meeting the expectations of the state auditor's office and other regulatory agencies.	Poor internal controls.
1	Gross failure in meeting the requirements of local board policy, your state laws and regulations, and your state accounting manual	Failure to teach state ASB law to students or advisors or coaches.	Not complying with the written directions of the state auditor's office and other regulatory agencies.	Poor internal controls resulting in evidence of criminal actions, cover-up, and/or misconduct.

If you scored 14 or above, congratulations! Your organization is in great shape. If you scored 13 or below, you might want to consider making changes to the policies and procedures in your school.

*Associated Study Body Law
Source: Fortin 2000, 18.

3. *Clubs*—science club, chess club, key club, etc.
4. *Athletics and Intramurals*—including revenue from "gate" and expenditures (Cuzzetto 1999, 4)

Each school needs to provide clear directions for:

- Forming clubs or classes,
- Establishing and preparing budgets,
- Requesting initial funds,

- Requesting the right to hold activities (including fund-raisers),
- Scheduling activities to the students' best interest,
- Dealing with parent/booster groups,
- Requesting the expenditure of funds, and
- Reporting financial status. (Cuzzetto 1999, 5)

The school should also determine whether a club is required to raise its own funds or whether they are allocated general student body funds. An aspect that often is overlooked is how assets will be handled upon dissolution of the club (Cuzzetto 1999). The club can stipulate in the bylaws that the assets of the club/class will be returned to the student council's general funds or transferred to another club upon dissolution. "For example, any money left from this year's graduating class may be transferred to next year's graduating class" (Cuzzetto 1999, 6).

The school board and student council should establish policies and procedures over the sales, revenues, and receivables. They should address:

- Approvals for all fund-raising activities,
- Scheduling of fund-raisers,
- Use of prenumbered forms for all activities,
- Authorization of change funds,
- Frequency of inventories for ongoing sales (store, etc.),
- Type of inventory (periodic or perpetual),
- Parental permission to participate,
- Limits to amount of merchandise to any student at one time,
- Process to transfer money between staff and/or students,
- Fines or grade holding for lost money or merchandise,
- Allowance for markdowns, giveaways, or promotional sales,
- Receiving and securing merchandise,
- Cost recovery allocation,
- Type of activities allowed (door-to-door, raffles, car washes, dances, etc.),
- Authorization for credit sales and collection policy and charge back, and
- Preparation of financial statements. (Cuzzetto 1999, 47)

Fund-raising teaches many leadership and business skills to club and activity members. Activity programs are expensive to maintain due to many factors, including insurance, advisor or coaches' salaries, equipment, and facilities. But activity programs are especially responsive to the developmental needs of students. Activities provide students with an outlet to actively pursue interests, become responsible, and acquire needed social skills. The research suggests that "student participation in activities does not occur at the cost of academic performance" (Buss 1998, 113). Participation is associated with many positive outcomes for the participants.

In closing:

As the school's student handbook says, students can count on encountering teachers who "like and respect young people, have broad interests, firm values, and sound training in their disciplines; and are enthusiastic about participating, beyond the classroom, in the social and personal growth of their students." (Sternberg 2000, 71)

Student respondents seem happy with the way in which their activities programs are organized. They would, however, like to see their advisers adequately compensated to attract more qualified sponsors. According to Stan Levy, "These people give much time and effort and should be paid accordingly for their professional services." (Rough 1994, 13)

12

WHAT WOULD A SCHOOL WITHOUT STUDENT ACTIVITIES BE LIKE?

When teachers realize the interdisciplinary nature of the curriculum and that learning occurring outside the classroom complements classroom learning, they can make connections that help students. "Student leaders today learn goal setting, decision making, problem solving, how to deal with diversity, teamwork, and communication skills. They serve as positive role models for their peers. High school is the optimum time to develop those leadership skills" (Wolff, Cummins, and Fiscus 2000, 17).

"What once may have started as 'something to do' activities have turned into programs that enhance and enrich the lives of students and their communities" (Fiscus 1999a, 13). At the 1919 annual convention of the National Association of Secondary School Principals, it was proposed that a national honor society be formed responding to the growing movement in schools to emphasize athletics and only strictly academic activities. The National Honor Society was founded in 1921 based on the fundamental virtues of character, leadership, scholarship, and service. According to Brogue and Jacobson (1940), by 1939, between two-thirds and three-fourths of all schools had some form of student government.

"Typical clubs of the decade included student government, foreign affairs, NHS, camera/photography club, drama, band, music, radio, movie/cinema club, art and architecture, and creative writing (scribblers) clubs" (Fiscus 1999a, 15). The focus of these clubs was on individual needs, specifically to develop "good citizenship, qualities such as leadership, poise, initiative, cooperation, proper attitude, special abilities, and social traits" (Fiscus 1999a, 16).

Over the decades to the present, the focus of student activities and the level of student involvement have changed with the times. Defining historical events such as war, environmental awareness, and political concerns have changed the focus and the nature of the activities. Some activities such as clubs, athletic teams, student government, and music groups continue to be popular. The role of student council at the local level today is supported by the National Association of Student Councils, which believes:

- Empowered students are vehicles for positive change in their school and community.
- Student leaders have the responsibility to be positive role models.
- Student councils play a vital role in preserving knowledge of and practice in the democratic process.
- Leadership training programs are essential to allow developing leaders to achieve their full potential.
- Involvement in state and national programs enhances the local school's leadership development program.
- Student council programs are stronger when all students are encouraged to participate.
- Every secondary school should have a student council. (Fiscus 1999a, 20)

As the United States becomes more diverse, schools are being forced to have a more multiethnic focus. Schools today need to assist in the assimilation of minorities, especially a dramatic growth in the Hispanic population. Census figures show that from 1990 to 2000, the number of Americans of Hispanic origin grew by almost 60 percent. Hispanics now comprise 12.5 percent of the total U.S. population. The African American population (including those who identified themselves as members of more than one race) increased about 16 percent, and now make up about 12.9 percent of the total population. The Asian American population almost doubled since 1990 to comprise 4.2 percent of the total population (Reid 2001). Even states like Iowa with traditionally homogeneous populations are seeing changes in their racial composition and 140 languages are now spoken in New Jersey classrooms. "Only about 10 percent of the 723,000-student Los Angeles district, the nation's second-largest school system, is made up of white, non-Hispanic students" (Reid 2001, 19).

President Bush's No Child Left Behind Act defines seven performance-based titles to support and assist elementary and secondary education in America. The titles are:

I. Improving the academic performance of disadvantaged students
II. Boosting teacher quality
III. Moving limited-English-proficient students to English fluency
IV. Promoting informed parental choice and innovative programs
V. Encouraging safe schools for the twenty-first century
VI. Increasing funding for Impact Aid
VII. Encouraging freedom and accountability. (*No Child Left Behind* 2001, 4)

The administration's education reform agenda relating to making schools safer for the twenty-first century is of interest to supporters of student activities. Combined into one performance-based grant are the Safe and Drug Free Schools program and the Twenty-First-Century Learning Centers program. Together, these programs will support before- and after-school learning opportunities, and violence and drug prevention activities. Four of the seven key components of this portion of the reform agenda are related to safety and character education:

- *Teacher Protection*—Teachers will be empowered to remove violent or persistently disruptive students from the classroom.
- *Promoting School Safety*—Funding for schools will be increased to promote safety and drug prevention during and after school. States will be allowed to give consideration to religious

organizations on the same basis as other nongovernmental organizations when awarding grants for after-school programs.

- *Rescuing Students from Unsafe Schools*—Victims of school-based crimes or students trapped in persistently dangerous schools will be provided with a safe alternative. States must report to parents and the public whether a school is safe.
- *Supporting Character Education*—Additional funds will be provided for Character Education grants to states and districts to train teachers in methods of incorporating character-building lessons and activities into the classroom. (*No Child Left Behind* 2001, 7)

How to proceed with this reform agenda is a concern for all schools in America. Huff's interviews of gang members provided the following data related to school safety:

- More than half of all respondents acknowledged that the members of their gangs assault teachers.
- About 70 percent admit that their gangs assault students.
- More than 80 percent stated that their gangs take guns to school, and nearly 80 percent also acknowledge that their gang's members have knives in school.
- More than 60 percent admitted that their gang's members sell drugs at school. (Huff and Trump 1996, 493)

In order to ensure that all youth become educated, responsible, and productive citizens, policies that address youth violence must be developed. As microcosms of society, schools are likely to have comparable problems (Huff and Trump 1996). If a community has gangs and gang-related problems, the community's schools will likely have them also.

It is imperative that school officials work with community officials to recognize, address, and prevent gang problems in school buildings (Trump 1998). What gang membership provides, says University of New Mexico researcher Gary LaFree, is "a kind of magical transformation" of lives that are mundane. "They get their own language. They get their own jacket. They get their own camaraderie" (Palting 1999, 53). Gangs provide a sense of belonging, self-esteem, and social/recreational involvement (Omizo, Omizo, and Honda 1997). Risk factors leading to gang membership are related to the following domains: community, family, school, peer group, and the individual (Howell 1998). School risk factors include the following:

- Academic failure
- Low educational aspirations, especially among females
- Negative labeling by teachers
- Trouble at school
- Few teacher role models
- Educational frustration
- Low commitment to school, low school attachment, high levels of antisocial behavior in school, low achievement test scores, and identification as being learning disabled (Howell 1998, 5)

Delinquency is sometimes followed by gang membership. Researchers have found a correlation between peer delinquency and an individual's delinquency. Gang members, however, come from a variety of backgrounds (Esbensen 2000).

A gang is defined as a group of individuals (many times adolescents) who organize for criminal or delinquent acts. If gangs did not engage in criminal activities, they would be powerful adolescent networks providing a sense of purpose and socialization skills similar to those provided by school-sponsored organizations (Riley 1991). In the absence of student activities, joining a "gang" would be appealing to many students. The term *gang* would describe "A group of persons working together; a group of persons having informal and usually close social relations" as defined in Webster's dictionary (Riley 1991, 11).

Having a sense of limited life options is a major factor influencing a person's decision to join a gang. A lack of alternatives drives many young people into gang activity. With more choices and opportunities, students are more likely to develop the skills necessary to become productive and contributing members both in school and the larger society (Riley 1991). "But if viable options are not available or if students are not aware of them, then their life options are limited. In other words, you cannot choose if you have no choices. If schools, churches, and communities offer few choices, then gang membership may appear to be the best option" (Riley 1991, 20).

Some of the key factors that influence a person's decision to join a gang are power, pride, peer pressure, self-preservation, and money. Conventional, socially acceptable involvement in school and community activities can also satisfy those needs to some extent, just as they do for the overwhelming majority of school-aged youth (Riley 1991). Character education and school climate are important aspects of intervention strategies. It is important for students to feel welcome and wanted every day they come to school and for school personnel to genuinely care about them (Riley 1991).

Clearly, students must "bond" to the school. A strong attachment or bond helps to reduce the chances of delinquency and gang membership on the part of the individual. When students are successful and feel good about their abilities, they view education as a ladder to a successful career. Successful students also exhibit more prosocial behaviors at school. "These students generally are not interested in becoming gang members, and their behaviors are less deviant" (Dukes, Martinez, and Stein 1997, 159).

More than half of all American families with children under thirteen need some form of nonparental care due to the economic realities of contemporary society. This has increased the demand for supervised in-school activities beyond the normal hours of the school day. Relatives look after many of these children but five to seven million of them must look after themselves. After-school programs offer children a secure and productive environment. Quality after-school programs can also help improve a student's academic and social skills. They also help keep young people out of trouble (After School Corporation n.d.).

Children who do not participate in after-school programs and spend their time in unstructured, unsupervised activities are at a greater risk for poor grades, truancy, substance abuse, and other destructive behavior. The risk of these behaviors is even greater for low-income children. Well-designed and managed after-school programs offer participants activities not always available during the school day—opportunities to engage in active, hands-on, informal learning. They help students develop creativity, problem-solving, and team-building skills through the arts, technology, and athletics. After-school programs may also involve children in community service, mentoring, and tutoring other students, activities that improve academic performance and enhance career aspirations. They also provide an opportunity for children to develop meaningful relationships with adults (After School Corporation n.d.).

Will high schools come to the point where students do most of their work over the web or through distance-learning courses?

> Starting in January [2000], the Kentucky Virtual High School will become the country's first statewide program offering online high school courses and will include advanced offerings in foreign languages, math, and science. The courses will be available to adults working toward passing the General Educational Development test, people learning English as a second language, home school students, homebound students and youths in the juvenile justice system. (Rosen 1999, 1)

What are the capabilities of virtual high schools? Virtual high school classes allow students to "Join a class composed of students from different states and countries chatting and learning together yet never leaving their homes! Virtual courses, virtual student lounges, virtual yearbooks, and virtual graduations; is this the education of the future" (Chaika 1999, 1)? In addition to Kentucky, Florida, as well as several other states, also now offer online classes.

Proponents of virtual high schools assert that they level the playing field. Geographic location and economic circumstances are no longer a hindrance to a quality education. For example, rural schools that don't have a wide selection of course offerings can allow students to take courses (like Latin) online (Keegan 2000). In districts with few advanced placement students, they can join other AP students online. It also allows students to take classes at their own pace—one student could log on every day, while another might log on only on weekends (Keegan 2000). Students can attend classes at any time, twenty-four hours a day, seven days a week.

The Virtual High School in the Hudson Public Schools (Massachusetts) was launched in 1996. This program is a joint venture with the Concord Consortium through a five-year, $7.5 million grant from the U.S. Department of Education.

> For some schools, the ability to schedule the VHS NetCourse during any period has substantially eased the challenges of scheduling these students into the regular courses they need and desire. . . . Communication in a NetCourse is asynchronous—that is, the teacher and students are not on-line at the same time but rather post entries in response to previous entries or assignments. The teacher never meets his or her students face-to-face. Discussions and assignments require written or multimedia communication rather than verbal dialogue. (Berman 1999, 13)

In short, a group of students studies the same course materials within a given time frame, according to their own personal scheduling preference.

Net courses can also be synchronous, which requires students to be online at the same time. The class "meets" electronically and live lectures and discussions take place. Synchronous courses can be difficult to schedule, however, and usually require simultaneous, two-way video and audio—but supporters point to the value of live interaction and discussion as part of the online course (Concord Consortium 1997). Is the complete virtual "schoolhouse" next?

> The Research Development Corporation is currently developing a virtual schoolhouse. The goal of the virtual schoolhouse is to be a repository of educational resources for students and teachers. These could be in the form of educational research articles, curriculum material, educational games, simulated laboratories, and forums for exchanging ideas. The goal is to provide the same types of resources found in an actual schoolhouse but without the constraints that educational resources, students, and

teachers be located at the same place at the same time. . . . When completed, the virtual schoolhouse will have the following components:

First, there would be a virtual library where teachers and students can read educational research findings, commentary, and other relevant educational publications.

Second, there will be a chat room, where teachers can discuss educational issues in real time.

Third, there will be a lecture hall where teachers and students can attend, at a distance, professional development lectures.

Fourth, there will be online resources such as tutorials and assessments. (Leddo 1997, 41)

Many nontraditional students, such as homeschooled students, are also able to take advantage of the virtual high school. Some of these students take all of their classes online. Taking these courses can be an attractive alternative to going to school. Online courses and schools have made it easier for families to homeschool their children, which is legal in all fifty states. Organizations now offer advanced placement courses in addition to regular high school courses. One such provider is class.com. It is the online version of the Independent Study High School of Nebraska. It is an accredited distance education high school run by the University of Nebraska that offers courses by mail at a cost of about $200 to $300 per student per semester (Guernsey 2001).

The American Federation of Teachers published guidelines in January 2000 suggesting that online courses make up no more than half a college student's educational program. Although the AFT has not yet studied high school online course offerings in depth, it is likely that the 50 percent limit or a lower percentage would be recommended (Guernsey 2001).

Students take virtual high school courses for a number of reasons. Sometimes they cannot schedule a particular course or they would like to accelerate. Is the virtual high school for everyone? "When kids get together in schools," said Barbara Stein, a senior policy analyst for the National Education Association, "they see people who may look different, who have different backgrounds, whom they have to learn to live and work with together" (Guernsey 2001).

Lowell Monks, coauthor of *Breaking Down the Digital Walls*, has indicated that "Any time we start doing telecommunication as a means of education, we enter an environment that is extremely diminished," he says, adding that it takes away body language, facial expression, tone of voice, and easily discernible sarcasm" (Engler 2000, 55). Are we moving to a condition of "horseless classrooms"—classrooms with no teacher present? With the availability of electronic equipment required to access Internet resources, students are "auto-educating" themselves in their homes via access to television channels, radio stations, and websites (Bossert 1997).

Most educators believe that traditional schooling will always be more beneficial and have wider appeal than the virtual classroom. Most people are just not willing to abandon the traditional classroom and school. Many see the benefits of virtual schools as an addition to the regular classroom—not a replacement for it (Keegan 2000). The potential also exists for students to feel isolated in an electronic learning environment. The common stereotype is "the loneliness of the long distance learner" (Eastmond 1995, 46). Distance learning can be both isolating and highly interactive, but electronic connectedness is different from classroom interaction. Yet, students who take online courses like the quality of online courses, their interaction with students from around the country and sometimes around the world, and the ability to read and discuss other students' work (Berman 1999).

The Web-Based Education Commission chaired by Senator Bob Kerrey (D-Neb.) recently called for an immediate national focus on the Internet's potential to help transform learning and improve achievement. In this comprehensive analysis of education and the Internet, *The Power of the Internet for Learning: Moving from Promise to Practice,* the commission urged President Bush and the leaders of the new 107th Congress to embrace "e-learning" as a centerpiece of our national education agenda. The commission issued to government, industry, and the education community a seven-point call-to-action that forms the framework of a national e-learning agenda:

- Make powerful new Internet resources, especially broadband access, widely and equitably available and affordable for all learners.
- Provide continual and relevant training and support for educators and administrators at all levels.
- Build a new research and development framework around learning in the Internet age.
- Develop quality online educational content that meets the highest standards of educational excellence.
- Revise outdated regulations that impede innovation and replace them with approaches that embrace anytime, anywhere, any pace learning.
- Protect online learners and ensure their privacy.
- Sustain funding—through traditional and new sources—that is adequate to meet the challenge of realizing the education potential of the Internet. (Web-Based Education 2001, 1)

What will the "wired" classroom look like? When it opened in 2002, Westview High School (Poway, California) was touted to be the Ferrari of high-tech high schools.

It had a short range wireless network so students can access the Internet from their laptops anywhere on the school grounds. There were 400 personal computers for 1,000 students—with more PCs on the way—and numerous handheld devices, such as the Palm Organizer from Palm, Inc. And there will be virtual classrooms, allowing students to log on from home to check assignments and participate in chat room discussions. These new tools have changed the way children learn. Students with access to the Internet can tap into a world of data that was unthinkable in the past. Kids participate in Internet classes that weren't available before, and interactive software helps them grasp arcane concepts. What's more, the Internet gives teachers a global database from which to call information, and allows parents to log on from home to see what their children are learning. (Tam 2001)

Founded in 1989, the University of Phoenix Online (www.uoponline.com) has an enrollment of 18,500 students and has graduated 8,000 students. It is accredited by the North Central Association and offers B.A., M.A., and Ph.D. degrees (Rewick 2001). Jones International University, Cordean University, and Capella University also have sizeable enrollments. However, "at only a fraction of schools is it possible to actually earn a degree online, and those are mostly degree-completion programs—the last two years of a degree program—or degrees, such as business and health care, for which there is a strong market demand" (Totty and Grimes 2001). The Massachusetts Institute of Technology is attempting to post almost all of its 2,000 courses on the web, free to anyone. MIT has announced a ten-year initiative for creating public websites for the courses and to post materials such as lecture notes, problem sets, syllabuses, and video lectures. Participation by faculty will be voluntary and web visitors will not earn college credit (Goldberg 2001). The president of MIT, Charles M. Vest said that he suspects, "in this country and throughout the world, a lot of really bright, precocious high school students will find this a great playground." And ultimately, "there will probably be a lot of uses that will really surprise us and that we can't really predict" (Goldberg 2001).

Will online learning and virtual high schools replace traditional high schools? William Bennett plans to provide a virtual curriculum for kindergarten through twelfth grade. His company, K–12, will target charter schools and might even develop "virtual" charter schools in states that allow tuition costs to be paid with tax dollars (Walsh 2001c). The online high school in Florida employs fifty-eight teachers and has an enrollment of 2,500 students. It is one of the largest and most established of online high schools in the United States (Trotter 2001). Its wide variety of courses and classes are open to any high school-eligible person in Florida. Online course work is a good alternative for self-motivated students who do not wish to attend the traditional high school. Yet approximately 25 percent of students who start courses are dropped from Florida High School courses by the end of the twenty-nine-day, no-fault withdrawal period (Trotter 2001). What about all the "off line" learning that takes place when students attend high school? Much of this learning takes place through student activities participation.

In 1983, in a "Statement on Student Activities," Scott Thomson, who was executive director of the National Association of Secondary School Principals at the time, stated,

> Student activities are a vital part of secondary school education. The opportunities for students to organize and plan, to assume leadership roles, to gain recognition and identity, to experience self-governance, to recreate physically and emotionally, and to mature socially come, to a significant degree, from the student activities programs. Students learn to work together in a band or on a yearbook staff. They can develop leadership skills as a club officer or newspaper editor. They learn to make decisions voting for class officers or serving on student council. These skills will be essential for a demanding future. (Thomson 1983, 1)

A more recent analysis is provided by Rocco Marano, director of NASSP's Department of Student Activities.

> Of course, student activities should be enjoyable, but, there are also valuable skills and lessons that can be taught to those who participate, such as goal setting, communication, organization, decision making, teamwork, conflict resolution, and tolerance. These are sometimes thought of as leadership skills, but they are really life skills that can be practiced as part of a club or organization and complement what is taught in the classroom. (Marano 2000b, 8)

Perhaps the most comprehensive list of general functions of extra-class activities was proposed by Miller, Moyer, and Patrick in 1956:

Contributions to Students:
1. To provide opportunities for the pursuit of established interests and the development of new interests
2. To educate for citizenship through experiences and insights that stress leadership, fellowship, cooperation, and independent action
3. To develop school spirit and morale
4. To provide opportunities for satisfying the gregarious urge of children and youth

5. To encourage moral and spiritual development
6. To strengthen the mental and physical health of students
7. To provide for well-rounded social development of students
8. To widen student contacts
9. To provide opportunities for students to exercise their creative capacities more fully

Contributions to Curriculum Improvement:
1. To foster or enrich classroom experiences
2. To explore new learning experiences which may ultimately be incorporated into the curriculum
3. To provide additional opportunity for individual and group guidance
4. To motivate classroom instruction

Contributions to More Effective School Administration:
1. To foster more effective teamwork between students, faculty, and administrative and supervisory personnel
2. To integrate more closely the several divisions of the school system
3. To provide less restricted opportunities designed to assist youth in the worthwhile utilization of their spare time
4. To enable teachers to better understand the forces that motivate pupils to react as they do to many of the problematic situations with which they are confronted.

Contributions of the Community:
1. To promote better school and community relations
2. To encourage greater community interest in and support of the school (Gholson and Buser 1983, 3–4)

A recent poll conducted by Phi Beta Kappa/Gallup shows the highest level of satisfaction with schools in the poll's thirty-three-year history. Schools were rated A or B by a majority of respondents for the first time. The results also showed an 11 percent increase in the A/B category, up from 40 percent in 1990 (Gewertz 2001b). Will this rating increase again in light of the tragedies of September 11, 2001? Schools can become "caring centers," "communities of connection and service," and "arenas for clarifying values" to help meet community needs (L. Smith 2001). However they change, schools have always been and will continue to be a means for supporting and extending academic learning. Without cocurricular activities, a significant portion of a school's objectives cannot be met (McKowen 1952).

In closing:

Cheryl Lange, a senior at Ironwood High School, Glendale, Arizona, stated: "Student leaders take pride in the clubs they join and help the clubs reach their full potential. Numerous activities on campus are directly run by the students. The blood drive, alcohol awareness week, assemblies, and Homecoming dance are a few examples which are a result of the diligent work and effort the student leaders put forth." (In What Ways Do Student Leaders 1999, 32)

"With the Internet, learning goes to the learner." (Mann 1999, 22)

"For every 10 kids who join gangs, nine do not graduate from high school. Seven out of 10 gang members end up dead or in prison by the age of 20. The average age that a kid joins a gang is 11 years old." (Wagner, Knudsen, and Harper 1999–2000, 47)

13

HOW SHOULD STUDENT ACTIVITIES BE ORGANIZED FOR MAXIMUM BENEFIT TO STUDENTS AND SCHOOL?

There is widespread agreement that schools should make it is easier for students and teachers to become well acquainted. Students should connect to their school and its purposes. Schools must become caring and learning communities. Building this kind of school community is more easily accomplished in small schools. It had been thought that bigger schools are more efficient due to economies of scale—increasing learning while saving taxpayers money. Actually, the opposite seems to be true: large schools are more expensive to operate (Sergiovanni 1995).

Regarding school size, small is better. This is especially evident when a decrease in size changes the relationships between students and teacher (i.e., teacher collaboration, student visibility, and learning communities). Size alone is not the issue. It is also important to focus on the relationships in the school and foster a more collaborative and personalized teaching that takes into account individual experiences (Klonsky and Klonsky 1999).

Big high schools are always composed of small schools created by students for survival. However, only two small groups of kids are able to join the subgroups within the school where the adults are significant members: the academic stars and the star athletes (Meier 1996). Performing arts students may sometimes form a third subgroup. "But, the vast majority of kids—probably 70 to 80 percent—belong to enclaves that include no grown-ups. A few loners belong nowhere" (Meier 1996, 12).

Seven reasons why small schools work best are as follows:

1. *Governance*. Ideally, a school's total faculty should be small enough to meet around one common table.
2. *Respect*. Students and teachers in schools of thousands cannot know one another well.
3. *Simplicity*. Keep the organizational side simple.
4. *Safety*. Anonymity breeds not only contempt and anger but also physical danger.

5. *Parent Involvement*. Schools are intimidating places for many parents; parents feel like intruders, strangers, outsiders.
6. *Accountability*. No one needs long computer printouts, statistical graphs, and educational mumbo-jumbo to find out how a teacher, kid, or school is doing when the scale is right. Parents can simply walk around the school, listen to teachers and kids, look at young people's work, and raise questions.
7. *Belonging*. In small schools, the other 70 percent belong. Every kid is known; every kid belongs to a community that includes adults. Relationships are cross-disciplinary, cross-generational, and cross-everything else. (Meier 1996, 12–14)

As schools grow larger, more kids get cut from an athletic team or don't get the lead in a school play unless the cocurricular offerings are changed. Some suggested strategies to maintain the percentage of students involved in cocurricular activities (athletic, fine arts, club, and intramurals) are:

- Create a pyramid of teams for each sport that involves a try-out-and-cut roster approach. For example, it makes sense for us to run multiple levels of soccer, baseball, and basketball in grades 9 and 10.
- Provide more intramural activities and allow the programs to share in the use of athletic facilities.
- Support involvement in community service projects by providing bus transportation and adult supervision after school.
- Identify a process for students to start a new club or organization within the school. (Berkey 1996, 25)

Schools have become larger, as the following quote illustrates: "In 1958, about 4,000 American high school seniors were enrolled in graduating classes of more than 100 students and 17,000 were enrolled in graduating classes of fewer than 100. By 1990 there were about 8,000 high schools with graduating classes of fewer than 100 students and 12,000 high schools with graduating classes of more than 100 students" (Marshak 1995, 31).

Social interaction in large schools is often anonymous, making discipline difficult to exercise because anonymous students can blend into the crowd if they wish to ignore reprimands and escape punishment. "Creating self-contained units within the building, each comprising a small set of students and adults, can produce the personalized contacts and positive relationships that result in well-controlled discipline and serious academic climates" (McPartland and Jordan 2001, 29).

Some students' lives outside the school are lacking any sense of caring, thus intensifying the problems associated with attending a large school. Children who feel little sense of belonging view themselves as outcasts in their home environment and expect the same from schools (Keaster, Downing, and Peterson 1995). Schools need to be aware of the needs of at-risk students and make certain that they do not treat any student as an outcast.

Clearly, schools must become more personal for students. According to Dyer (1996), all students must have at least the following:

1. An adult advocate—a person to help the student academically and to help when needs, concerns, and problems arise.

2. A progress plan—an individualized education plan to ensure that the graduation requirements are understood and met as well as high school goals and expectations.

3. Accommodation for learning styles—teachers that understand students' learning styles and adjust methods of instruction accordingly.

4. High schools with fewer than 600 students—composed of learning communities or "houses" in which faculty and students stay together for their entire high school career. (Dyer 1996)

However, in 1990, "89 percent of the students were enrolled in the high schools with more than 100 students in the graduating class; 64 percent were in high schools with more than 800 graduating students" (Marshak 1995, 31).

Regardless of size, every high school should send all students a clear message that it is ready and able to help them meet their responsibilities. Likewise, all students should acknowledge their obligation to obtain the full advantage of their education and be willing to contribute to the school (Sternberg 2000). One means of making a large school smaller is to develop a school- or schools-within-a-school.

An example of a school-within-a-school is the academy program at Parsippany High School and Parsippany Hills High School (Parsippany, New Jersey). The program "combines cross-disciplinary curricula with teamwork, community involvement, and portfolios to benefit students who might not otherwise excel" (Konet 2001, 19). The program involves students in four components for personal and academic success. The four components are:

1. *Academic requirements* invite all students to strive for academic excellence. The academy offers courses in English, mathematics, science, and social studies. These offerings approach honors and AP curricula in rigor.

2. *Team participation* includes both athletic and nonathletic collaboration with others. Students may play on an athletic team, be part of a drama production, or be a contributing member of some other group effort.

3. *Community service* lies at the heart of the academy philosophy. Participating in the community complements students' academic experiences.

4. *Portfolios* demonstrate the growth and development of intellectual skills, and each academy student is required to keep a portfolio of selected work from all classes and school activities. (Konet 2001, 19–20)

According to Konet, everyone strives to do his personal best through significant achievement in the four components. The community involvement component consists of two parts.

First, there is a 40-hour per year community service requirement. . . . Second, students must attend at least six cultural events every year. . . . Team participation in the Academy means "using the body as an instrument of learning." There are a number of ways to satisfy this requirement besides participating in organized school sports. Taking a role in the school play, being involved in religious activities at one's place of worship, or participating in an academic team are ways to satisfy this requirement. Students must participate for 100 hours and meet the following three criteria:

- "Personal best" is required for success
- The student's personal best is not enough for success—it is the result of the team effort that means success or failure
- The body and mind are used as instruments of learning. (Konet 2001, 21–22)

Many districts have turned to before-school and after-school programs to help students be successful. These programs offer students an extended school day with opportunities for academic support, participation in cultural and technological enrichment programs and, many times, recreational activities. Research on middle and high school students in quality, after-school programs reveals better academic performance, behavior, and school attendance and higher expectations for the future than students who do not participate (de Kanter 2001).

The number of after-school programs has increased rapidly because of three major societal trends. First, many young people are home alone because of working parents. Also, adults are not home in the neighborhood. Second is the realization that all children can learn if given extra learning opportunities. Extended-day programs help close the achievement gap by providing needed experiences. Third, after-school crime and victimization of young people has increased greatly in recent years. "Teen crime is highest between the hours of 3:00 and 6:00 P.M." (Kugler 2001, 5).

Quality, after-school programs include tutoring, community service, technology classes, and career development (Kugler 2001). In Wellington, Kansas, Unified School District 353 operates a high school after-school evening program from 6:30 to 10:00 P.M., "so as not to compete with after-school athletics and clubs. Students have access to computers and can work with tutors, mostly district teachers, in an informal setting" (Pardini 2001, 15). The Milwaukee Public Schools wanted to establish marching bands and forensic, chess, and drama clubs at schools throughout the city. Despite an anticipated budget deficit of $14 million, officials allocated $1.2 million for the district's after-school program. Willie Jude, Milwaukee's deputy superintendent, successfully argued that "giving students, especially those in the middle and high school, a chance to participate in activities they love can provide a strong incentive to stay in school. That's critical in Milwaukee where the dropout rate in 1999–2000 was 10.4 percent and high school attendance rate fell to 77.7 percent last fall" (Pardini 2001, 12).

Full-service community schools—schools that provide health and social services to children and families—are emerging in some urban areas. "Schools and community agencies form partnerships to provide seamless, one-stop environments. Schools are open extended hours, on weekends, and during the summer as safe havens for youth development and community use" (Dryfoos 1998, 39). According to the U.S. Departments of Education and Justice (2000), children and teens who are unsupervised during after-school hours are much more likely to use alcohol, drugs, and tobacco, engage in criminal and high-risk behaviors, get poor grades, and drop out of school than those who have the constructive activities supervised by responsible adults after school. The absence of after-school opportunities means that an estimated five to seven million latchkey children return home alone after school. According to the American Youth Policy Forum (1999), about 35 percent of twelve-year-olds are regularly left alone while their parents are working (U.S. Departments of Education and Justice 2000).

Several final points regarding the value of after-school programs are found in "Working for Children and Families: Safe and Smart After-School Programs":

When the "healthiness" of a community is measured by the degree of social problems present in the high school student population, communities with well-attended, structured activity programs were five times more likely to be ranked among the healthiest communities. The 1995 study defined social problems as "the prevalence of problem behaviors, such as drug and alcohol use, sexual activity, depression, and school problems" (U.S. Departments of Education and Justice 2000, 12). In these communities, most students (over 50 percent) participated in sports, clubs, and community organizations. In the least healthy communities, only 39 percent of youth participated in similar activities. If students are not participating in activity programs outside school, the activity of choice is watching television. Students watch alone 50 percent of the time—and almost all of what they watch is not appropriate for them (Snyder and Sickmund 1999).

As an extension of the school's curriculum, the primary goal of student activities should be to involve all students. A comprehensive activity program would include student government, student publications, drama, music, service clubs, sports, intramurals, cheerleading, honor societies, school assemblies, and other special interest groups (Grady 1981). Each program should be governed by an "Activity Philosophy," such as the one of Township High School District 211 (Illinois), which states:

> The Board of Education and professional staff have a responsibility to develop individual students to be productive citizens. Recognizing that the best interests of society and the best interests of the individual are compatible, it is our belief that schools should provide students with the opportunity to develop skills that will enable them to lead productive lives in our democratic society.
>
> Our student activity program, therefore, is an integral part of our education plan. Activity groups may be organized in order to enhance current curricular offerings; to provide a particular service to the school community; or to engage in interscholastic activities.
>
> Participation in student activities will encourage each individual to develop:
>
> - Concern for others by organizing service projects and volunteer programs, and developing teamwork.
> - Goal setting and accomplishment skills.
> - An ability to work and socialize cooperatively with peers.
> - Skills necessary for contributing positively to society.
> - Social and cultural interests for an active, productive, and culturally diverse lifestyle.
> - A positive self-image realized through a sense of accomplishment.
> - An ability to participate in the decision-making process, assisting others to feel competent and to have a sense of loyalty to their school environment.
> - Broad and varied programs that will meet the needs and interests of all of our students.
> - Interpersonal communication skills through experiences that build character and enable students to meet personal challenges. (Township High School District 211 1997, 3)

The person in charge of the student activities program is many times an assistant or associate principal or it could be a full- or part-time "student activities director" with job responsibilities similar to these:

- Supervise student government activities
- Coordinate all nonathletic activities in the school
- Monitor all club budgets and activities
- Assist in identifying and supervising activity advisors
- Maintain a calendar of events
- Publish periodic announcements of activities
- Coordinate the use of the gymnasium, auditorium, or other assembly areas on the campus
- Coordinate arrangements for speakers, performers, and other school guests
- Coordinate and arrange for transportation related to student activities
- Plan the school's awards assemblies

- Supervise school fund-raising activities
- Maintain activity records
- Assist in planning and supervising schoolwide events, such as homecoming festivities, dances, carnivals, etc.
- Arrange for publicity and announcements of school activities in the local press
- Assist in the arrangements for chaperones, security personnel, and use of facilities
- Meet regularly with club sponsors and student representatives
- Meet with sales representatives regarding student activities
- Enlist the aid of parent and faculty volunteers
- Prepare the budget for the activities office
- Assign bulletin board space throughout the building. (Grady 1981, 4–5)

A job description might look as follows:

Putnam City School District

Title:	Activities Director
Qualifications:	1. Certified personnel with five years experience
	2. A background as head class sponsor or major club advisor for three years
Reports to:	Building Principal
Supervises:	All student organizations and school master calendar
Job goal:	To give direction to the student activities program, the student officers and advisors/ sponsors; to maintain an accurate calendar for the school's activities and usage of its facilities.

Performance responsibilities:
1. Establishes, maintains, and coordinates the school master calendar.
2. Coordinates and assists in planning all school assemblies.
3. Schedules the usage of any of school facilities by any group and contacts the appropriate people involved—i.e., security, custodial, cafeteria.
4. Instructs and assists sponsors of all school organizations.
5. Coordinates all club activities within the school.
6. Coordinates with the athletic director the use of the gym and the other sporting events as to available dates and possible conflicts.
7. Coordinates all fund-raising activities of school organizations and those of the parent booster organizations.
8. Assists in any community/district special events at school site.
9. Coordinates with vendors regarding rings, photographs, caps and gowns, graduation announcements, and the like; also ensure that information is distributed by class advisors to students and that announcements are made as to selling and distribution dates.
10. Schedules all field trips, secures district buses for those trips, and assists adult in charge in preparing for trips—e.g., permission forms, excused lists, possible challenges, etc.
11. Ensures that the eligibility list is correct and published.
12. Ensures that the excused absence list is correct and published.
13. Coordinates the procedures and selection of student awards, honors, and scholarships. Maintains a file of procedures and results.

14. Publishes a monthly activity calendar that is distributed to the staff, district offices, and wherever the principal directs.
15. Maintains a file listing all clubs, advisors, and organizational constitutions.
16. Involved with coordination/overseeing all schoolwide elections or voting.
17. Acts as a liaison with all parent associations and reunion groups.
18. Works closely with all involved in promoting school spirit, cooperation, and sportsmanship within the school.
19. Involved with commencement/baccalaureate activities.
20. Involved with leadership development throughout the school.
21. Assists the administration in any manner as directed by the building principal. (Putnam City Schools n.d.)

The success or failure of the student organization or activity rests squarely in the hands of the advisor. An advisor's (sponsor's) job description might be as follows:

Each organization should constantly look for ways to be innovative and positively impact the school's environment. Since each club has its own purpose, it is important to discover unique ways to ensure the organization's success. We expect our activity sponsors to:

- Work cooperatively with the activity director. The activity director will assist the sponsor in evaluating projects and in the facilitation of the organization's achieving its goals successfully.
- Facilitate the planning, organizing, and implementing of regular meetings. These are held to determine future projects and activities. The minimum number of meetings is specified in the sponsor's job description.
- Incorporate an executive board to act as a steering committee. It may be possible that this group meets more frequently than the entire club to ensure maximum efficiency at regular club meetings.
- Utilize special committees. Such organization in the club's operation will allow more students to exhibit leadership within the organization. Committees usually report at regular meetings and must be carefully directed by the advisor.
- Maintain accurate club records. These records include financial transactions, club participation, appropriate transportation requests, and any other administrative tasks involved with the organization.
- Promote observance among all students of personal safety, protection of school property, and respect for individual civil rights. The sponsor is responsible to provide for the proper supervision and safety of students while participating in club activities. (Township High School District 211 1997, 4)

Another example of a sponsor's job description is as follows:

The Sponsor is delegated responsibilities for the participants and activities of his/her activity. The Sponsor is responsible for ensuring that the students involved are properly trained and organized and that suitable supervision is provided. Furthermore, the Sponsor has primary responsibilities to ensure that activities are conducted to serve the best interests of students of the Gateway School District and that all district regulations and guidelines are thoroughly understood and observed.

Areas of Responsibility

1. Shall be present for the complete duration of activity sessions, meetings, and events; and shall guarantee the supervision of all students participating during these times.
2. Shall instruct all participants in the proper techniques, skills, and knowledge appropriate to the activity.
3. Shall instruct participants in the safe and proper use and care of all equipment and facilities required for the activity.
4. Shall supervise the proper usage of, and provide reasonable safeguards for, the maintenance, cleanliness, and full return of any and all assigned equipment.
5. Shall complete, in the form prescribed and within the times specified, all records, requisitions, budget requests, statistics, etc., as may be required for the administration of the activity.
6. Shall have a current knowledge of school district regulations and guidelines (and any regulations of a parent organization) and ensure the compliance of all participants with same.
7. Shall work to ensure that participation in the activity does not negatively affect academic performance.
8. Shall establish, publish, and enforce reasonable rules for participation, acquaint the students with these rules and the consequences of noncompliance. (Gateway School District 2001)

Performance responsibilities at Gateway are presented in table 13.1.

An annual agenda must be developed to ensure an effective activities program. Planning the agenda entails teamwork and cooperation among many stakeholders. One district committed to excellence in cocurricular activities established and funded a Department of Student Activities and Athletics. The department's mission is to organize, support, facilitate, and coordinate all non-music-related student activities (Roland 2001).

County funds provided to the department are placed in two separate budgets, one for athletics and one for nonathletic activities. The nonathletic budget contains money to:

- Pay supplements for academic games and competition sponsors
- Pay for high school graduation ceremonies
- Cover the expenses of in-county games and academic competitions
- Help students with travel expenses to state and national competitions
- Help support the programs of the Broward County Association of Student Councils, the Broward Chapter of the National Honor Society, and the Broward Chapter of the Future Educators of America
- Fund the Broward County Student Volunteer Service Program. (Roland 2001, 11)

The Department of Student Activities and Athletics is the sponsoring agency of the Broward County Association of Student Councils (BCASC), the Broward County Chapter of the National Honor Society (BCNHS), and the Broward County Chapter of the Future Educators of America (BCFEA). Membership in the BCASC consists of middle level and high schools and the organization meets once per month from August to May with six of those meetings scheduled during the school day. The BCASC elects the student adviser of the School Board of Broward County, sponsors a number of countywide service projects, holds an annual one-day convention, and has developed a comprehensive awards program for middle level and high schools. (Roland 2001, 11–12)

Sometimes a school or district can sponsor an interclub conference or workshop, an activity that can bring together various student leaders—student council, class, NHS, clubs—to work cooperatively.

Table 13.1   Performance Responsibilities at Gateway School District

Responsibility	Guidelines	Performance Indicator
INSTRUCTION	• Provides knowledge and skill that is current and appropriate to the activity	• Instructs participants in the use of proper techniques and skills • Instructs participants in safe and proper use and care of equipment and facilities
SUPERVISION	• Supervises or provides for appropriate supervision of participants during activities • Supervises use of equipment • Promotes and maintains standards for academics and character development	• Present for complete duration of an activity, meeting, or event • Maintains an inventory of all equipment possessed and/or distributed, and monitors return in appropriate condition • Establishes and publishes rules for participation • Communicates and enforces consequences of noncompliance for academics, participation, and behavior
ADMINISTRATION	• Works within the rules and regulations adopted by the school administration for student activities • Maintains accurate records for the collection and distribution of funds	• Meets timelines for requisitions, budget, statistics, records, etc. • Works with administration to develop schedules for activities, transportation and facilities • Records for collection and payments of activity funds adhere to school policy • Complies with policy for issuing awards or honors and maintaining operational guidelines
FAIR AND EQUITABLE TREATMENT	• Promotes and maintains fair and consistent treatment for all participants • Adheres to local, state, and federal regulations with regard to civil rights	• Advertises the activity and actively recruits participants • Communicates progress of participants to parents when appropriate • Treats all participants in a non-prejudiced manner • Complies with regulations dealing with race, origin, sex and disability

Source: Gateway School District 2001, n.p.

This is an excellent way for club members to understand the functions of other clubs while allowing student leaders to pool resources, share ideas, and exercise leadership and plan service (Marano 1999). Collaborations can take many forms. Consider the following:

- First, determine which model [of collaboration] will be the most effective superstructure, and then start the planning process. One method might involve the total cooperation between two or more groups from start to finish.
- Another type of collaborative activity necessitates a different model. A large school may have many different service groups with varying sizes and organizational abilities. In such a case, the student council might serve as a guiding force in a collaborative activity, taking on a larger share of the planning, while smaller or newly formed groups assume less labor-intensive assignments.
- A third model requires even less common planning but may still yield common results. The individual groups can still hold their individual projects, but with all donations going to the selective beneficiary. (Bloomstran 2001a, 5)

Working cooperatively is beneficial to each group and may also enhance creativity. Groups working together on various endeavors can benefit the entire student body as well as the individual groups. With greater participation in an activity, groups become more involved in it. If the activity involves profit sharing, decisions need to be made at the start regarding group shares (Bloomstran 2001a).

Clearly, when the student activities program is in place and activities are taking place—in a coordinated collaborative manner—the following questions should be asked relative to each activity:

- Is the goal of the activity relevant to the goals of the curriculum?
- Do large numbers of students benefit from the activity?
- Do the costs of the program match the benefits gained?
- Are the revenues sufficient to support costs effectively? (Christensen 1984, 2)

A procedure to answer the above questions is shown in appendix A. It is hoped that all students involved on a student activity "team" will also benefit from the following:

1. Getting Acquainted—Team members should know each other well and feel comfortable with each other. Take time to understand each other's needs, differences, and behaviors without labeling them as good or bad.
2. Goal Setting—Teams need purpose. Strive to set goals and objectives that are satisfying and agreeable to all members of the team.
3. Communication—Productive teams need to communicate effectively.
4. Conflict Management—Prior to a conflict, a team should establish a problem-solving method that can be used when problems arise.
5. Group Roles—Increase team strength by teaching members the roles and duties of other members.
6. Focusing—Successful teams keep their mission in the forefront.
7. Recognizing Talents and Resources—Utilize and recognize the talents and resources of your team. (Fortin 1998, 26)

There should also be a set of rules governing participation in cocurricular activities for students. A sample set, developed in the Windsor Central School District (New York), is shown in appendix B.

An example of policies and procedures from Township High School District 211 (1998, appendix A–C) is shown in appendix C.

A template for a student handbook of extracurricular activities information and eligibility (from *A Comprehensive Guide to Developing Student Handbooks for New York State Schools 2001–2002*, 39–40) is shown in appendix D.

For many students, participation in student activities is an important component of their school experience. A strong and comprehensive student activities program benefits the entire school community in many ways. Leadership begins when a student is elected to office. Schools need to provide student leadership training opportunities in and outside the school district to support students elected to office. Many schools have started leadership classes and enroll appropriate students. To ensure successful programs, schools need to provide ongoing training for student officers who can apply skills learned in their clubs and organizations (Baker 1993).

To motivate students, consider the following keys to success:

- When planning an activity, give a great deal of thought to the needs of the job and the characteristics of the students involved. Too many times, we ask for volunteers or railroad a student into a leadership position and then wonder why the result is unsuccessful.
- Ensure that the students you ask to do a job are motivated to see it to completion. Break down the larger tasks into smaller ones so younger leaders can do them and feel good about their success. They will be ready for bigger tasks next time.
- Ensure students catch the "vision" of what you are trying to accomplish and how it fits into the entire picture. We all like to feel a part of something exciting and greater than ourselves.
- Develop an effective method for monitoring progress and keep on top of things. Know exactly what is going on. Always evaluate the process as part of an experience, never single out or condemn a student who is unsuccessful.
- Reward and recognize the accomplishments of those involved. Open new doors for students—give them an adventure.
- Never be afraid of failure. Ensure that your administration and staff members understand that the student council is a learning tool. Failure can lead to growth.
- As an advisor, one must demonstrate, by personal example, enthusiasm and excitement, concern and caring, and dedication and the ability to trust students to be successful. This takes time and perseverance.
- Remember, if it isn't fun, students won't be back. (Savard 1993, 22)

Students complete a great number of projects as part of the student activities program. The success of the projects depends in large part on the planning. Always consider the eleven Ws:

- *What* are you planning to do?
- *Why* do you want to do this project?
- *When* and *where* will the activities take place?
- *Who* will benefit from the project?
- *Who* needs to approve the project?

- *When* will the basic planning be done?
- *What* funds are needed? *When* will the money be needed? *Who* will arrange for getting the money?
- *What* kind of publicity is needed and *when* is it needed?
- *What* committees are necessary? (List the committees, tasks, chairpersons, and deadlines.)
- *Who* deserves special thank-yous? *Who* will write the thank-you notes and *when* will it be done?
- *Will* the project be worthwhile? How will you know? (Chmielewski 2000, 22)

In closing:

In our America, you and I will work together, side by side, in an atmosphere of mutual respect. We won't notice or care about our differences, but rather we will focus on what we have in common . . . like our need for safety, love, dignity, and respect. (Smith 1998, 32)

"Our human resources are our competitive edge," John Naisbitt continued. "In this regard, no country in the world is better positioned for the future that the U.S. We have the richest mix of racial, ethnic, and global experience, which yields creativity." (Adkins 1989, 17)

I've discovered that I'm now more impressed with people who are kind than with people who are smart and I have a great deal to learn from those who are kind. (Smith 2000, 53)

14

WHAT IS THE IDEAL VERSUS TYPICAL PROFILE OF THE TEACHER-ADVISOR TO STUDENT ACTIVITIES?

Class advisors are responsible to oversee student participation in those activities and projects in which a particular class is involved. Oversight of this participation includes attending all class activities, monitoring class activities, class treasurer oversight, budget planning and preparation, encouragement of parent support groups when appropriate, and assisting in organizing the group to ensure fulfillment of class responsibilities. It also involves acting as a guiding force to enable the class to meet its goals, instilling good leadership skills, promoting class unity and cohesiveness, utilizing the democratic process, promoting appropriate parliamentary skills at both class and committee meetings, and assisting in the planning and development of both short and long term goals for the class.
(Brunswick 1996)

Township (Illinois) High School District 211 (1989, 1–2) uses the following descriptions for sponsors in its handbook:

The major responsibilities of the Student Council sponsor include:

• Plan and organize all council events
• Provide leadership training experiences and exposure to the parliamentary process
• Work to strengthen cooperation among students, faculty, administration, and community
• Promote student involvement in activities beneficial to the school and student body
• Supervise students involved in council activities
• Oversee the correct and responsible use of council funds

Key duties (in operation of the student council):

- Oversee weekly meetings of the: executive board, council, and standing committees
- Advise council members on the organization of annual Homecoming activities, dances, and other council-sponsored events
- Encourage participation in council events
- Meet regularly with the principalship to provide current information about council activities
- Maintain accurate and current files on all council activities
- Arrange participation in the programs of the Northeast District, Illinois Association of Student Councils, and the National Association of Student Councils
- Organize and supervise periodic school elections
- Initiate the selection, purchase, care and storage of equipment and supplies
- Arrange for the use of building facilities and transportation
- Maintain financial and inventory records
- Plan recognition awards for council participants
- Coordinate fund raising events
- Arrange for publicity of council events
- Execute other duties and assignments as required

Successful student organizations are made possible by willing, patient, creative advisers. Henrico County Public Schools (n.d., 31–32) describes the advisor's role as that of:

- Planner—As a planner, the adviser helps the student group set its goals without wasting excessive time in discussion.
- Consultant—As a consultant, the adviser helps students to find answers, but he need not answer each question directly.
- Counselor—As a counselor, the adviser often helps to mold the attitudes and character of students.
- Evaluator—As an evaluator, the adviser is concerned with the process as well as the product of the group.
- Teacher—As a teacher, the adviser is to work with and through students to carry out a phase of their civic education and enhance leadership skills.

In summary, the activity advisor is to be the student leaders' leader!

When the classroom learning process meets students' emotional needs, students are more likely to be genuinely involved in learning. When teachers build strong relationships with their students, they create an environment that is supportive and one in which quality, collaborative learning can take place (Rogers, Ludington, and Graham 1998). Six standards that support relationship-centered teaching are:

- *Standard 1: Safe.* For students to place a priority on learning, they must feel safe from both physical danger and embarrassment.
- *Standard 2: Valuable.* Students are more apt to engage fully and produce quality work if they perceive that what they are doing has value.
- *Standard 3: Successful.* To maintain intrinsic motivation, students need evidence of success in achieving either mastery or significant progress toward mastery.
- *Standard 4: Involving.* Students are more motivated to learn when they have a meaningful stake in what's going on.

- *Standard 5: Caring.* Students respond positively to being liked and to being accepted and respected members of the class.
- *Standard 6: Enabling.* To create a motivating context, teachers must constantly seek out best practices that enable students' learning and ensure students' attainment of standards. (Rogers and Renard 1999, 35–37)

Obviously, the same six standards apply to activity advisors as they develop a relationship with students.

When students are asked to list the qualities that the best teachers should possess, about two-thirds said, "Teachers' ability to explain things clearly and spend time to help students." Approximately half the students said, "Being fair to their students, treating students like adults, relating well to students, and being considerate of student feelings" (Dyer 1996, 5). A good teacher is a leader, not a manager. Leaders help others meet challenges through coaching and advising. They also listen to, support, and care as much about those under their leadership as they do about the product being produced (Volp 1995).

Good advisors make effective use of committees in order to organize and run student activities. Having several people participate in the activity leads to greater involvement from the entire student body. Committees generate new ideas for student activities (Keck 1997). Talented staff members are a resource that sometimes goes unnoticed because they are never asked to participate. The following key points help keep staff members involved:

- Communicate with staff members to get and keep them involved.
- Look for hidden talents of teachers who are willing to share their expertise if given the opportunity.
- Plan activities well in advance to give teachers time to adjust their schedules.
- Show your appreciation with small gifts or notes to teachers.
- Tell faculty members the positive aspects and intended results of an activity.
- Gain teacher approval for all activities.
- Project a positive attitude when presenting an idea to the staff.
- Remember to say thank you. (Prothro 1993, 35)

People tend to lend support to activities that they have helped create. Faculty member involvement with committees makes them part of the student activities team as well. Through participation in student activity programs, many students achieve a level of school involvement that a strictly academic program would not bring about (Vornberg 1998). Through involvement in activity programs, students often become more interested in academic courses; are able to practice leadership skills; can socialize with peers, interact with teachers in a setting outside the classroom, and get recognition; and have a venue for healthy use of their leisure time (Vornberg 1998).

One way to help new advisors is to partner them with experienced advisors. Just like the mentoring relationship among veteran and student teacher-advisors can also benefit from mentoring. Advisors should feel that they are prepared for their advising duties and are supported by more experienced staff and administrators (Solter 2000). The early 1970s saw the emergence of formal mentoring programs for beginning teachers. These programs have tripled in number since that time (Darling-Hammond and Sclan 1996).

Mentoring programs are likely to expand during the next decade due to a convergence of three trends that will result in a large influx of new teachers: an increasing number of children entering American schools, a growing proportion of teachers who will be retiring, and continuing efforts to reduce class size. . . . Mentoring enables a veteran teacher to establish a special relationship, certainly professional and often personal, with a novice teacher just entering the profession or an experienced teacher new to the school. (Ganser 1999, 10)

Simply put, mentoring is the relationship of seeking and receiving advice from a respected, experienced person. Informal mentoring occurs when one person explains the how and why of something to another person. A formal mentoring program involves an organized and systematic relationship between a helper and helpee (Heller and Sindelar 1991). Good mentors are excellent teachers and truly interested in the success of their mentees. Mentor and mentee must also be a good "match"—able to work together. Coaching is a form of short-term mentoring in a particular skill or activity and is a valuable skill for advisors. Mentoring can also be used to accomplish many worthwhile goals, among them improving racial harmony and promoting social change (White-Hood 1993).

Mentoring programs for new teachers come in all sizes and shapes. However, they all share the common goal of helping beginning teachers make a smooth transition from college student to tenured teacher.

Learning to teach takes years. Although the learning begins in teacher preparation programs, it continues to a greater extent in the schools. School systems are becoming aware of the critical role they play in nurturing the potential of their new recruits. Schools that are successful in retaining new teachers and in helping them reach a high level of instructional competence do so by providing a systematic, orderly process of induction. These systems realize that experienced colleagues do influence the development of beginning teachers, and they make every attempt to provide positive influences through formal assigned mentors. (Blank and Sindelar 1992, 22)

Six basic but essential qualities of the good mentor are:

- The good mentor is committed to the role of mentoring. The good mentor is highly committed to the task of helping beginning teachers find success and gratification in their new work.
- The good mentor is accepting of the beginning teacher. At the foundation of any effective helping relationship is empathy.
- The good mentor is skilled at providing instructional support. Beginning teachers enter their careers with varying degrees of skill in instructional design and delivery.
- The good mentor is effective in different interpersonal contexts. All beginning teachers are not created equal, nor are all mentor teachers. . . . Good mentor teachers recognize that each mentoring relationship occurs in a unique, interpersonal context.
- The good mentor is a model of a continuous learner. Beginning teachers rarely appreciate mentors who have *right* answers to every question and *best* solutions for every problem. . . . Good mentor teachers are transparent about their own search for *better* answers and *more effective* solutions to their own problems.
- The good mentor communicates hope and optimism. . . . Good mentor teachers capitalize on opportunities to affirm the human potential of their mentees. (Rowley 1999, 20–22)

Fifteen percent of all new teachers will leave teaching after their first year of teaching—two and a half times the overall teacher turnover rate. This fact makes mentoring programs especially important for new staff (Schlechty and Vance 1983). Furthermore, within five years of starting their teaching career, one-third will leave the profession (Delgado 1999). When working with teachers and advisors in the mentoring process, four principles provide guidance for program planners:

1. People want to and will grow personally and professionally if the environment and conditions meet their needs. Providing these conditions is one of the responsibilities and challenges of staff development.
2. Dignifying people is essential in all aspects of staff development.
3. Support, reinforcement, and practice are essential in transferring workshop knowledge into teachers' use in their classrooms.
4. Teacher choice and ownership through self-analysis in the mentoring experience offer the greatest chance for growth. (Hofsess 1990, 21)

Teachers who have attained higher levels of professional development teach so that students will demonstrate higher levels of thinking and academic skill development (Odell 1990). These teachers expect more from their students. Their students respond by setting and achieving higher standards.

Good advisors also exhibit these qualities and their students respond accordingly. The demands and responsibilities for advisors have changed with the times. For example, field trips often use an airplane instead of a bus and last a week instead of a day or two. Students may also need passports and luggage for the field trip (Biederman 2001). New activities are started due to student interest with the help of supportive school staff members.

The stock club at John P. Stevens High School in Edison, New Jersey, is an example. "Stock Club itself didn't exist until two years ago, when five juniors started getting together to dissect the market with a math teacher named Charles Babich. Last year, membership bulged to 88, and this year it surged to 192. Members ran the gamut of personality and market awareness, but only a sprinkling of girls belonged" (Kleinfield 2001).

CNBC, the financial cable network, has also become involved by sponsoring a stock market contest for student groups across the United States. Enrollment is open to teams from grades 4 through 12 and currently about 13,500 schools are involved.

A good measure of the effectiveness of a student activities program is the level of student participation. Programs should provide many opportunities to meet the needs of a diverse student body. Increasing participation is a major challenge in some schools. One response to this challenge has been the creation of special need clubs, such as ethnic or bilingual clubs. The building principal's leadership is key to the success of the student activities program in any school. Encouragement and direction from the principal helps advisors feel supported. This is especially true for staff development programs and activities that promote student clubs and organizations (Vornberg 1998).

Many times, students, parents, and faculty members have ideas and insights that can be used to improve student activities programs. A review of the programs by a committee of these persons, along with the principal, can be a powerful vehicle for improvement. If this group is formed into a site-based, decision-making council, they can respond to needs and make program recommendations over a long period of time. The site-based team may also be able to assist with fund-raising to support the activities program and help involve more individuals in program evaluation (Vornberg 1998).

A comprehensive student activities program must help all students grow into healthy, productive adults. In order for this to occur, basic human needs must be met during adolescence. Students must:

- Find a valued place in a constructive group
- Learn how to form close, durable human relationships
- Feel a sense of worth as a person
- Achieve a reliable basis for making informed choices
- Know how to use the support systems available to them
- Express constructive curiosity and exploratory behavior
- Find ways of being useful to others
- Believe in a promising future with real opportunities

Meeting these requirements has been essential for human survival into adulthood for millennia. But in a technologically advanced democratic society—one that places an increasingly high premium on competence in many domains—adolescents themselves face a further set of challenges. They must:

- Master social skills, including the ability to manage conflict peacefully
- Cultivate the inquiring and problem-solving habits of mind for lifelong learning
- Acquire the technical and analytical capabilities to participate in a world-class economy
- Become ethical persons
- Learn the requirements of responsible citizenship
- Respect diversity in our pluralistic society (Carnegie Council on Adolescent Development 1995, 10–11)

The work of the Carnegie Council has focused attention on the challenges faced by children ages ten to fourteen. This developmental stage can be a rewarding time for personal growth and development. It is also an age when individuals adopt behavior patterns that can have long-term significance. Still, no institution by itself can guarantee that adolescents will become responsible, decent, thoughtful, and competent adults. It is the interaction and cooperation of institutions that will be crucial. Working together, they can address the underlying causes that lead to millions of young people becoming involved in serious health-threatening behaviors.

Health-damaging behaviors as well as health-promoting behaviors in adolescents tend to cluster. Common factors that contribute to problem behaviors in adolescents are academic difficulty and the absence of strong, sustained guidance from concerned adults. Because the influences on adolescents are complex, the basic requirements for healthful, positive development must be met through the combined efforts of a several key institutions, starting with the family and including schools and a wide range of neighborhood and community organizations (Carnegie Council on Adolescent Development 1995).

At the middle level, advisors can help students by developing support systems for moral development. Middle school students' moral development can be supported through programs that focus on:

- Conflict resolution—middle school students need to learn conflict resolution techniques and use them to resolve issues peacefully.
- Cultural sensitivity—schools are more culturally diverse and so is our society. Tolerance, acceptance of others' opinions, and an awareness of other cultures are critical skills that young people need.

- Mentoring—the development of personality, goals, and aspirations is related in large part to a young person's peers and the significant adults in their lives.
- Service projects—the school can encourage students to participate in service projects to provide a positive outlet for the energy of middle school students and to engage them in hands-on projects. (Korsak 2000)

Some states, including Massachusetts, Mississippi, and North Carolina, have spent a great deal of money recently to attract and recruit teacher candidates, many of whom will become the next generation of activity advisors. Yet, most states leave teacher recruitment to individual school districts. Incentives that are offered to candidates tend to be small and are only available to a few. Scholarships and loan programs are two common incentives. The incentives usually do not address the real problems that discourage young people from entering the teaching profession, such as poor salaries, unfavorable working conditions, and lack of merit pay systems (Olson 2000). Without a larger pool of candidates, districts will continue to compete against each other for the same individuals, whether or not incentives are offered.

One long-range solution to the shortage of teacher candidates is the establishment of teaching clubs and other programs for middle and high school students that encourage young people to consider a teaching career. These programs also would ensure that students are prepared for college by taking the appropriate high school courses. About 75 percent of South Carolina's high schools offer an honors course through the Teacher Cadet program. South Carolina also supports middle school teaching clubs. These clubs encourage minority students and others who have not traditionally considered an education career to consider becoming a teacher (Olson 2000). The results from South Carolina are encouraging. About 40 percent of the students involved in teaching clubs become teachers and three-quarters of them stay in South Carolina to teach. Several other states and urban districts now offer similar programs.

Who will be the cocurricular advisors in the future? The young students that enter teaching will make up the majority. Will there be enough new teachers ready and willing to accept the role of student activity advisor? Only time will tell, but the two issues are clearly related. The future health of public education in America depends upon the current success of our efforts. If there aren't enough teachers, can there be enough activity advisors?

The ideal advisor is someone who can help students learn the following lessons through their involvement in student activities. In the words of one student,

1. *Trust*—I learned that I could trust others for help, support, and assistance and that others could trust me for the same.
2. *To Be Myself*—I learned that I have a lot to offer others and that diversity is OK—it makes us all stronger. We are all different pages of the same book.
3. *Perseverance*—I learned to persevere and stick to my goals and to be flexible in achieving the standards I set for myself. I learned not to give up or take the easy route.
4. *To Believe in Myself*—I learned to believe in myself—that I can make a difference, that I can accomplish difficult tasks. I can help at least one starfish everyday!
5. *Friends*—I learned to make new friends, to talk with others and to listen. I learned some valuable lessons in how to be a friend and to be part of a team. I also learned that others have a lot in common with me.
6. *Risks*—I learned to take risks and that it is OK to fail. No gains can be achieved without taking risks. When I stumbled, *I fell forward not backward*.

7. *Road Map*—I could have gotten to my goal sooner if I had a road map. I wouldn't have been "lost" along the way. Next time I will plan my activities ahead of time. I'll be better prepared—to succeed.

8. *Problem Solving*—I learned to think more on my own and to solve problems for myself. I also learned to help others solve their problems. I CAN HELP OTHERS!

9. *Communication*—I learned to communicate to let others know how I feel and what I mean. I learned to listen to what others said and to compromise, to work out an acceptable solution for all.

10. *Fun*—I learned to have fun and laugh at things that I did and others did. Not to laugh at others, but to laugh with them. I smiled a lot. It made my work more enjoyable and learning a lot easier.

In closing:

School failure, substantial time spent "hanging out," and other related factors combined are three to eight times more likely to predict risky behavior among teens than race, income, and family structure combined. (School Failure 2001, 1)

In April of 2001 the Urban League released results from a random survey of 200 corporate executives from Fortune 1000 companies that show these business leaders value character, leadership abilities, and effective communication much more than test scores, grades, or advanced degrees when determining employees' potential. (Gehring 2001, 3)

WHAT WILL STUDENT ACTIVITY PROGRAMS LOOK LIKE IN FIVE, TEN, OR FIFTEEN YEARS?

America's future and hope depend directly on the education of our children—on young men and women with the skills and character to succeed.

—G. W. Bush, 2000

Oddly, over the next twenty years, the greatest demand for school construction will be in communities that have not even been named yet.

—H. J. Hodgkinson, 2000

Nothing is distributed evenly across the United States. Not race, not religion, not age, not fertility, not wealth, and certainly not access to higher education.

—H. J. Hodgkinson, 2000–2001

It is projected that, in the next decade, five states will have a 25 percent increase in students and nine states will have a decline. Almost all the increase in student diversity is projected to occur in only 200 of the 3,068 counties in the United States. Sixty percent of the increase will be composed of Hispanic and Asian populations. Currently, about 43 percent of the Asian population lives in three cities: Los Angeles, San Francisco, and New York (Hodgkinson 1999). Changes in student demographics depend upon where you live in a particular state. According to Hodgkinson (2000–2001),

About one-quarter of Americans live in big cities, half live in suburbs, and a quarter live in small towns or rural areas. If you live in a central city in the eastern half of the country, you can expect almost no enrollment increases and some decreases. Those who can, flee to the suburbs. The inner suburban ring (where there is nothing between you and the city limits) will see a major increase in student diversity—more minorities, more immigrants, more students learning English as a second language (ESL), and more students from poverty. Teaching in an inner suburb will increasingly resemble teaching in an inner city. The second suburban ring (with one suburb between you and the city) will see some expansion in student enrollments, especially as you reach the beltway, which used to contain growth—like a belt—but is now the jumping-off place for growth. In these areas, parents do not commute to the central city; they live in one suburb and work in another. Finally, enrollments in small towns or rural areas will be flat. But these places will have increasingly large percentages of elderly people. Older residents tend to "age in place," and whereas the young move away, some elderly do seek out small-town life. (Hodgkinson 2000–2001, 6–8)

The majority of the American population lives in only nine states—California, Texas, Florida, New York, Pennsylvania, Ohio, Illinois, Michigan, and New Jersey—but only three states, California, Texas, and Florida, are experiencing rapid population growth (Hodgkinson 2000–2001).

What should be the major emphasis of schools? Most teachers (48 percent) say public schools should emphasize academics. But most of the public (46 percent) say student responsibility should be the main emphasis (Langdon and Vesper 2000). In the 2000 Phi Delta Kappa/Gallup Poll of the public's attitudes toward the public schools, respondents were asked to indicate how important each purpose of public education is from a list (Rose and Gallup 2000). The results are presented in table 15.1.

The following questions were also asked: *In your opinion, which is the primary purpose of the schools—to teach the basic subjects, such as English, math, and science, or to provide a balanced education in which the basics are only one factor?* The results are presented in table 15.2.

Do you consider extracurricular activities as important as the academic subjects, or do you consider them as only a supplement to the academic subjects? The results are presented in table 15.3.

Survey results also indicated that 76 percent of respondents believed that more emphasis should be given to "racial and ethnic understanding and tolerance" in high schools.

Another Phi Delta Kappa/Gallup Poll of the public's attitudes toward the public schools found that the availability of extracurricular activities (band/orchestra, theater, clubs) was very important or fairly important to 91 percent of the respondents. However, quality of teaching staff, maintenance of

Table 15.1   How Important Is Public Education?

	Importance of Purpose	
	Mean	Rank
To prepare people to become responsible citizens	9.0	1
To help people become economically self-sufficient	8.6	2
To ensure a basic level of quality among schools	8.5	3
To promote cultural unity among all Americans	8.0	4
To improve social conditions for people	7.8	5
To enhance people's happiness and enrich their lives	7.5	6–7
To dispel inequalities in education among certain schools and certain groups	7.5	6–7

Source: Rose and Gallup 2000, 47.

Table 15.2 What Is the Basic Purpose of Schools?

	National Totals %	No Children in School %	Public School Parents %
Teach the basic subjects	29	29	28
Provide a balanced education	69	69	70
Don't know	2	2	2

Source: Rose and Gallup 2000, 47.

Table 15.3 What Is the Role of Extracurricular Activities?

	National Totals %	No Children in School %	Public School Parents %
As important as academic subjects	42	40	46
A supplement to academic subjects	56	58	52
Don't know	2	2	2

Source: Rose and Gallup 2000, 47.

student discipline, curriculum, and size of classes were the aspects of schools that are of greater importance to respondents than extracurricular activities (Rose and Gallup 1999). A majority of respondents (74 percent) felt that homeschooled students should also have the opportunity to participate in public school extracurricular activities. Table 15.4 shows other topics that respondents also felt should be taught to students.

The thirtieth annual Phi Delta Kappa/Gallup Poll surveyed the biggest problems facing public schools. These results are presented in table 15.5.

Table 15.4 Topics That Should Be Taught in Public Schools

	National Totals	
	1999 %	1993 %
Honesty	97	97
Democracy	93	93
Acceptance of people of different races and ethnic backgrounds	93	93
Caring for friends and family members	90	91
Moral courage	90	91
Patriotism/love of country	90	91
The Golden Rule	86	90
Acceptance of people who hold different religious beliefs	—	87
Acceptance of people who hold unpopular or controversial political or social views	71	73
Sexual abstinence outside of marriage	68	66
Acceptance of people with different sexual orientations—that is, homosexuals or bisexuals	55	51
Acceptance of the right of a woman to choose abortion	48	56

Source: Rose and Gallup 1999, 51.

Table 15.5   Biggest Problems Facing Public Schools

	National Totals	
	1998 %	1997 %
Fighting/violence/gangs	15	12
Lack of discipline/more control	14	15
Lack of financial support/funding/money	12	15
Use of drugs/dope	10	14
Overcrowded schools	8	8
Concern about standards/quality of education	6	8
Difficulty getting good teachers/quality teachers	5	3
Pupils' lack of interest/attitudes/truancy	5	6
None	3	2
Don't know	16	10

Source: Rose and Gallup 1998, 51.

Ninety percent of the respondents felt that extracurricular activities (as part of a young person's education) were seen as very important or fairly important. Fifty-three percent of respondents felt that there was about the right amount emphasis on sports (Rose, Gallup, and Elam 1997).

Clearly, for many young people, "understanding other cultures, possessing multicultural flexibility, may well be today's most important core competency to acquire. . . . The Census Bureau predicts that by the year 2066, half of Americans will trace their roots to places other than Western Europe" (Mavrelis 1998, 18).

Many immigrants who arrive in America today speak languages other than English that are "new" to schools. In many California school districts, from thirty to fifty foreign languages and dialects are represented in the student population. Population projections indicate continued growth in diversity in the future (Noguera 1999).

Currently, 93 out of every 100 children are being born in Asia, Africa, and Latin America; European birthrates are dropping, reflecting a change from the early twentieth century when one-third of the world's population was European born. From 1900 to 1910, 97 percent of all immigrants to the United States were from Europe. Today, 85 percent of immigrants come not from Europe but from Asia and Latin America. "By the end of 1998, Anglos had become a numerical minority in 243 U.S. counties, with 42 making that transition within the past five years" (Cortes 1999, 13). Hispanics and Asians will account for 61 percent of the growth in the U.S. population between 1995 and 2023. The increasing diversity, however, will be concentrated to a small number of areas (Hodgkinson 1999). The global movement of people, communications technologies, and worldwide, overnight transportation make diversity a reality to all of America.

A means of helping students understand others who are different from them is through cultural programming. Such programming teaches students to look at the world in a new way—a useful skill in today's world. The following are some suggestions for cultural programming:

- *Create a new position on the student council*. This cultural programmer could plan several events throughout the year.
- *Assess your activities program*. Give your student leaders a chance to review their program and make sure it is culturally sensitive and aware.

- *Recruit student leaders*. If the student council members are not diverse culturally, you could recruit students from all segments of the school population for committee positions.
- *Take it one step further*. Multicultural programming must go beyond the traditional black history month or diversity day. While these activities have value, we should also foster cultural "meshing" ceremonies or events that help participants discover similarities as well as unique features of differing cultures.
- *Offer a varied program*. Work to sponsor projects that bring together disparate people and school organizations for a common cause. In the drive to achieve a shared goal, students often find they have more in common with people who are culturally different from them than they thought.
- *Educate your participants*. Multicultural programs are *about* the particular culture being celebrated, not *for* it. Often, cultural programs are attended only by people who happen to be of the culture being discussed. It is important to make sure that the school community understands these programs are for all cultures to come and discover together. (Garrett 1995, 21)

The lack of sensitivity to and understanding of other groups on the part of staff or students is one of several factors that can lead to school violence (Mills 1998). Suggested long-term strategies for violence prevention programs that could involve the student activities program are:

- Train teams to problem solve using school-based data.
- Implement before- and after-school programming.
- Establish research-based conflict resolution programs for students, parents, and school staff.
- Use instructional approaches and curriculum materials that improve achievement, promote daily application of positive values and conflict resolution skills, reduce student alienation, and encourage respect for student diversity.
- Use schools within schools, block scheduling, and mentoring programs, and increase the use of paraprofessionals to create more opportunities to work directly with students.
- Foster collaboration among school, home, and community for peaceable schools.
- Train staff to de-escalate aggressive acting out students.
- Create support groups for parents and staff.
- Involve students and staff in educational programs that emphasize diversity. (Mills 1998, 2)

Every school should encourage positive relationships between students and staff. Research shows one of the most critical factors in preventing student violence is the existence of a positive relationship with adults who offer students guidance, support, and direction. Some students need assistance to overcome feelings of isolation and encouragement to develop social connections (Dwyer, Osher, and Warger 1998).

Effective schools communicate to students and the greater community that all children are valued and respected. There is a deliberate and systematic effort—for example, displaying children's artwork, posting academic work prominently throughout the building, respecting students' diversity—to establish a climate that demonstrates care and a sense of community. (Dwyer, Osher, and Warger 1998, 4)

Offering extended-day programs and promoting good citizenship and character education are two key strategies that can be used by schools to be responsive to all children and, therefore, safe schools (Dwyer, Osher, and Warger 1998).

Family configurations take a variety of forms in contemporary America society. Schools must take this into consideration when trying to involve parents in programs and events. Schools must also ensure that the diversity of student groups is represented in activities and during assemblies. It is important to recognize all groups of students, not just one group (athletes) or a few groups (career clubs, for example). If this is the case, other groups will feel that they are not important and do not belong to the school community. School assemblies and pep rallies are wonderful opportunities to promote multiculturalism and the inclusion of all students (Sapon-Shevin 2000–2001).

Advances in technology are making the physical distance between classrooms, schools, and school districts inconsequential at the state, national, and international levels. Diverse groups of students and teachers can be brought together through e-mail and the Internet. This technology allows schools to offer classes and resources that it might not otherwise have been able to provide (Ganser 1998). In many cases, these new resources can support the school's multicultural education efforts.

"In 1984, 1989, and 1996, teachers were asked to name the biggest problem with which the schools in their communities must deal. The problem they identified most often throughout these years was lack of interest and support from parents" (Langdon 1997, 214). The use of technology can help school districts overcome this problem. District websites can provide up-to-date information about school programs and activities. Adult education courses in technology use can also bring community members into the schools who might never otherwise visit.

In order to have a lasting effect on a child's character, it is imperative that school values be reinforced at home. These values must be agreed upon by the school and the community in order to put into practice effective programs that support moral development (Lickona 1988).

In 1966, James S. Coleman undertook a massive study to determine how much of children's achievement was associated with the school and how much with what Lawrence A. Cremin, the late president of Teachers College at Columbia University, called "the other educators." It turns out that only 30 percent is due to school characteristics and the other 70 percent is from the family, the media, and the peer group. (Mann 1999, 22)

Asked to judge the importance of six measures of school effectiveness, 69 percent of teachers say good citizenship is very important, but 82 percent of the public says the school's high school graduation rate is very important. Only 15 percent of teachers say standardized test scores are a very important indicator of school effectiveness, whereas 50 percent of the public says they are a very important measure (Langdon 1999).

The U.S. economy has evolved from a manufacturing-based economy to a more complex, technology-dependent economy that requires workers to have better academic skills. "Even though 70 percent of high school graduates are enrolling in college right after high school, more than a quarter of those college freshman—29 percent—require costly remedial education" (Viadero 2001b, 12). Schools have also assumed more caretaking roles because many more children come from nontraditional homes. Single-parent households—particularly single-mother households—tend to have lower incomes than two-parent households. The negative impact of a lower household income on children, aside from poverty, influences education attainment and the likelihood of staying in school (Trotter 2001a).

Intergenerational programs can create a richer family life for many students since many young people today are less likely to interact with older family members. These programs also help overcome stereotypes held by both the young and the old (Hopkins 2000).

"Reliving the USO Years," an annual spring dance event, is an intergenerational activity of the Pattonville School District in St. Louis County, Missouri. Programs such as these are part of the district's comprehensive effort to link young and old (Halford 1998). As people age, they become more distanced from the public schools. "Indeed, 40 percent of the U.S. adult population has no daily or even weekly contact with school-age children. . . . Helping seniors see education as a civic responsibility isn't merely a matter of urging them to support school bond issues, social researchers say, but a matter of reuniting generations" (Halford 1998, 49–50). The best intergenerational programs make it possible for seniors and children to establish personal relationships over a period of time.

In addition to cognitive knowledge, young people need good interpersonal skills, a strong sense of values, and a positive but accurate self-image in order to succeed socially and professionally. "While schools usually subscribe to these characteristics in their goals and statements of philosophy, few address them directly or substantially in the learning experiences they offer youth" (Cawelti 1989, 30–31). More and more, jobs require mathematics ability, reading, problem solving, and technical knowledge as well as the skill to work with others as a team or group member. To be successful, students must be proficient in the following skill areas:

- Job-related skills—These are skills required to perform specific job tasks.
- Basic skills—These are skills outlined in two reports, the Secretary's Commission on Achieving Necessary Skills, commonly known as the *SCANS Report*, published by the U.S. Department of Labor in 1990, and a 1996 report by the RAND Corporation.
- Career decision-making skills—Throughout our lifespan, the decisions we make about careers and leisure are critical to our sense of well-being. (Ettinger 1998, 28)

During the 1990–1991 school year, the state of Michigan piloted a portfolio program to determine the skills that all students should have to enter and advance in the workforce. The Michigan Employability Skills Task Force wanted to assist students to discover and record the skills that would help them become employable. The general skills that need to be developed in all students were found to be:

Academic Skills
- Read and understand written materials
- Understand charts and graphs
- Understand basic math
- Use mathematics to solve problems
- Use research and library skills
- Use specialized knowledge and skills to get a job done
- Use tools and equipment
- Speak in the language in which business is conducted
- Write in the language in which business is conducted
- Use scientific method to solve problems

Personal Management Skills
- Attend school/work daily and on time

- Meet school/work deadlines
- Develop career plans
- Know personal strengths and weaknesses
- Demonstrate self-control
- Pay attention to details
- Follow written and oral instructions
- Follow written and oral directions
- Work without supervision
- Learn new skills
- Identify and suggest new ways to get the job done

Teamwork Skills
- Actively participate in a group
- Know the group's rules and values
- Listen to other group members
- Express ideas to other group members
- Be sensitive to the group members' ideas and views
- Be willing to compromise if necessary to best accomplish the goal
- Be a leader or a follower to best accomplish the goal
- Work in changing settings and with people of differing backgrounds (Stemmer, Brown, and Smith 1992, 33)

Students should also leave school having developed the ability to solve problems or to make something that is valued in one or more cultures. The intelligences that students should develop, according to Howard Gardner, are:

- *Linguistic intelligence* is the capacity to use language, your native language and perhaps other languages, to express what's on your mind and to understand other people.
- People with a highly developed *logical–mathematical intelligence* understand the underlying principles of some kind of causal system, the way a scientist or a logician does; or can manipulate numbers, quantities, and operations, the way a mathematician does.
- *Spatial intelligence* refers to the ability to represent the spatial word internally in your mind, the way a sailor or airplane pilot navigates the large spatial world, or the way a chess player or sculptor represents a more circumscribed spatial world.
- *Bodily kinesthetic intelligence* is the capacity to use your whole body or parts of your body—your hand, your fingers, your arms—to solve a problem, make something, or put on some kind of production.
- *Musical intelligence* is the capacity to think in music, to be able to hear patterns, recognize them, remember them, and perhaps manipulate them.
- *Interpersonal intelligence* is understanding other people. It's an ability we all need, but is at a premium if you are a teacher, clinician, salesperson, or politician.
- *Intrapersonal intelligence* refers to having an understanding of yourself, of knowing who you are, what you can do, what you want to do, how you react to things, which things to avoid, and which things to gravitate toward.

- *Naturalist intelligence* designates the human ability to discriminate among living things (plants, animals) as well as sensitivity to other features of the natural world (clouds, rock configurations). (Checkley 1997, 12)

According to *Breaking Ranks: Changing an American Institution*, a report of the NASSP study of the restructuring of the American high school, produced in partnership with the Carnegie Foundation for the Advancement of Teaching, the nine purposes of high schools are:

I. High school is, above all else, a learning community and each school must commit itself to expecting demonstrated academic achievement for every student in accord with standards that can stand up to national scrutiny.
II. High school must function as a transitional experience, getting each student ready for the next stage of life, whatever it may be for that individual, with the understanding that, ultimately, each person needs to earn a living.
III. High school must be a gateway to multiple options.
IV. High school must prepare each student to be a lifelong learner.
V. High school must provide an underpinning for good citizenship and for full participation in the life of a democracy.
VI. High school must play a role in the personal development of young people as social beings who have needs beyond those that are strictly academic.
VII. High school must lay a foundation for students to be able to participate comfortably in an increasingly technological society.
VIII. High school must equip young people for life in a country and a world in which interdependency will link their destiny to that of others, however different those others may be from them.
IX. High school must be an institution that unabashedly advocates in behalf of young people. (NASSP 1996, 2)

More recently, the American Association of School Administrators produced a report, "Preparing Schools and School Systems for the Twenty-first Century." The characteristics of schools and school systems capable of preparing students for a global knowledge/information age are:

- The definitions of "school," "teacher," and "learner" are reshaped by the digital world.
- All students have equal opportunity for an outstanding education, with adequate funding, no matter where they live.
- Educators are driven by high expectations and clear, challenging standards that are widely understood by students, families, and communities.
- A project-based "curriculum for life" engages students in addressing real-world problems, issues important to humanity, and questions that matter.
- Teachers and administrators are effectively prepared for the global knowledge/information age.
- Students, schools, school systems, and communities are connected around the clock with each other and with the world through information-rich, interactive technology.
- School systems conduct, consider, and apply significant research in designing programs that lead to constantly improving student achievement.

- Students learn to think, reason, and make sound decisions and demonstrate values inherent in a democracy.
- School facilities provide a safe, secure, stimulating, joyous learning environment that contributes to a lifelong passion for learning and high student achievement.
- Leadership is collaborative, and governance is focused on broad issues that affect student learning.
- Students learn about other cultures, respect and honor diversity, and see the world as an extended neighborhood.
- Schools promote creativity and teamwork at all levels, and teachers help students turn information into knowledge and knowledge into wisdom.
- Assessment of student progress is more performance based, taking into account students' individual talents, abilities, and aspirations.
- A student-centered, collaboratively developed vision provides power and focus for education community-wide.
- Continuous improvement is a driving force in every school and school system.
- Schools are the crossroads and central convening points of the community. (American Association of School Administrators 1999, 7–15)

What will student activity programs look like in five, ten, and fifteen years as they evolve to meet the challenges of twenty-first-century schools? Consider the following responses:

The best answer to the question, "What will student activities look like in 5, 10, 15 years?" is a short one. They cannot look like they do today. The longer answer lies in explaining why. Student activities are a microcosm of school life. The kinds of activities reflect the values of the school that sponsors them. The traditional sports teams, service groups, and academic interest groups have traditionally held the interest of much of our student population. As society has become more complex, we have an increasingly complicated student body; one not so easily entertained or engaged. The school must value this changing student body. Although in years past we have always had students who are not as involved as we would like, they have historically had more of an indifference rather than a violent negativity. In the past few years, we have seen a radical shift in the climate of our schools. What this means is that the traditional ways of engaging students in our schools through student activity participation must be examined. Apparently, not all students feel a connection to the school community and a pride in being one of its members. Generally speaking if there is a bond and a sense of belonging to something, chances are there won't be a violent reaction against such a source. This is relevant to students and a feeling of belonging to their school. If school is a positive experience, there is less likelihood of turning against it. Although schools have undergone tremendous change in their academic structure and philosophies, student activities do not seem to reflect such change. In the past, it was always easy to concentrate on the bright and athletic because the loner or the marginal student simply left the school alone. They believed that the school held nothing for them and they found their identity and value in other facets of their life. However, today we have no choice but to address those who are not active participants in school life because they are demanding our attention, through violence directed toward the school.

Student activities in the future need to become more diverse to recognize the talents and interests of all students. Not all students are athletic in traditional ways. Today's athlete may be a skateboarder, an extreme skier, or snowboarder. There has been a movement toward inclusion of different sports that were not always so mainstream, like lacrosse and soccer. However, schools should not be so resistive toward change for fear that our traditional sports may be downplayed. Recognizing the need to create new athletic opportunities would contribute to a stronger sense of acceptance by the school. There needs to be more emphasis on diversity, as our schools are reflecting more and more the global nature of our communities. In years past, our communities reflected the families that worked at the local plant or family business. We were very homogenous. Today, with the increase of on-line business, and traditional jobs becoming passé, we find our families moving to places simply to find employment or being able to live anywhere and work out of their home. Thus our communities reflect the heterogeneous nature of the world even though it still may look like small town America. Due to the instant access of information we have through the Internet we now have more information than ever before from all parts of the globe. World problems and issues have found us in our homes and schools. Student activities cannot ignore this information influx and need to take an active role in addressing world issues. The world is now their backyard. The local efforts in helping our community can be tied into larger world efforts. For example, there was a young child in Illinois who was being bullied and a school in Colorado found out and sent students to the school as a group to show support for this youngster. This demonstrates the outreach role that student activities could be playing in the future. Instead of school versus school rivalry as it used to be, school and school collaboration working on issues of importance to all students will be the new model.

There are many ways that student activities can become more progressive and inclusive but it will rely on those leaders of the schools to take the initiative and demand change. As we have seen in the unfortunate events in our schools in the last few years, schools cannot ignore the challenge of changing. Changing student activities will better prepare all our students for the ever-changing world they will enter after high school.

Jan D'Onofrio
New Hartford Senior High School

What will student activities look like in 5, 10, 15 years? There is no simple answer. Indeed, it is a very good question to ask in light of the many changes facing the educational system in the next 5, 10, to 15 years.

Before we can look into the future, I think we need to understand the role of student activities: what they are, who administers them, and the impact they have on student life. Student activities are generally divided into two categories—athletics and other activities including clubs and special interest groups. Up until a few years ago, these activities were referred to as "extra" curricular activities because they were seen as an "add on" to a school's overall program. In recent years, however, these activities are referred to as "cocurricular," seen now as a critical component of a school's overall program. While this may seem like a matter of semantics, it is indicative of the true understanding and the importance that activities play in the life of school children.

What are some of the typical student activities found in most schools today? The following list, although not inclusive, includes some of the most common activities: Math Club, Language Clubs, Journalism, Science Club, Chess Club, Service Clubs, Yearbook, Speech and Debate, Computer Club, Honor Societies.

Classroom teachers have typically served as advisors to these clubs as part of their regular teaching assignment. And this is perhaps the first area of concern as we look to the future. A brief historical glance at the role of the teacher includes these references: teaching is a "service" profession, and one does not "go in it for the money," because "the children are more important than anything." Are these references still applicable today? Are they even fair? As an administrator, I see the changing face of the teaching profession—and the impact on student activities. If teachers at one time were expected to be expert in the subject they taught, today they must be experts not only in the academic area, but also in technology, adolescent psychology, parenting, life skills, and conflict resolution. They must also serve as a student activity advisor. Are these expectations realistic? I hear teachers expressing dissatisfaction with what they are asked to do—whether it is salary related or in terms of time commitment. While many veteran teachers are still willing to sacrifice their own family time and ignore the financial compensation for serving as an advisor, recent hires are not as inclined to take on the additional responsibilities. With so many veteran teachers reaching retirement age, the availability of teachers to advise/supervise the cocurricular activities is dwindling. I think the issue of availability is a critical one.

Will the range of current clubs meet the needs of students in the future? Has the shift to integrating technology into most areas of education created a need for new club offerings? Who will take charge of these new opportunities? Are parental expectations changing? These are critical questions—with uncertain answers.

Although we can't predict the future, we can certainly address the issue of student activities in teacher preparation programs. I believe teachers need to be fully aware of the all-encompassing role they will play as they enter the profession. Being skilled—or even expert—in an academic discipline is simply a piece of the puzzle—but it is not enough to successfully meet the needs of the changing face of education. Teaching candidates need to understand they will be asked to serve as mentors, student advisors and club advisors. Teachers will need to be willing to look beyond the traditional school day to meet the expectations put before them.

Given the role of tomorrow's teacher, will there be candidates? Will our brightest students choose this honorable profession, or will they go elsewhere, where the time, energy and passion they put into work will reward them more handsomely?

As we look ahead, as we see the "old guard" retiring and taking with them a longstanding attitude about teaching, are we prepared for tomorrow's educators and a new approach to the teaching profession?

When we consider the future of student activities and the broad range of programs that might need to be offered to reach students from all walks of life, will we have the advisors to lead them? I believe these issues are inextricably tied together.

Marsha Hirsch
Pembroke Hill School

To make any accurate predictions about the future of student leadership and cocurricular activities, one must consider the recent evolution student activities have undergone. It has been only ten years since I was a student leader in my high school. At that time, we believed our student council to be extremely high functioning and important to our school. As president, I thought my role was absolutely imperative to the smooth operation of the school. In retrospect, I realize how insignificant planning the dances, pep rallies and homecoming really were. Some of our community service was helpful to residents and had a positive impact, but I now reflect on the superficial nature of our role as "leaders." Who did I really lead? What did I lead them to? Did the administration really need our input? What impact did this have? The answers were disappointing. Further reflection brought me to our regional student leadership conferences with students from our county. I was disenchanted by my thoughts. Just a decade ago, student *leadership* appeared to be a misnomer in my school community.

Next, I considered my role as a student council and class advisor over the past five years. Dramatic changes have taken place since my days in high school. Students now have the opportunity to attend state and national conferences. They network with students from around the country and even the globe. Workshops are now focused on leadership skill development and training students to improve worthwhile, marketable skills. Opportunities for leaders have increased considerably. Students also have a much more active role in the school community. Although dances and other events certainly still take place, community service and leadership skill development are at the heart of student organizations. Today, student leaders have become active participants in some of the decision making in the school district. Student input is sought in many forms including school and district-wide committees, surveys and informal discussions. In many ways, students are leading the educational process. In addition, challenges and problems faced by contemporary society have forced student leaders to take a prominent leadership role in the school community. School violence, drugs, alcohol, suicide and even terrorist attacks have prompted student organizations to mobilize and take action. In my school, after the events of September 11, the school administration immediately turned to student leaders to coordinate efforts. I do not believe the climate of schools a decade ago would have allowed students to take the central role in organizing school response to such events. Non-violence pacts, peer mediation, and counseling have become part of the job descriptions for student leaders. Truly, it is not just dances and pep rallies any more.

The massive infusion of technology into society has also changed the anatomy of student leadership. Methods of communication have advanced to such a degree as to make the world and consequently schools seem much smaller. I now communicate with student leaders via e-mail and instant messaging for much of my correspondence. This has dramatically changed the face of student activities. Such accessibility and flexibility allows a greater variety of student activities and initiatives. A major barrier to student organizations, time and opportunity to interact, has been reduced significantly. Not only does this facilitate student-advisor interaction, it also allows greater contact between student leaders. They communicate not only with leaders from their own school, but rather have vast networks of peers from around their region, state and even the nation. The last state conference I attended illustrated this very well. It was like a reunion for the students who I thought did not even know one another. In fact, they had communicated electronically for months before even meeting face-to-face. I felt like the one who needed ice-breaking activities.

I believe the changes that have occurred over the past several years will serve as the groundwork for radical changes in student activities in the future. In five years, these changes may not become totally evident. The evolution experienced over the past several years may simply expand and become better articulated. The role of student leaders will be further refined and adjusted. Leadership organizations and conferences will continue to grow and be adjusted to have more of the substance student leaders and their advisors desire. Tragedies and societal problems will continue to dictate the involvement of student leaders. Technological advances will further assist in student activities making them more effective and efficient.

In a decade and beyond, I think the changes in student activities will be more easily recognized. I believe there are three areas in which changes will take place. First, since more than fifty percent of sitting school administrators will retire in the next five years, I think the role of student leaders will increase even further. I think new school administrators will better realize the need for and value of student activities in schools. They may recognize that student activities are a major ally in reaching high standards. They will understand what a tremendous resource positive student leaders can be and realize what problems are created when student leaders are not properly utilized. Secondly, I believe student leaders and student organizations will have greater responsibility for the safety, health and psychological well being of schools. Teachers and administrators are already overwhelmed with standardized testing and other assessment issues. I believe the thirst for accountability will only increase. This will leave a void in areas where counseling and other forms of assistance are necessary for the at-risk student population which I think will continue to increase in number. The solution may be to make greater use of student organizations. I think that peer mediation, tutoring, counseling, conflict resolution, character education, and service learning will be a critical component of student activities in the future. I assert that the role of student leaders will be taken to the next level. Flowery community service projects and insignificant events will be replaced with more meaningful, essential functions in the school community. Finally, I believe technology will surpass our wildest imagination. Meetings will be held electronically, virtual conferences will become common and data will be shared in forms not currently conceivable. Student leaders working closely with one another to perform increasingly important functions may never be in physical proximity. Travel may be revolutionized to make travels across the nation seem like a trip across town. I think technology may be the single greatest factor in shaping the appearance of student activities, but the soul will remain the same: kids doing great things to help other kids and their communities.

If someone had told me what student activities would be like today when I was in high school, I certainly would have been skeptical. It is difficult to imagine. I believe the key to the growth of student activities is to embrace opportunities for change and expansion of our role while holding on to the basic ideologies that prompt students to act as leaders. No matter what changes in student activities take place, advisors must continue to help cultivate the very best from our students. If we keep our eye on the ball, future developments will only enhance what we already achieve every day.

Jason Andrews
Windsor Central High School

"What will student activities look like in 5, 10, 15 years?" There are many factors that will shape the future landscape of student activity programs. As with any component of the educational curriculum, the vision of the school district and the leadership within each school building will serve as a major driving force. It will be incumbent on school administrators and teachers to continue to exercise their creativity and remain steadfast to their strong personal commitment to student leadership development, particularly in light of increased demands to prepare students for demonstrating competence on statewide proficiency exams. School personnel that recognize and support the successful partnership between academics and activities will best prepare students for the challenges of this century and will serve as models for other districts to emulate.

Today's successful student activities programs can and should serve as an anchor for envisioning future activity programs for our students. Specifically, consideration should be given to the following areas:

1. *Purpose/Mission of the Student Activities Program:* Student activity programs will need to have a well-defined mission statement that reflects the diverse needs of the students it will be serving. For those programs with an already defined purpose, careful examination should be given to reviewing its mission to ensure that it truly reflects the current needs of its student population. Thought should also be given to how students are receiving information and its impact on their socialization and learning. Over the past three years, the Internet, technology, 24-hour news shows have all changed the way we communicate and decipher information. Students are being inundated with information and being asked to respond to issues and events that are often challenging and beyond comprehension. The purpose of any student activity program will be shaped by future global events and advisors will need to be guides and support students through often sensitive issues. Programs will need to expand beyond fund-raising and spirit-building efforts and emphasize awareness and service. Service should include three areas: to their fellow students—what are their peers' needs and how can they respond; service to their school—what needs to occur to make their environment an optimal place for inclusion and education, emotional and social growth for all its students; and service to their community—what events are happening around them in a more global sense and what can they change, influence, and/or simply develop an understanding for on how it impacts their life. Finally, students will need to be given real opportunities to assume leadership roles that test their skills, encourage growth in areas of weakness, offers rewards and consequences for their actions and truly prepares them for their place in an ever-changing, challenging world.

2. *Scheduling:* There needs to be a regularly scheduled time and place for students and advisors to meet during the school day to truly prepare them for their roles as student leaders within the building and the outside community. Optimally, that can be accomplished through block scheduling or some other creative form of class offerings; i.e., a leadership class. Such scheduling serves a multi purpose. First, it makes a statement that student activities is a cocurricular activity. Second, it provides a weekly or biweekly block of purposeful time during the school day where all interested students and advisors can plan, organize, and carry out the goals and objectives of its program. Third, it provides credibility to its purpose and doesn't compete with students' other responsibilities such as sports programs, part-time jobs and personal family obligations.

3. *Compensation for Advisors:* In some cases, advisors are being asked to take on more and more responsibility without additional compensation and certainly in most cases, at an increased risk to their own personal liability (transporting students to events, serving in loco parentis at overnight events). In the same way that coaches for athletic programs are compensated, advisors need to be recompensed as well. Transportation to events, workshops and conferences need to be provided by district vehicles in again the same way it is offered to team sports. Finally, district insurance policies need to be reviewed and updated to ensure they cover the full range of responsibilities their advisors assume when working with students. Valued employees such as advisors should not be left unprotected in a highly litigious environment.

4. *Advisor Training:* Advisors need to be equipped with the skills to help them properly fulfill their roles as advisors. New advisors are often at a loss on what their role is and how to best serve their students. Advisors need the flexibility to attend workshops and conferences offered to student activity advisors for support and a sharing of ideas. In addition to advisor training, it is critical that teachers be provided training, instruction, and/or guidance in counseling skills. Given the issues that students are confronting today and in the future, advisors need an expanded skill set to deal with such challenging issues as terrorism, school shootings, hate, fear and violence on many levels. Advisors need to be trained in individual and group counseling skills. They need to have access to and time spent with crisis intervention professionals. Since advisors are often the

first adults to observe how students are processing and responding to challenges and their environment, it becomes critical that they feel adequately equipped to counsel. While schools no longer serve as safe havens from problems of the "outside world," our obligation to keep students safe remains as strong and as important as ever.

Elena M. Zongrone
Duxbury, Massachusetts

In closing:

The nurturing of cultural tolerance is often overshadowed by media coverage of intolerance. (Richardson 1995, 39)

It is easier to look at others and criticize, harder to look at ourselves and change. However, it is vastly more effective to change ourselves. (Perrin 1999, 27)

16

LEGAL ISSUES AND CONSIDERATIONS FOR COCURRICULAR ACTIVITIES

When the public was asked if extracurricular activities were as important as academic subjects, 42 percent indicated that they are as important as academic subjects, 56 percent indicated they are a supplement to academic subjects, and 2 percent didn't know (Rose and Gallup 2000).

Students have many outlets for expression when they become involved in student activities. The Supreme Court ruled in *Tinker vs. Des Moines Independent Community School District* (1969) that student expression may take place in an orderly, nondisruptive manner (Buss 1998). Two subsequent cases further addressed the issue of free speech and somewhat restricted the expression granted in *Tinker*. In the first, *Bethel School District #403 vs. Fraser* (1986) "the Court ruled that the school had the right to control the *manner* of the students' lewd and disruptive speech even if it did not have the right to control its content as established in *Tinker*" (Buss 1998, 110). In the second, the Supreme Court ruled in *Hazelwood School District vs. Kuhlmeier* (1988) that "the [school] newspaper was a part of the curriculum and not an open forum for unrestricted student expression" (Buss 1998, 110).

The implications of the *Bethel* and *Hazelwood* decisions for schools are summarized by the National Association of Secondary School Principals:

- The First Amendment free speech rights of students are not as extensive as those provided for adults.
- The decision as to what speech is inappropriate in the public school properly rests with the school board.
- The courts will intervene to protect the First Amendment rights of students only when the school's decision to control student expression is made without a valid educational purpose.
- The school and its organs of communication are not public forums unless school officials have, by policy or by practice, clearly established that they are to be available for use by the general public. (NASSP 1988, 7 quoted in Buss 1998, 110)

The Supreme Court has cited three criteria for school-sponsored student publications that make them *not* a public forum. The criteria are:

1. Is it supervised by a faculty member?
2. Was the publication designed to impart particular knowledge or skills in student participants or audiences?
3. Does the publication use the school's name or resources? (Student Press Law Center n.d., quoted in Hoover 1998, 49)

In keeping with Supreme Court rulings, if the school is the publisher of any publication that is not a public forum, it may control the expression in the publication (Hoover 1998). Specifically, "In the role of publisher, school officials are permitted to make editorial decisions about the paper, so long as they are reasonably related to legitimate pedagogical concerns" (Gill 1991, 255). However, the amount of editorial control retained by students depends upon several factors, as the following three examples illustrate:

- Underground paper: A school cannot control the content.
- Sponsored paper but a public forum: A school's right to control content is restricted.
- Sponsored paper in a limited public forum: A school can control the content if it goes against the school's educational mission. (Bell 2001, 3)

Congress passed the Equal Access Act in 1984. It states that if a school receives federal aid and allows "non-curriculum related" student activity groups to meet on the school campus after or before instructional hours or at lunchtime or during activity periods, an open forum has been established. As such, it "must grant equal access, without discrimination, to any noncurriculum student group that seeks to exercise and express religious, political, philosophical, or other content views at their meetings" (Buss 1998, 111). The act represents three main concepts: nondiscrimination, protection, and preservation. Nondiscrimination requires that student groups be granted equal, nonpreferential treatment. Protection requires that student meetings be initiated, led, and controlled totally by students. Preservation refers to locus of control—"that schools retain the authority to establish reasonable time, place, and manner restrictions for student clubs as long as the restrictions are both uniform and nondiscriminatory" (Taylor 2000, 69). A noncurriculum-related club or activity is one whose "roots" cannot be traced to the school curriculum. School officials usually make the determination as to whether a club or organization is curriculum or noncurriculum related. The definition of "curriculum related" cannot be based on arbitrary conditions, nor can it exclude clubs for reasons such as the group's subject matter or composition (Taylor 2000). The determination of curriculum related or not by the school may be challenged by an individual or group.

According to provisions of the EAA [Equal Access Act], the meetings of these noncurriculum student groups must be voluntarily initiated by students; not be sponsored by the school; employees of the school or school system cannot be present at the meetings; the student group cannot interfere with the orderly conduct of school affairs; and nonschool persons cannot direct, conduct, control, or regularly attend the meetings of the student group. (Buss 1998, 111)

A school is not required to create a limited open forum and may ban all clubs. One such case of banning all clubs occurred in Salt Lake City where the board of education, attempting to preempt establishment of the Gay-Straight Alliance, voted 4 to 3 to eliminate all cocurricular clubs so that it would still be in compliance with the Equal Access Act and the *Mergens* criteria (Buss 1998).

In the 1990 *Mergens* decision (*Board of Education of the Westside Community Schools vs. Mergens*),

> The Supreme Court ruled on two issues: whether the EAA violates the establishment clause and whether any of Westside's clubs were noncurriculum related as defined by the EAA. The Court decided that the EAA was constitutional and did not lead to the establishment of religion. It also ruled that the Westside did have noncurriculum-related clubs. This meant the school must allow the religious club to meet since the other clubs could also gather. (Buss 1998, 111)

A curriculum-related club was defined by the Court as one that meets the following criteria (Cary 1992, 20–21; Mahon 1990, 544):

1. The content is taught or soon to be taught in a regularly offered course. A Latin Club is directly related if Latin is taught in the curriculum.
2. The subject matter concerns the body of courses as a whole. The student council is directly related to the social studies curriculum.
3. Participation is required for a particular course. If students in a journalism course must work for the newspaper, a direct relationship exists.
4. Participation results in academic credit. If a student's grade in chorus depends on participating in a set number of after-school concerts, a direct relation exists. (Buss 1998, 111–12)

On June 11, 2001, the Supreme Court ruled 6 to 3 that school districts must give children's Bible clubs access to school facilities on an "equal footing" with other community organizations. Justice Clarence Thomas wrote in the majority opinion that the Milford Central School District (Milford, New York) "engaged in 'viewpoint discrimination' when it excluded the club [Good News Club] from the after-school forum." The courts further held that by allowing the religious club into its "limited public forum," the district would not violate the First Amendment's prohibition against a government establishment of religion (Walsh 2001b, 1). The Good News Club is an after-school Christian group for six- to twelve-year-olds.

The Milford Central School Districts' facilities-use policy permitted the schools to be used by outside organizations. However, the use of the facilities for a religious purpose would not be allowed (Worona 2001a). The K–12 building is the only public school in the community for the 530-student district. In 1993, the Supreme Court had held in *Lamb's Chapel vs. Center Moriches Union Free School District* that a school district would be discriminating on the basis of viewpoint if it permitted its facilities to be used for presentations on family issues and parenting from all but religious points of view.

> In *Lamb's Chapel*, the Court rejected the school district's claim that it could not allow any group to use school facilities for religious purposes without violating the Establishment Clause of the First Amendment, which requires that there be a separation between church and state. The Court concluded that there was no realistic danger that the community would think that the district was endorsing religion or any particular creed, and any benefit to religion or to the church would have been no more than incidental.

In *Good News*, the district maintained that, notwithstanding the *Lamb's Chapel* decision, school districts may distinguish between religious "viewpoint" (or prayer) and religious "instruction" when making decisions as to which groups may properly be excluded from using school district facilities. The Supreme Court disagreed, reversing a divided three-judge panel of the Second Circuit of the U.S. Court of Appeals, which had held that the Milford district did not violate the constitutional rights of the Christian youth organization. Judge Thomas pointed out that teaching character development and morals was a permissible purpose under the school district's policy; he concluded that excluding the club because it proposed to teach those subjects from a religious perspective was the same type of viewpoint discrimination that the Court had struck down in *Lamb's Chapel* and *Rosenberger*. (Worona 2001b, 1, 8)

The Supreme Court has established that teaching about religion can be an acceptable part of the school curriculum. However, this teaching in public schools should be academic in nature and part of an academic course. Students may, on their own, pray and distribute religious literature on school property. However, neither activity may be disruptive or infringe on the rights of others—students or staff. The school may also determine how literature may be distributed in a reasonable manner (Thomas 1999).

Some suggested guidelines for public school administrators in the area of religious activity are:

1. The school's harassment policy should include protection from religious harassment.
2. Teachers and administrators should not support, either through their own participation or through classroom announcements, forms of student religious activities such as meetings at the flagpole or group prayer sessions.
3. Free speech permits the government to control time, place, and manner of expression, and school officials may want to designate certain locations in a building for forms of student expression such as distribution of literature.
4. School officials should include religion in their diversity statement to ensure that all religions and religious beliefs will be given equal protection and recognition. (Mawdsley 1998, 16)

In 1992, the issue of prayer at cocurricular school activities reached the Supreme Court. "In *Lee vs. Weisman*, a student challenged a state law that allowed principals to invite clergy to offer the invocation and benediction prayers at middle and high school graduation ceremonies. . . . The Supreme Court held that the government involvement was sufficient to rise to the level of creating a 'state-sponsored and state-directed religious exercise in a public school'" (*Lee vs. Weisman*, 505 U.S. 577, 112 S.Ct. 2649, 2655 [1992] in Okun 1996, 29). At least five federal courts since *Lee vs. Weisman* have rendered decisions on the issue of prayer at cocurricular activities with no clear findings.

Other than the U.S. Constitution, there is no federal statutory law that directly governs the issue of prayer in schools. This past summer, [1995] however, President Clinton issued a directive ordering a statement be distributed to every school district in the country explaining that "the law gives students the right to pray privately or to express religious views in homework assignments." . . . In addition, the statement reiterated that "school officials may not mandate or organize prayer at graduation." The statement was advisory only, without the force of law, and was intended to be a "neutral recital of current law" rather than advocating new policies. (*Washington Post* 1995, quoted in Okun 1996, 32)

Central to the issue of student-led prayer in public schools are the establishment clause and the free exercise clause of the First Amendment. The establishment clause prohibits schools from supporting religion, and the free exercise clause permits students to exercise their religious freedoms (Essex 2001).

The Supreme Court has developed three tests to determine whether conduct conforms with the First Amendment's prohibition of an establishment of religion: *Lemon vs. Kurtzman* (1971) tripartite test (government conduct must have a secular purpose, must neither inhibit nor advance religion, and cannot foster an excessive entanglement); endorsement (see *Wallace vs. Jaffree* 1985); and psychological coercion (*Lee vs. Weisman* 1992). (Mawdsley 2001, 23)

Graduation prayers led by clergy remain unconstitutional. The Supreme Court ruled in 1992 that they are an "establishment of religion." However, student-led prayers are another matter when they are student initiated (Walsh 2001d). "Although the Supreme Court has not addressed the issue, a consensus seems to be emerging in the lower courts that a school does not violate the establishment clause if a student speaker, on his own initiative, begins to pray or express a religious viewpoint. The real difficulty arises when the student asks for audience participation" (Thomas 1999, 16).

The following are some recommended best practices for public school educators:

1. No school personnel should indicate actively or passively a time for prayer or "private meditation."
2. Music teachers should be careful in their selection of music. However, certain religious music is traditional and proper for its academic value. The same is true for art teachers.
3. No public school should display religious articles, photographs, paintings, or other forms of art unless there is a clear, academic reason for such display.
4. No teacher should award extra points to students for attending outside religious functions.

Conversely, the following guidelines accommodating religious practices are offered:

1. Students who wish to bow their heads, fold their hands, or otherwise pray silently, and who are not being disruptive, should not be admonished.
2. Students who wish to distribute religious material during noninstructional time, and who are not being disruptive, should be allowed to do so.
3. Students who wish to leave the public school during the day to attend religious instruction elsewhere may be allowed to do so with parental permission and the principal's consent.
4. Students may not be penalized for observing their respective religious holidays. (Murray and Evans 2000, 81–82)

Regulations regarding students with disabilities represent different legal issues. In 1975, President Ford signed into law the Individuals with Disabilities Education Act (IDEA), which required school districts to educate students with disabilities in the least restrictive environment. Under IDEA, school districts are required to ensure:

1. That, to the maximum extent appropriate, children with disabilities are educated with children who are nondisabled; and

2. That special classes, separate schooling, or other removal of children with disabilities from the regular educational environment occurs only when the nature or severity of the disability is such that education in regular classes with the use of supplementary aids and services cannot be achieved satisfactorily (IDEA Regulations, 34 C.F.R. § 300.550[b]). (Yell 1998, 70)

The Individuals with Disabilities Education Act was not reviewed until twenty-two years later when President Clinton signed into law Amendments of 1997 (Morrissey 1998). The Individuals with Disabilities Education Act, the Federal Rehabilitation Act (Section 504), and the Americans with Disabilities Act (ADA) are laws that protect the educational rights of students with disabilities and uphold students' rights to participate in school athletics (Goedert 1995). IDEA regulations require that schools "shall take steps to provide nonacademic and extracurricular services and activities in such a manner as is necessary to afford children with disabilities an equal opportunity for participation in those services and activities" (34 C.F.R. §300.308 [1993], quoted in Goedert 1995, 405).

Under equal opportunity to participate in athletics, a school system must offer the services it provides during a normal school day, to allow all students access to extracurricular activities. The Individuals with Disabilities Education Act prohibits schools from denying students access to sports participation due to disabilities. But unless stipulated in the students' IEP, the school has no obligation to waive or adjust eligibility rules to permit such participation. These eligibility rules "may include maximum age limits or restrictions on the number of semesters of participation, minimum grade averages, school attendance and residence and enrollment requirements, transfer rules, and amateur status assurances" (Goedert 1995, 411). Reasonable accommodation cases heard by the Supreme Court do not require an agency because of Section 504 "to lower or effect substantial modifications of standards to accommodate a handicapped person" or to impose "undue . . . administrative burden [or] fundamental alteration in the nature of [a] program" (Pottgen, 40 F.3d at 929, citing Davis, 442 U.S. at 413, and Arline, 480 U.S. at 287 n.17, quoted in Goedert 1995, 415). But if a student meets objective criteria but is not allowed to participate due to a disability, then accommodations must be considered. Even if a student with disabilities cannot meet the eligibility standards or lacks the skill for interscholastic play, there may be other opportunities for participation. Some schools have intramural programs for students who do not meet the requirements for higher-level team competition (Goedert 1995).

The following are general recommendations to follow for school administrators:

1. Work cooperatively with athletic associations to advocate and develop sound waiver policies.
2. Develop district policies and procedures to facilitate individualized decision making for the exceptions.
3. Streamline but maintain the considered, individualized aspects of the decision-making process for lower-stakes decisions.
4. Keep the channels of communication and dispute resolution open with the parents.
5. Include provisions for participation in extracurricular activities in IEPs or Section 504 plans only when necessary.
6. Develop alternative ways for students to participate meaningfully in extracurricular or other activities. (Sullivan, Lantz, and Zirkel 2000, 266)

There are four areas of possible legal concern when students take field trips: instruction, supervision, transportation, and emergencies. Field trips are probably the most risky of all school-related activities. A number of potential problems arise when students are taken away from the school and its supervision and routines (Kelly 1998). The field trip release forms need to be "instructive," providing comprehensive information and details to parents and guardians. The form should provide a statement for "liability release" that is signed by an adult in parental relation to the child. This permission allows the child to attend the field trip and releases chaperones and the school district from liability claims against individuals. Students on a field trip are supervised by the adult chaperones and by the person in charge, who directs and oversees the chaperones. Chaperones are expected to provide the same high level of supervision as students would receive if they were in school. Transportation is another area of legal concern, especially when students provide their own transportation using private vehicles. The issue is whether the student drivers will be considered agents of the school should a mishap occur. The last area of concern is emergencies and how to prepare to handle misbehaving students (Mawdsley 1999).

> The right—and obligation—to control the behavior of students in school has been established under the common-law doctrine called *in loco parentis*. The Latin phrase means "in place of the parent." A Nebraska court defined the doctrine, stating that "general education and control of pupils who attend public schools are in the hands of principals and teachers. This control extends to health, proper surroundings, necessary discipline, promotion of morality, and other wholesome influences, while parental authority is temporarily suspended." (*Richardson vs. Brahan*, 249 N.W. 557 [Neb. 1933], quoted in Kelly 1998, 63)

Suggestions for administrators are as follows:

1. Field trip forms should be sent out for parent signature three to four weeks prior to the trip. This amount of time gives teachers the opportunity to talk with parents whose children may have special needs.
2. Return of the signed form is a condition for student participation. Whether or not the form exculpates liability, a well-prepared form eliminates subsequent parent complaints about the purpose of the trip, and offers parents a vehicle for providing useful information to the teachers.
3. If private cars are to be used, parents should be notified to contact their insurance companies before agreeing to drive to ascertain their liability coverage.
4. The person responsible for emergency safety features for the trip should be designated. This person should have not only a list of all safety/medical equipment but also a list of emergency phone numbers and a map indicating the nearest medical facilities. (Mawdsley 1999, 31)

The Supreme Court has upheld testing of student athletes for drug use and the Louisiana High School Athletics Association has put in place a statewide requirement for testing (Basler 2000). However, according to the National Federation of State High School Associations, only about a thousand of the nation's 25,000 public high schools test their student athletes for drugs. Some schools that previously had tested have stopped testing for a variety of reasons, including costs (Basler 2000). The testing of nonathletes has met with mixed results in the courts. A federal appeals court did not uphold an Oklahoma school district's testing policy that provided testing of all students engaged in cocurricular activities. Testing was found to be a violation of the Fourth Amendment's prohibition against unreasonable searches (Walsh 2001a). "Districts seeking to impose random drug testing as a condition of joining in a school activity 'must demonstrate that there is some identifiable drug abuse problem among a sufficient number of those subject to the testing,' U.S. Circuit Judge Stephen H. Anderson said in the majority opinion" (Walsh 2001a, 7). However, the legal landscape on this issue remains unclear.

> Last year [1999], the Colorado Supreme Court struck down the drug testing program of a Colorado school district, which was challenged by a member of the marching band. But a federal appeals court upheld a drug-testing program in Cave City, Arkansas, for students who wish to participate in extracurricular activities. Also last year, the U.S. Supreme Court refused to hear a challenge to an Indiana high school's policy of testing students engaged in extracurricular activities. The court had upheld drug testing for athletes in 1995, in part because sports involved potentially dangerous activities. (Basler 2000)

Any school district or postsecondary institution of higher education that receives federal funding must comply with Title IX laws, which prohibit gender discrimination. A complaint of a Title IX violation can be made directly to the school, the Department of Education's Office for Civil Rights (OCR), or by filing a lawsuit in federal court (Tungate and Orie 1998). The penalties for violations may include the loss of federal dollars, a required program to correct violations ordered by the court, and having to pay both compensatory and punitive damages. Athletic programs are frequently the targets of OCR complaints by individuals (Tungate and Orie 1998).

> With respect to school athletes, the U.S. Department of Education in 1979 issued "Intercollegiate Athletics Policy Interpretation" and a further clarification in 1996, the general principles of which also apply to elementary and secondary interscholastic athletic programs. The Policy Interpretation and subsequent clarification provide a three-part test to assess whether an institution is violating Title IX in the area of interscholastic sports. A school district need only pass one part to be in compliance.

> The three parts are:

> 1. Whether interscholastic level participation opportunities for male and female students are provided in numbers substantially proportionate to their respective enrollments.
> 2. Where the members of one sex have been and are underrepresented among interscholastic athletes, whether the institution can show a history and continuing practice of program expansion that is demonstrably responsive to the developing interests and abilities of the members of that sex.
> 3. Where the members of one sex are underrepresented among interscholastic athletes, and the institution cannot show a history and continuing practice of program expansion as described above, whether the district can demonstrate that the interest and abilities of the members of that sex have been fully and effectively accommodated by the present program (44 CFR § 71413 *et seq.*; "Clarification of Intercollegiate Athletics Policy Guidance: The Three-Part Test" [1996]). (New York State School Boards Association, 2000, 442)

In response to the threat of lawsuits, many school districts, in conjunction with their insurance carriers, have developed risk management programs. These programs attempt to balance the costs of a program against the potential liability. "The biggest concern, I think, is to make sure that the district is proactive, to keep the element of play safe," says Tom Rende, assistant superintendent of the Lenape, N.J., Regional High School District (Mac 1998, 42). One area in which there has been an increase in lawsuits involves student-teacher or student-coach sexual relationships. However, the cause of the increased number of cases may be, in part, due to better reporting (Mac 1998). However, an *Education Week* national study in 1998 revealed 244 cases of inappropriate behavior in a six-month period of time. The behavior reported ranged from "unwanted touching to years-long sexual relationships and serial rape" (Shoop 1999, 10). Seventy percent of the cases involved teachers, but other school personnel (such as principals, librarians, janitors, and bus drivers) were also implicated. Eighty percent of the accused were men and students were found to have made up claims in only two of the 244 cases (Shoop 1999).

The following is a list of six steps for school personnel to follow. These guidelines will help reduce the chance of inappropriate behavior by school personnel:

1. Acknowledge that teacher-to-student sexual abuse is a serious problem.
2. Ensure there is a board-approved policy that specifically describes inappropriate behaviors and makes it clear that sexual harassment and sexual abuse will not be tolerated.
3. Pay attention.
4. Don't make judgment errors because of bias.
5. Conduct appropriate training for all staff members and students.
6. Ask the right questions in the preemployment process. (Shoop 1999, 11–12)

The number of homeschooled students in the United States has increased to an estimated one million and continues to grow (Gewertz 2001a). In New York State, homeschooled students are ineligible for participation in interscholastic sports. Section 135.4(c)(7) of the Regulations of the Commissioner of Education addresses this issue. However, a school district may allow participation of homeschooled students in cocurricular activities and intramural athletics, should they exist (New York State Education Department 2001). However, regulations regarding participation by home-instructed students in cocurricular activities and athletics vary widely by state and by type of school; charter school students may be able to participate in activities of the district's schools. May a school district suspend or exclude a student from participation in cocurricular activities? In New York State, school boards have the right to institute reasonable academic standards as eligibility prerequisites for cocurricular activities. "In addition, a school district does not discriminate against a student athlete, if the discipline imposed on the athlete is more severe than the penalty imposed on nonathletes involved in the same disciplinary incident" (New York State School Boards 2000, 386). An athlete can be suspended from school and from a team for a number of games in excess of his school suspension. The courts have found that participation in noninstructional activities is not a constitutional right. However, suspensions from cocurricular activities may only be imposed according to fair procedures that provide students and parents the opportunity to appear informally before the authorizing body that imposed the penalty in order to discuss the conduct being reviewed (Hogan and Sarzynski 1998).

The standard of just cause is suitable for determining if a procedure is "basically fair." The following questions will serve as a guide:

1. Did the school district, through the teacher or administrator, give the student forewarning or foreknowledge of the possible or probable disciplinary consequences of the student's conduct? If

not, was the conduct such that it would be reasonable to assume the student knew his actions were wrong?

2. Did the district, before administering discipline, make an effort to discover whether or not the student had, in fact, violated or disobeyed a rule or order or participated in the inappropriate conduct?
3. Was the district's investigation conducted fairly and objectively?
4. Has the district applied its rules, orders, and penalties evenhandedly and without discrimination?
5. Were the student and parent given an opportunity to informally appear before the person or body authorized to impose discipline in order to discuss the conduct being reviewed?
6. Is the degree of discipline to be administered by the district reasonably related to the seriousness of the offense and the record of the student?

If the answer to every one of these questions is in the affirmative, then it would be safe to say that the action was with just cause and that the procedure is basically fair (Hogan and Sarzynski 1998, 32–33).

Provided that the rules of participation do not discriminate against students or treat them differentially, a school board has wide latitude regarding the rules and regulations for cocurricular activities (Yurek 1996). Courts generally uphold a school's right to limit participation in cocurricular activities for infractions of school rules. If an activity is not required and carries no credits, the courts have found that students are not entitled to participate (Yurek 1996). In addition, regardless of what the legal system does, school officials can punish a student or conduct their own investigations independent of the legal system. In relation to student activities, there is no "double jeopardy" because the concept only applies in a criminal setting (Strope 1998). Some recommendations for administrators to follow:

- Spend less time writing rules.
- Have rules that are known and understood by all constituencies.
- Avoid letting legal foundations intrude on sensible administrative practices.
- Look (and be) fair. (Strope 1998, 41)

The principal and staff of the school must establish and maintain a standard of reasonable care to keep children safe. Key to reasonable care is proper supervision. Litigation against a principal for lack of supervision or leadership negligence falls under the description of torts, which are "wrongful acts, not including a breach of contract or trust, which result in injury to another's person, property, reputation, or the like, and for which the injured party is entitled to compensation" (*Black's Law* 1996, quoted in Permuth and Permuth 2000, 35). Over the past ten years, the more than one thousand legal cases concerning student activities have centered on two areas: a student's right to participate and an administrators' role to lead and supervise (Permuth and Permuth 2000). The principal is responsible for the following three issues related to cocurricular activity:

1. The principal is responsible for the development of appropriate rules of conduct for the successful operation of a school.
2. The principal is responsible for the promulgation of appropriate rules of conduct for the operation of the school.
3. The principal is responsible for the enforcement of appropriate rules of conduct for the successful operation of the school. (Permuth and Permuth 2000, 35–36)

By the year 2005, it is estimated that the number of U.S. children and teenagers going online will increase to more than 13 million from just under 9 million in 1999 (Aidman 2000). Many of these 13 million teenagers will use their knowledge and creative talents to develop a website. Unfortunately, some of these sites will post negative remarks about school personnel, policies, or events. However, unless the posted material causes substantial disruption at the school, the students' actions are beyond the reach of the school. "Student websites that are not developed or hosted by the school are generally beyond the school's control" (Bell 2001, 4).

Attendance is another area of frequent legal concern. If a student misses class for several days due to participation in a school activity, that student is still missing class. Currently in New York State, a board of education cannot distinguish between legal and illegal absences (Hogan and Sarzynski 1998). The only exception appears to be illness. However, students should be given the opportunity to make up the work they missed. Of course, some students will make up the work and some won't.

In June 2000, the Supreme Court ruled that the Boy Scouts of America could exclude homosexuals. The court ruled that private groups may discriminate in their acceptance of members on the basis of sexual orientation. The ruling stated that a private organization has the First Amendment right of expressive association, which allows exclusion of those with conflicting viewpoints to its own (Walsh 2000b). The ruling did not address the related issue of excluding homosexuals. As a result, many school districts must make decisions about whether or not to allow the Boy Scouts to use their facilities. School districts will respond with varied facilities-use policies. Some school districts will continue to allow the Boy Scouts to use their facilities but will restrict other activities such as recruitment. Other districts will revoke their status as a school-sponsored or chartered organization (Randall 2000). The major dilemma surrounding this issue is whether it is possible to teach children tolerance and respect for differences while continuing to support an organization that promotes discrimination and intolerance towards homosexuals (Brodsky 2000). Schools must be attentive to antidiscrimination policies concerning the use of school facilities. Schools must consider whether the intended use is "nonexclusive" and "open to the general public" when groups such as the Boy Scouts refuse to allow certain members of the community (i.e., homosexuals) to participate in the group (Worona 2000, 17). Since the Boy Scouts are led by adults not associated with the school, the group is not subject to the Equal Access Act—a federal law that prohibits schools from selectively denying noncurricular clubs. The law requires schools that receive federal aid to treat noncurricular student groups equally (Walsh 2000a). A student-led, noncurricular group such as a chess club would come under the protection of the law. The law regarding the use of school by outside groups is very different from the law regarding student-led groups that wish to use the schools in the time periods before school hours, after school hours, at lunchtime, or during activity periods (Worona 2000).

A recommendation for administrators to follow: Consult your school attorney when in doubt regarding any of the above issues or any other legal issues.

In closing:

The first laws making school attendance compulsory appeared in 1642 and 1647 in New England. They came to be known as the Old Deluder Laws because of their function. Satan was the Old Deluder, and because the devil finds work for idle hands to do, it seemed wise to teach young people to read and write, primarily to keep the devil away. (Hodgkinson 1996, 19)

Twenty percent of U.S. kids are below the poverty line today—exactly the same percentage as 15 years ago—even though most of the nation is less segregated and wealthier. (Hodgkinson 2000–2001, 9)

APPENDIX A

EVALUATION PROCEDURES FOR STUDENT ACTIVITIES

1. **Program Name**. Enter the name of the program.
2. **General Purpose**. Rate the stated purpose for each program listed.
   1 = Congruent with district/school philosophy.
   2 = Moderately congruent with district/school philosophy.
   3 = Lacks general congruency with district/school philosophy.
3. **Number of Participants.** Rate the number of students participating for each program listed.
   1 = High levels of participation in all grades.
   2 = Moderate participation across and within grade levels (some grades not represented and/or limited participation in specific grades for which the activities are intended).
   3 = Minimal participation across, as well as within, grade levels.
4. **Costs per Participant.** On a separate worksheet, list the total per-pupil costs for each program. List them in ascending order beginning with the lowest. Next, divide the list into three ranges of cost that represent the most homogeneous category for each range.
   1 = Lowest range
   2 = Moderate range
   3 = Highest range
5. **Revenue per Pupil.** On a separate worksheet, list the total revenues per pupil for each program. List these figures in descending order beginning with the highest. Next, divide the list into three ranges of revenue that represent the most homogeneous category for each range.
   1 = Highest range
   2 = Moderate range
   3 = Lowest range
6. **Total.** Enter the total rating for each program listed. The total is determined by adding the individual ratings to each category.
   TOTAL = [(2) + (3) + (4) + (5)]
7. **Average.** Enter the average rating for each program listed. The average rating is determined by dividing the total by the number of categories added.

$$\text{AVERAGE} = \frac{Total}{4}$$

Each school district should determine procedures for judging the results of assessments, such as the one shown in table A.1. For example, using the four categories listed here (general purpose, number of participants, cost per pupil, and revenue per pupil, the average ratings can be interpreted as follows:

1 = Programs that closely agree with school district philosophy, allow for high student participation across grade levels, are low in per-pupil costs, and are high in revenue per pupil.

2 = Programs that moderately agree with the above criteria.

3 = Programs that have little in common with the above criteria. Programs that are high in per-pupil revenue should not be automatic targets for reduction or elimination, but the maintenance of such programs should be based upon full awareness of the cost/revenue ratio involved. (Christensen 1984, 3)

Table A.1   Student Activities Program Assessment (Composite Rating)

(1) PROGRAM	RATINGS				COMPOSITE RATING	
	(2) Purpose	(3) Participation	(4) Costs	(5) Revenue	(6) Total	(7) Average

Source: Christensen 1984, 3.

APPENDIX B

RULES GOVERNING PARTICIPATION IN COCURRICULAR ACTIVITIES FOR STUDENTS—WINDSOR CENTRAL SCHOOL DISTRICT (NEW YORK)

I. The policies governing participation in the Windsor Central High School Cocurricular Program are established as a code, which each participant must honor for the privilege of participating in any cocurricular activity.

II. A participant's first priority must be towards academic schoolwork. Any student involved in the cocurricular program who needs extra academic help will be excused from all meetings, rehearsals and/or activities after school for that help with a faculty member. The student should let his or her advisor know ahead of time and return to the scheduled activity with a pass from the faculty member who was supporting the student. No student participant will be disciplined for missing or arriving late to a practice when the reason for such absence or lateness concerns the student's pursuit of improvement of academic performance by meeting with a teacher. In addition, no sanction will be imposed on any participant by any advisor related to the participant's absence from an activity due to class enrichment field trips or another academic exercise sponsored or approved by the Windsor Central School District.

III. Expectations
    A. Participants in cocurricular activities are required to attend all meetings and/or rehearsals or activities as scheduled.
    B. Violation of the school's discipline code as regards the use or possession of tobacco will result in a three-week suspension from participation in an activity in which the student participates. If a student is involved in a limited activity, one that only meets for a set number of weeks

rather than all year (i.e., musical), a violation of this rule will result in a three-day suspension from that activity.

C. The use or possession of alcohol is prohibited. Students found guilty of using alcohol shall be suspended from involvement in the cocurricular program for five weeks for the first offense and will be removed from all participation in cocurricular activities for the remainder of the school year for a subsequent offense. If a student is involved in a limited activity, one that only meets for a set number of weeks rather than all year (i.e., musical), a violation of this rule will result in a one-week suspension from that activity. A student will be removed from participation in cocurricular activities for the remainder of the school year for a subsequent offense. The student will also be referred to the Student Assistance Counselor Program before returning to participate in the cocurricular program.

D. The use, possession, and sale or gift of any drug or controlled substance is prohibited by the Student Discipline Code of the Windsor Central School District. All students participating in cocurricular activities must abide by the entire Student Discipline Code. In addition, no student participating in cocurricular activities may use, possess, sell, or give any drug or controlled substance, at any time unless such drug or controlled substance is prescribed to the student by a duly licensed physician in the State of New York or is a recognized, commercially available, over-the-counter medication taken off school premises for a purpose intended by the manufacturer of such medication. Students found in violation of this rule will be immediately suspended from involvement in the cocurricular program for the remainder of the year. The student will also be referred to the Student Assistance Counselor Program.

E. The giving or selling of drugs is prohibited. The giving or selling of alcohol to another student is prohibited. Students found guilty of either of the above infractions will result in the immediate suspension from involvement in the cocurricular program for the remainder of the year. The student will also be referred to the Student Assistance Counselor Program.

F. School attendance: Participants in any scheduled cocurricular event such as meetings, rehearsals, or scheduled activities must be in school for at least the morning session or afternoon session of the school day. The end of the morning session and the beginning of the afternoon sessions is 11:30 a.m. Attendance in school at either session on Friday is necessary for a Saturday event. Extenuating circumstances will be given consideration for relief.

G. Good citizenship is an expectation and important concept for students to follow if involved in the cocurricular program. Students involved in the cocurricular program are expected to represent their activity and the school with pride and positive citizenship qualities. (For example, no insubordination, stealing, destroying school property, rudeness, etc.)

H. Any student who asks for help with any of the above concerns without being caught in violation, will be referred to the Student Assistance Counselor Program without consequence.

I. Additional rules and consequences, other than those cited above, may be established by the advisors. Participating students are also advised that the Discipline Code of Windsor Central High School applies to all students participating in the cocurricular program.

The policy concerning participation in the cocurricular program must be reviewed by the participant and the parent of the participant. They will each be required to sign the policy statement prior to participation in a cocurricular activity. A copy will be returned to the participant and parent. Signatures indicate that the parent and participant have read and understand the rules under which a student may participate in the cocurricular program and agree to participate in accordance with the rules.

Parent signature: _____ Date: _____

Student signature: _____ Date: _____

If applicable, _____ is a limited activity.

(Brunswick 2000, n.p.)

APPENDIX C

ATHLETIC AND COMPETITIVE ACTIVITY POLICIES AND PROCEDURES FOR DISTRICT 211 (ILLINOIS)

One purpose of the athletic and competitive activity program is to provide students with wholesome competition on an interscholastic level. A necessary corollary to this purpose is the development in students of a sense of dedication and the establishment of high standards of conduct and attitude. Because participants represent their school, they are expected to represent high standards of morality and conduct. Student conduct is expected to be exemplary the year around.

In order to participate in the athletic and competitive activity programs, the student and his/her parents shall be required to attend a mandatory preseason meeting at which parents and the student will be informed about training and participation rules and the function of the Athletic/Activity Board.

Misconduct among participants shall include offenses such as the possession or use of tobacco in any form, possession or use of alcohol or drugs, theft, dishonesty, and other misconduct. Students who are found to be involved in such misconduct will face disciplinary action according to procedures outlined in section B, Disciplinary Procedures. When alcohol or drugs in any form are present at student parties, it is recommended that students involved in athletics or activities leave the party immediately.

A participant who admits to a drug, alcohol, or tobacco related problem to a school staff member before a reported rule violation occurs will be referred to the principal. The principal will hold a conference with the student and his/her parents. After considering all information pertinent to the student's problem, the principal will decide the best course of action to help the student. The principal will confer with the Director of Student Activities at the district office before releasing the decision.

A. THE ATHLETIC/ACTIVITY BOARD

The Athletic/Activity Board is the disciplinary arm of the athletic and competitive activity program. It is composed of the following individuals:

> Athletic/activity director—Chair
> Selected members of the coaching/activity staff
> District 211 central administration representative

The Student Assistance Program Coordinator will receive notification of all Board meetings. When there is a need for the Athletic/Activity Board to meet because of a rule infraction by a student in a competitive activity, the director of student activities will serve on the Board in lieu of the division head for athletics.

The Board shall meet after a request has been presented to the athletic/activity director by the activity sponsor or coach to consider a disciplinary case involving an athlete or individual in a competitive activity (Cheerleaders, Chess Club, Debate Team, Flag Squad, Math Team, Model United Nations, Pom Pom Squad, Scholastic Bowl Team, Science Bowl Team, Science Olympiad, Special Olympics, Speech Team, Student Congress, Water Polo, and Worldwide Youth in Science and Engineering Club). The Athletic/Activity Board shall weigh the evidence that is presented and, after considering the best interests of the student and the school, make a decision on the disposition of the student's case.

DISCIPLINARY PROCEDURES

After a participant has been given an opportunity for due process and there is reason to conclude that the student has violated Athletic/Activity Policies based upon available information, he/she will be suspended from practices and/or competition pending a disciplinary review and decision by the Athletic/Activity Board. The parent will be notified in writing of the rule violation and will be requested to attend a Board meeting related to their student. The Board will meet at the earliest opportunity but no later than ten school days from the date of written notification of the Board meeting to consider the status of the student and render a decision. Generally, the following process will be observed for both in/out-of-season violations.

1. The Athletic/Activity Board verifies that the participant has been made aware of rules of the sport or activity.
2. Upon notice to the administration, either verbal or written, of an alleged violation of the rules, the student will be informed by the athletic/activity director of the nature of the offense and suspended from practice and/or competition. The athletic/activity director will notify the student to appear at a meeting of the Board. Parents will be notified of the rule violation and requested to appear at the meeting. If the violation occurs out of season, the participant will be informed by the administration and the same procedures will be followed.
3. The Athletic/Activity Board will meet to review the situation. The Board may invoke one or more of the following:

    a. Dismiss the charges.

    b. Place the student on probation for a specific length of time.

    c. Invoke a suspension.

        1. A minimum penalty for first violation of possession/use of alcohol, tobacco in any form, or drugs will be 25% of the scheduled contests. (Tournaments, multiples, invitations, and doubleheaders count as one contest at the participant's level of competition).

        2. When a suspension is invoked for a drug, alcohol, or tobacco violation, the student must attend and successfully complete an educational program recommended by the Athletic/Activity Board. The cost of educational programs will be the responsibility of the student's parent.

        3. The penalty for theft and dishonesty will be established by the Board after review of the severity of the infraction.

        4. When a suspension is invoked, the Athletic/Activity Board will determine the season in which the penalty will begin.

    d. Drop the student from the sport or activity for the remainder of the season.

    e. Drop the student from participation in athletics or activities for the remainder of his/her time in high school.

  4. The decision of the Board will be communicated in writing to the parent of the student.

C. GENERAL RULES

Suspected violation and/or rumors are to be directed to the student's immediate coach or sponsor. It is hoped that the coach or sponsor can serve in a counseling role and directly inform the participant of the allegations and the importance of correcting an improper image. The District Director of Student Activities should be consulted if any doubt exists regarding the convening of an Athletic/Activity Board.

Cocurricular Activities Code of Conduct

Participation in cocurricular activities is a privilege extended to all students in District 211. It is an opportunity for students to develop character, leadership skills, self-discipline, teamwork, and cooperation.

With this opportunity comes the responsibility that students exhibit behavior that does not infringe upon the privileges of others or reflect poorly upon themselves or the school.

With this in mind, I understand that I am expected to adhere to the following code of behavior as a participant in the school activities program:

- I will display respect, consideration and courtesy for students and staff and their property.
- I understand that any behavior expected of me during the regular school day must also be exhibited at all school activities and meetings.
- I will refrain from the use, sale, possession of drugs, alcohol, tobacco, or other illegal substances.

- I understand that I will be held accountable for the rules of the activity I am joining as communicated by the sponsor before the activity begins.

Where violations to the above code of conduct occur, regular school penalties apply.

I have read the above activity code of conduct and agree to abide by it while participating in the school activities program.

_____   _____   _____
           Student Signature   I.D. #   Date

As parent (guardian) of _____, I have read the above code of
                                    Student Name

conduct. I understand that while my student is a participant in the student activity program of High School District 211, he/she must abide by the activity code of conduct.

_____   _____
Parent Signature

                                                   Date

Approved by the Board of Education: 1/17/91

APPENDIX D

EXTRACURRICULAR AND COCURRICULAR ACTIVITIES— CENTERBURG SCHOOL (ILLINOIS)

Centerburg School offers a variety of cocurricular and extracurricular activities for students. Participation in such activities provides students with experience in building social relationships, developing interests in an academic area, and gaining an understanding of the responsibilities of good citizenship.

Members of school clubs and teams are public representatives of the school district. Centerburg students who participate in extracurricular activities are expected to conform to standards that meet or exceed those in the school district code of conduct.

I. *Academic Standards*
   1. In order to remain eligible for participation in the above-named activity, district students must maintain a _____% grade point average (GPA). If the student's GPA drops below this percentile, he/she will be placed upon probation for two weeks; during this time, the student's GPA must improve to the acceptable level, or he/she will not be allowed to participate in the activity for the remainder of the season/school year (whichever is appropriate).

II. *Behavior Standards/Code of Conduct*
   1. A student agrees to abide by the district-wide Student Code of Conduct and understands that a violation of the code may result in suspension from the above-named activity in addition to any penalty given by the district.
   2. The student agrees to refrain from the use, possession or sale of alcohol, drugs and/or tobacco products, *on or off campus*, during the time that he/she participates in the above-named activity.
   3. The student agrees to abide by any further conditions imposed by the activity advisor/coach during the time that he/she participates in the above-named activity.

III. *Participation/Training Standards*

Certain activities require a minimum level of participation/training, as established by the activity advisor/ coach. The student agrees to these conditions (*provided by activity advisor/coach*) and realizes that failure to maintain this minimum level of participation may result in suspension from the activity.

A student will be ineligible to participate in an extracurricular and/or interscholastic activity when one of the following occur:

1. The student is deficient in meeting academic requirements.
2. The student is found truant.
3. The student is given the equivalent of a full day of in-school suspension.
4. The student is suspended from school.
5. The student's behavior does not meet the standards set by the school.

No student can participate in any cocurricular activity or interscholastic activity on a day when he or she is absent from school.

Each year, the school will send home guidelines for student participation in extracurricular activities. These guidelines must be read and signed by all student participants and their parents. For questions regarding extracurricular activities, please contact the district athletic director at 555-2222.

(from *A Comprehensive Guide to Developing Student Handbooks for New York State Schools 2001–2002*, 39–40)

REFERENCES

34 Code of Federal Regulations, section 300.308 (1993).

Abrams, I. 1999. Hightower Trail Middle School celebrates every month! *Schools in the Middle* (March): 9–13.

Adair, J. 2000. Tackling teens' no. 1 problem. *Educational Leadership* (March): 44–47.

Adkins, G. 1989. Megatrends author foresees the millennium. *Educational Leadership* (September): 16–17.

Adler, J. 1995. Activities teach leadership skills for life. *Leadership for Student Activities* (December): 40–41.

After School Corporation. n.d. *3:00 p.m.: Time for after school*. New York: After School Corporation.

Aidman, A. 2000. Children's online privacy. *Educational Leadership* (October): 46–47.

Aimone, L. 2000. Building school spirit. *Leadership for Student Activities* (September): 12–13.

Alderman, M. K. 1990. Motivation for at-risk students. *Educational Leadership* (September): 27–30.

Allison, B. 1979. Student activities as the ultimate academic department. *NASSP Bulletin* 63, no. 426:95–98.

American Association of School Administrators. 1999. *Preparing schools and school systems for the twenty-first century*. Arlington, Va.: American Association of School Administrators.

American Youth Policy Forum. 1999. *More things that do make a difference for youth*. Washington, D.C.: American Youth Policy Forum.

Andrus, E. 1996. Service learning: Taking students beyond community service. *Middle School Journal* 28, no. 2 (November): 10–18.

Anticoli, D. J. 1996. Performance based assessment: Re-instituting fairness in our student evaluation system. *High School Magazine* (March–April): 46–49.

Aubrey, L. 1996. Developing student leaders in theater. *Leadership for Student Activities* (December): 19–20.

Baker, K., J. Jacoby, and P. Gugliuzza. 2000. The fourth R. *Principal Leadership* (October): 42–43.

Baker, V. L. 1993. Taking the lead in student activities. *The High School Magazine* (December): 20–23.

Baltrinic, B. 1998. Character counts! *Leadership for Student Activities* (October): 27–29.

Bandura, A. 1986. *Social foundations of thought and action*. Englewood Cliffs, N.J.: Prentice Hall.

Basler, G. 2000. SV joins national debate on drug tests for student athletes. *Press and Sun Bulletin* (January 30): 1A.

Bell, A. 2001. *The First Amendment: Do you practice what you teach? A legal memorandum*. Reston, Va.: National Association of Secondary School Principals.

Bennett, B. 2001. Teaching the 4th and 5th Rs: Respect and responsibility. *On Board* (April 9): 17.

Berger, J. 2000. Does top down, standards-based reform work? A review of the status of statewide standards-based reform. *NASSP Bulletin* 84 no. 612 (January): 57–65.

Berkey, T. B. 1996. Making big schools smaller. *The High School Magazine* (June–July): 22–26.

Berkow, I. 2001. A champion who continues to not give up. *New York Times*. February 17, D9.

Berman, S. 2000. Service as systemic reform. *The School Administrator* (August): 20–24.

Berman, S. H. 1999. The reality of virtual learning. *The School Administrator* (April): 12–16.

Berreth, D., and S. Berman. 1997. The moral dimensions of schools. *Educational Leadership* (May): 24–27.

Biederman, M. 2001. Not just a permission slip, but a passport as well. *New York Times*. April 11, B3.

Biemiller, A., and D. Meichenbaum. 1992. The nature and nurture of the self-directed learner. *Educational Leadership* (October): 75–80.

Biernat, N., and E. Klesse. 1989. *The third curriculum: Student activities*. Reston, Va.: National Association of Secondary School Principals.

Billig, S. H. 2000a. Research on K–12 school-based service learning—The evidence builds. *Phi Delta Kappan* (May): 658–64.

———. 2000b. The effects of service leaning. *School Administrator* (August): 14–18.

Bishop, B. 1999. The Columbine challenge. *Leadership for Student Activities* (September): 39–42.

Black's Law Dictionary. 1996. 7th ed. St. Paul, Mo.: West.

Blank, M., and N. Sindelar. 1992. Mentoring as professional development: From theory to practice. *Clearing House* (September–October): 22–26.

Bloom, B. S., ed. 1956. *Taxonomy of educational objectives: The classification of educational goals: Handbook 1, cognitive domain*. New York: Longman.

Bloomstran, S. 2001a. Collaborating for successful activities. *Leadership for Student Activities* (May): 4–7.

———. 2001b. Learning to lead. *Leadership for Student Activities* (January): 4–8.

Bonstingl, J. J. 2001. Are the stakes too high? *Principal Leadership* (January): 8–14.

Bossert, P. J. 1997. Horseless classrooms and virtual learning: Reshaping our environments. *NASSP Bulletin* 81, no. 592 (November): 3–15.

Bowman, D. H. 2001. High school bands join the march to Bush inauguration. *Education Week* (January 27): 25.

Boyte, H. C., and N. Skelton. 1997. The legacy of public work: Educating for citizenship. *Educational Leadership* (February): 12–17.

Breaking ranks on teaching values. 1998. *Leadership for Student Activities* (October): 21.

Breaking ranks: Cocurriculars essential to changing an American institution. 1996. *High School Magazine* (September–October): 4–6.

Breeding, M. A. 1998. Get your hands dirty: Learning leadership skills by doing. *Leadership for Student Activities* (March): 28–29.

Brendtro, L., and N. Long. 1995. Breaking the cycle of conflict. *Educational Leadership* (February): 52–56.

Brodsky, B. 2000. A former Boy Scout leader speaks. *On Board* 1, no. 21 (December 11): 5.

Brogue, E. B., and P. B. Jacobson. 1940. *Student council handbook*. Reston, Va.: National Association of Secondary School Principals.

Brooks, L. 1994. Promoting peaceful resolution: Implementing a peer mediation program. *High School Magazine* (September): 27–28.

Brown, B. B. 1988. The vital agenda for research on extracurricular influences: A reply to Holland and Andre. *Review of Educational Research* (Spring): 107–111.

Brown, D. F., and J. Varady. 1997. Reexamining the writings of Dr. Seuss to promote character development. *Middle School Journal* 28, no. 4 (March): 28–32.

Brown, J. B. 1996. Can leadership be taught? Lessons that linger. *Leadership for Student Activities* (April): 17–19.

Brunswick, D. J. 1996. *Job descriptions: Windsor Central School District*. Windsor, N.Y.: Windsor Central Schools.

———. 2000. *Rules governing participation in co-curricular activities*. Windsor, N.Y.: Windsor Central Schools.

Building school spirit is building school esteem. 2000. *Leadership for Student Activities* (September): 14.

Burton, B. 1997. Spirit works . . . Turn it on! *Leadership for Student Activities* (September): 18–21.

REFERENCES

Bush, G. W. 2000. Gov. George W. Bush's plans for education in America. *Phi Delta Kappan* (October): 122.

Buss, D. C. 1998. The student activity program: Its place in the secondary school. In *Annual review of research for school leaders*, edited by P. S. Hlebowitsch and W. G. Wraga. New York: Macmillan.

Butterfield, F. 2001. Students, mindful of Columbine, break silence to report threats. *New York Times*. February 10, A1.

Cairn, R., and S. Cairn. 1999. Service learning makes the grade. *Educational Leadership* (March): 66–68.

Calabrese, R. 1989. Alienation: The secondary school at-risk. *NASSP Bulletin* 73, no. 514 (February): 72–76.

Canfield, J. 1990. Improving students' self-esteem. *Educational Leadership* (September): 48–50.

Caplan, J. G. 1998. *Critical issue: Constructing school partnerships with families and community groups*. North Central Regional Educational Laboratory, at www.ncrel.org/sdrs/areas/issues/envrnment/famncomm/ pa400.htm.

Caplan, J. G. 2000. Building strong family-school partnerships to support high student achievement. *Informed Educators Series*. Arlington, Va.: Educational Research Service, 1–8.

Carnegie Council on Adolescent Development. 1995. *Great transitions—Preparing adolescents for a new century*. New York: Carnegie Corporation.

Cary, J. M. 1992. Legal issues related to extracurricular activities. *Law School Bulletin* 23: 15–23.

Cates, P. 2000. Reinventing Lubbock High School. *High School Magazine* (May): 23–27.

Cawelti, G. 1989. Designing high schools for the future. *Educational Leadership* (September): 30–35.

Center for Human Resources. 1996. *An orientation to the school-to-career vision*. Waltham, Mass.: Brandeis University.

Chaika, G. 1999. Virtual high schools: The high schools of the future? *Education World* (March 1): 1–4.

Checkley, K. 1997. The first seven . . . and the eighth: A conversation with Howard Gardner. *Educational Leadership* (September): 8–13.

Childress, H. 1998. Seventeen reasons why football is better than high school. *Phi Delta Kappan* (April): 616–19.

Chmielewski, T. R. 2000. Student leadership: A checklist for success. *Leadership for Student Activities* (October): 19–23.

Christensen, D. D. 1978. *Planning and evaluating student activity programs*. Reston, Va.: National Association of Secondary School Principals.

———. 1984. *Managing Student Activities*. Reston, Va.: National Association of Secondary School Principals.

Christenson, S. L. n.d. *Home-school collaboration: Building effective parent-school partnerships*, at www.cyf-c.umn.edu/Learn/home.html.

Clinton says schools can't bar religion. 1995. *Washington Post*. 13 July, A1.

Cobb, C. D., and J. D. Mayer. 2000. Emotional intelligence: What the research says. *Educational Leadership* (November): 14–18.

Colburn, J. J. 2000. School spirit. *Leadership for Student Activities* (September): 4–7.

Colvin, R. 2000. Losing faith in self-esteem. *School Administrator* (February): 28–35.

Commission on National Community Service. 1993. *What you can do for your country*. Washington, D.C.: Commission on National Community Service.

The Concord Consortium. 1997. Fully synchronous netcourses. *Concord Consortium,* October, at www.concord.org (accessed April 11, 2001).

Conrath, J. 1986. Effective schools must focus on potential dropouts. *NASSP Bulletin* 70, no. 494 (February): 46–50.

Conyers, J. G. 1996. Building bridges between generations. *Educational Leadership* (April): 14–16.

Cooke, G. J. 1995. Choice not chance: Strengthening school transitions. *Schools in the Middle* (February): 8–12.

Cortes, C. E. 1999. The accelerating change of American diversity. *School Administrator* (May): 12–14.

Couch, C. 1996. Guidelines for conducting a community service project. *Leadership forStudent Activities* (January): 23.

REFERENCES

————. 1966. Joining forces adds impact. *Leadership for Student Activities* (January): 20–22.

Crockett, M. J. 1995. Creating successful schools for all early adolescent learners: No easy answers. *NASSP Bulletin* 79, no. 575 (December): 42–51.

Curry, T. 2000. Organizing a successful fundraiser. *Leadership for Student Activities* (November): 19–20.

Cuzzetto, C. E. 1999. *Student activity funds: Procedures and controls*. Reston, Va.: Association of School Business Officials International.

D'Onofrio, J. 1999. The breakfast club. *Leadership for Student Activities* (November): 22–25.

Daggett, W. R. 2001. *The 12 guiding principles of exceptional character*. Rexford, N.Y.: International Center for Leadership in Education.

Darling-Hammond, L., and E. M. Sclan. 1996. Who teaches and why: Dilemmas of building a profession for the twenty-first century. In *Handbook of research on teacher education*, 2nd ed., edited by J. Sikula, T. J. Buttery, and E. Guyton, 67–101. New York: Macmillan.

Davalos, D. B., E. L. Chavez, and R. J. Guardiola. 1999. The effects of extracurricular activity, ethnic identification and perception of school on student dropout rates. *Hispanic Journal of Behavioral Sciences* 21, no. 1 (February): 61–77.

de Kanter, A. 2001. After-school programs for adolescents. *NASSP Bulletin* 85, no. 626 (September): 12–21.

Delgado, M. 1999. Lifesaving 101: How a veteran teacher can help a beginner. *Educational Leadership* (May): 27–29.

Dempsey, C. W. 2001. *A letter from Cedric W. Dempsey, NCAA President, NCAA 2001*, at www.ncaa.org/eligibility/cbsa (accessed June 14, 2001).

DesMarais, J., Y. Yang, and F. Farzanehkia. 2000. Service-learning leadership development for youths. *Phi Delta Kappan* (May): 678–80.

Dewey, J. 1964. My pedagogic creed. In *John Dewey on education: Selected writings*, edited by R. D. Archambault. New York: Modern Library,

Dick, M. W., and M. Thomas. 2000. How are student activities funded at your school? *Leadership for Student Activities* (November): 40.

Dickman, D., and J. A. Lammel. 2000. Getting to the core of student athletic standards. *Principal Leadership* (October): 30–32.

Dobosz, R. P., and L. A. Beaty. 1999. The relationship between athletic participation and high school students' leadership ability. *Adolescence* 34, no. 133 (Spring): 215–20.

Dowty, S. 1996. Building a solid foundation: Involving middle level activities. *Leadership for Student Activities* (March): 24–25.

Drape, J. 1999. Deserted but determined—Lehigh's Jean, abandoned at 13, is beating the odds. *New York Times*. October 22, D1.

Dryfoos, J. 1998. The rise of the full-service community school. *High School Magazine* (October): 38–42.

Dukes, R. L., R. O. Martinez, and J. A. Stein. 1997. Precursors and consequences of membership in youth gangs. *Youth and Society* (December): 139–65.

Duvall, L. 1995. Changing the world. *Leadership for Student Activities* (January): 17–19.

Dwyer, K., D. Osher, and C. Warger. 1998, August. *Early warning, timely response: A guide to safe schools*. Washington, D.C.: U.S. Department of Education.

Dyer, T. J. 1996. Personalization: If schools don't implement this one, there will be no reform. *NASSP Bulletin* 80, no. 584 (December): 1–8.

Eastmond, D. V. 1995. *Alone but together: Adult distance study through computer conferencing*. Cresskill, N.J.: Hampton Press.

Eccles, J. S., and B. L. Barber. 1999. Student council, volunteering, basketball, or marching band: What kind of extracurricular involvement matters? *Journal of Adolescent Research* 14, no. 1 (January): 10–43.

Educational Research Service. 1999. *Creating a caring school community*. Arlington, Va.: Educational Research Service.

REFERENCES

Edwards, A. T. 1997. Let's stop ignoring our gay and lesbian youth. *Educational Leadership* (April): 68–70.

Egger, K. 1998. Multicultural clubs: The need for multicultural clubs. *Leadership for Student Activities* (February): 30–31.

Elias, M. J. 2001. Easing transitions with social-emotional learning. *Principal Leadership* (March): 20–25.

Engler, N. 2000. Distance learning in the digital age. *Harvard Education Letter*: 51–59.

Esbensen, F. 2000. Preventing adolescent gang involvement. *Office of Juvenile Justice and Delinquency Prevention Bulletin* (September). Washington: U.S. Department Of Justice.

Essex, N. 2001. Handling student-led prayer at school events. *School Administrator* (May): 48.

Ettinger, J. 1998. Shaping tomorrow's workforce today. *High School Magazine* (March–April): 26–31.

Extracurricular participation and student engagement. 1995. *ERS Spectrum*, no. 3 (Summer): 12–15

Farr, J. 1997. Spirit club improves school climate. *Schools in the Middle* (November–December): 16–17.

Feifer, S. D. 1998. Celebrating "The acts of kindness experience." *Schools in the Middle* (May–June): 16–17.

Fertman, C. I., and J. A. van Linden. 1999. Character education: An essential ingredient for youth leadership development. *NASSP Bulletin* 83, no. 609 (October): 9–15.

Fibkins, W. L. 1999. Guiding students who become star athletes. *Leadership for Student Activities* (February): 37–38.

Finney, M. R. 1997. Service learning in Maryland: Making academics more relevant. *NASSP Bulletin* 81, no. 591 (October): 37–44.

Fiscus, L. 1995. *Leadership curriculum guide*. Reston, Va.: National Association of Secondary School Principals.

———. 1999a. Back to the future. *Leadership for Student Activities* (April): 12–22.

———. 1999b. "Hey! What about us?" *Leadership for Student Activities* (November): 16–21.

———. 1999c. Supporting academics. *Leadership for Student Activities* (October): 16–21.

———. 2000. Seamless leadership. *Leadership for Student Activities* (March): 13–15.

Fitzpatrick, K. A. 1991. Restructuring to achieve outcomes of significance for all students. *Educational Leadership* (May): 18–22.

Fitzsimmons, W. R, and M. M. Lewis. 1996. Cocurricular activities and the quest for college. *High School Magazine* (September–October): 18–19.

Fogarty, R. 1999. Architects of the intellect. *Educational Leadership* (November): 76–78.

Follman, J., and K. Muldoon. 1997. Florida Learn and Serve 1995–96: What were the outcomes? *NASSP Bulletin* 81, no. 591 (October): 29–36.

Fort Worth Public Schools. 1990. *Competing in the new international economy*. Washington, D.C.: Office of Technology Assessment.

Fortin Jr., M. E. 2000. Managing the money. *Leadership for Student Activities* (November): 14–18.

Fortin, S. 1997. Abraham Maslow and school spirit. *Leadership for Student Activities* (September): 46–47.

———. 1998. Seven team-building strategies. *Leadership for Student Activities* (November): 25–27.

Frankfurt, K. 1999. Countering a climate hostile to gay students. *High School Magazine* (May–June): 25–29.

———. 2000. A place for everyone. *Principal Leadership* (October): 64–67.

Friedland, S. 1999. Violence reduction? Start with school culture. *School Administrator* (June): 14–16.

Galletti, S. 1996. Middle level and cocurricular programs: What makes a match? *Leadership for Student Activities* (September): 34–35.

Galley, M. 2000. Extra benefits tied to extracurriculars. *Education Week* (October 18): 8.

Ganser, T. 1998. Into the 21st century: Dissolving boundaries in schooling. *NASSP Bulletin* 82, no. 597 (April): 60–63.

———. 1999. Under their wing: Promises and pitfalls of mentoring. *High School Magazine* (October): 8–13.

Garber, M. P., and J. A. Heet. 2000. Free to choose service-learning. *Phi Delta Kappan* (May): 674–77.

Garrett, B. 1995. Diversity: The challenge of the 90s. *Leadership for Student Activities* (January): 20–21.

Gateway School District. 2001. *Supplemental contract applicants job description*. Monroeville, Pa.: Gateway School District.

REFERENCES

Gehring, J. 2001. Corporate leaders decry emphasis on SATs. *Education Week* (April 18): 3.

Gehrmann, T. 1998. Invest in your future! Experience excellence in a vocational student organization. *Leadership for Student Activities* (March): 17–20.

George, P. 2001. Implementing a schoolwide sportsmanship program: A true team effort. *Leadership for Student Activities* (May): 19–22.

Gerber, S. 1996. Extracurricular activities and academic achievement. *Journal of Research and Development in Education* 30, no. 1:42–50.

Gerzon, M. 1997. Teaching democracy by doing it! *Educational Leadership* (February): 6–11.

Gewertz, C. 2001a. Decision leaves Iowa student diploma-less. *Education Week* (May 2): 5.

———. 2001b. Public support for local schools reaches all-time high, poll finds. *Education Week* (September 5): 18.

Gholson, R E. 1985. Student achievement and cocurricular activity participation. *NASSP Bulletin* 69, no. 483 (October): 17–20.

———. 1996. Student activities: Jargon-free learning zone. *High School Magazine* (September–October): 20–22.

Gholson, R. E., and R. L. Buser. 1981. Student activities: A guide for determining who is participating in what. *NASSP Bulletin* 65, no. 445 (May): 43–47.

———. 1983. *Cocurricular activity programs in secondary schools*. Reston, Va.: National Association of Secondary School Principals.

Gill, A. M. 1991. In the wake of *Fraser* and *Hazelwood*. *Journal of Law and Education* 20: 253–69.

Glasser, W. 1993. *The quality school teacher*. New York: Harper Perennial.

Goedert, J. G. 1995. Schools, sports, and students with disabilities: The impact of federal laws protecting the rights of students with disabilities on interscholastic sports. *Journal of Law and Education* 24, no. 3: 403–21.

Goldberg, C. 2001. Auditing classes at MIT, on the web and free. *New York Times*. April 4, A1.

Goldman, J. P. 1991. User fees to the rescue? Pay-to-play measures trigger debate over free public schooling. *School Administrator* (October): 30–34.

Good grades on resume may not guarantee job. 1993. *USA Today*. 28 January.

Grady, J. B. 1981. Student activities: An extension of the curriculum. *Practitioner* 8, no. 1 (October).

Graf, O. L., and B. Henderson. 1997. Twenty-five ways to increase parental participation. *High School Magazine* (June–July): 36–41.

Greene, B., and S. Uroff. 1989. Apollo High School: Achievement through self-esteem. *Educational Leadership* (February): 80–81.

Grier, K. 1996. Teens making a difference through peer leadership. *Leadership for Student Activities* (October): 34–35.

Grinkmeyer, J. 1998. PantherQuest: The ultimate transition experience. *Leadership for Student Activities* (May): 26–29.

Guernsey, L. 2001. School time minus the face time. *New York Times*. February 15, G1.

Guzo, D. 1995. Food drive: A new look at a traditional project. *Leadership for Student Activities* (December): 44–45.

Haensly, P. A., A. E. Lupkowski, and E. P. Edlind. 1985–1986. The role of extracurricular activities in education. *High School Journal* 69, no. 2:110–119.

Halford, J. M. 1998. For significant support, turn to seniors. *Educational Leadership* (May): 49–51.

Hanks, M. P., and B. K. Eckland. 1976. Athletics and social participation in the educational attainment process. *Sociology of Education* 49, no. 4:271–294.

———. 1978. Adult voluntary associations and adolescent socialization. *Sociological Quarterly* 19, no. 3:481–90.

Hansen, J. M., and J. Childs. 1998. Creating a school where people like to be. *Educational Leadership* (September): 14–17.

Hardy, L. 1997. Pay to play—do fees for school sports undermine the American promise of free public education? *American School Board Journal* 184, no. 8 (August): 25–27.

Harned, P. J. 1999. Leading the effort to teach character in schools. *NASSP Bulletin* 83, no. 609 (October): 25–32.

Harris, I. M. 2000. Peace-building responses to school violence. *NASSP Bulletin* 84, no. 614 (March): 5–24.

Heiser, P. 2001. New York highly rated in standards and accountability. *On Board* 2, no. 2 (January 29): 9.

Heller, M. P., and N. W. Sindelar. 1991. *Developing an effective teacher mentor program.* Bloomington, Ind.: Phi Delta Kappa Educational Foundation.

Henderson, A. T., and N. Berla. 1995. *A new generation of evidence: The family is critical to student achievement.* Washington: Washington, D.C., Center for Law and Education.

Henrico County Public Schools. n.d. *Student activity advisor's handbook.* Richmond, Va.: Henrico County Public Schools.

Henze, R. C. 2000. A required curriculum for respect. *Principal Leadership* (December): 14–19.

Hereford, N. 1999a. A good sport! Middle school athletics can help kids put their best foot forward. *Middle Ground* (August): 25–28.

———. 1999b. Positive school climate—creating a place where people want to be. *Middle Ground* (October): 10–15.

Hertzog, C. J., and P. L. Morgan. 1999. Making the transition from middle level to high school. *High School Magazine* (January–February): 26–30.

Hodgkinson, H. J. 1996. Why have Americans never admired their own school? *School Administrator* (May): 18–22.

———. 1999. The uneven spread and blurring of student diversity. *School Administrator* (December): 13–14.

———. 2000. Reading the future of secondary schools. *High School Magazine* (May): 42–43.

———. 2000–2001. Educational demographics: What teachers should know. *Educational Leadership* (December–January): 6–11.

Hofsess, D. 1990. The power of mentoring: A moving force in staff development. *Journal of Staff Development* 11, no. 2: 20–24.

Hogan, J. B., and E. J. Sarzynski. 1998. *Hornbook of topics and forms pertaining to students.* Binghamton, N.Y.: Hogan and Sarzynski.

Holland, A., and T. Andre. 1987. Participation in extracurricular activities in secondary school: What is known, what needs to be known? *Review of Educational Research* 57, no. 4:437–66.

Holland, H. 1999. Diversity defined—Supportive middle schools search for the beauty within. *Middle Ground* (December): 6–10.

Holson, L. M. 2001. Talk about bang for the buck—An investment group for the professional athlete. *New York Times.* January 27, C1.

Home ownership made easier. 1996. *Leadership for Student Activities* (October): 20.

Honan, W. H. 2001a. Do big-money sports belong in college? *New York Times.* January 7, 19–21.

———. 2001b. Panel proposes a revamping of college sports. *New York Times.* June 27, A16.

Hoover, C. G. 1998. The *Hazelwood* decision: A decade later. *NASSP Bulletin* 82, no. 599 (September): 48–56.

Hopkins, G. R. 2000. How important are intergenerational programs in today's schools? *Phi Delta Kappan* (December): 317–19.

Hornbeck, D. 2000. Service learning and reform in the Philadelphia public schools. *Phi Delta Kappan* (May): 665.

Howell, J. C. 1998. Youth gangs: An overview. *Office of Juvenile Justice and Delinquency Prevention Bulletin* (August). Washington, D.C.: U.S. Department of Justice.

Huff, C. R., and K. S. Trump. 1996. Youth violence and gangs—School safety initiatives in urban and suburban school districts. *Education and Urban Society* 28, no. 4:492–503.

REFERENCES

IDEA Regulations, 34 C.F.R. 300.550 (b).

Illinois State Board of Education. 1997. *Illinois Learning Standards* (July). Springfield: Illinois State Board of Education.

In what ways do student leaders help govern your school? 1999. *Leadership for Student Activities* (February): 32.

International Society for Technology in Education, 2000. *National Educational Technology Standards for Students Connecting Curriculum and Technology*. Eugene, Oreg.: International Society for Technology in Education.

Jackson, A. W, G. A. Davis, M. Abeel, and A. Bordonaro. 2000. *Turning points 2000: Educating adolescents in the 21st century. A Report of Carnegie Corporation of New York*. New York: Teachers College Press.

Johnson, D. R., and R. C. Steigerwald. 1997. Developing a student fund activities handbook. *School Business Affairs* (October): 37–41.

Johnson, D. W., and R. T. Johnson. 1989–1990. Social skills for successful group work. *Educational Leadership* 47, no. 4 (December–January): 29–33.

Johnson, S. 1996. *Miami-Dade Community College* at www.mdcc.edu/servicelearning/def.html.

Jones, S. C., and J. Stoodley. 1999. Community of caring: A character-education program designed to integrate values into a school community. *NASSP Bulletin* 83, no. 609 (October): 46–51.

Jordan, W. J. 1999. Black high school students' participation in school-sponsored sports activities: Effects on school engagement and achievement. *Journal of Negro Education* 68, no. 1: 54–71.

Jurgensen, K., ed. 2001. Hoop dreams denied. Our view: NBA drafts high schoolers, leaving illusions for their peers. *USA Today*. June 29, 14A.

Kaiser, J. S. 1995. Eight months of activities—Unity through purpose. *Schools in the Middle* (February): 15–18.

Kanaby, R. E. 1996. Willing learners remove apathy from the equation. *High School Magazine* (September–October): 8–12.

Kaplan, B. 2000. Power to change. *Leadership for Student Activities* (May): 28–30.

Kaye, C. B. 1997. *Service learning—Raising service projects to the next level, A guide for student activity advisers*. Reston, Va.: National Association of Secondary School Principals and Quest International.

Keaster, R. D., H. D. Downing, and M. R. Peterson. 1995. At-risk students: Are schools contributing to the problem? *High School Magazine* (September): 33–37.

Keck, E. 1997. Committees are vital for major activities. *Leadership for Student Activities* (December): 36–37.

Keegan, D. 2000. Students and teachers experiment with virtual high schools, August 9. CNN.com from Civic.com.

Kelly, E. B. 1998. *Legal basics—A handbook for educators*. Bloomington, Ind.: Phi Delta Kappan Educational Foundation, 59–73.

Kessie, A. 2001. *Providence high school athletic information for 2001–2002*. Charlotte, N.C.: Providence Senior High School.

Kielsmeier, J. C. 2000. A time to serve, a time to learn: Service learning and the promise of democracy. *Phi Delta Kappan* (May): 652–57.

Kingsley, C. 1995. *An Overview of the Rapidly Changing Labor Market*. Waltham, Mass.: Center for Human Resources, Brandeis University.

Kinsley, C. W. 1997. Service learning: A process to connect learning and living. *NASSP Bulletin* 81, no. 591 (October): 1–7.

Kleinfield, N. R. 2001. Coping with homework and a bear market. *New York Times*. June 21, B1.

Klesse, E., and J. D'Onofrio. 1993. Involving students at risk. *Leadership for Student Activities* (October): 10–15.

———. 1994. *Student activities for students at risk*. Reston, Va.: National Association of Secondary School Principals.

Klima, S. M. 1997. Student activity period. *Leadership for Student Activities* (November): 24–26.

Klonsky, S., and M. Klonsky. 1999. In Chicago: Countering anonymity through small schools. *Educational Leadership* (September): 38–41.

Koerner, T. 1992. Student activity programs enhance education experience for nation's youth: A *Bulletin* special. *NASSP Bulletin* 76, no. 542 (March): 60–65.

Kolbe, G. C., and B. Berkin. 2000. Health and wellness after school. *Educational Leadership* (March): 40–42.

Konet, R. J. 2001. Striving for a personal best. *Principal Leadership* (February): 19–23.

Korsak, M. T. 2000. Support systems for moral and cognitive development. *Schools in the Middle* (May): 5–7.

Krystal, S. 1998–1999. The nurturing potential of service learning. *Educational Leadership* (December–January): 58–61.

Kugler, M. R. 2001. After-school programs are making a difference. *NASSP Bulletin* 85, no. 626 (September): 3–11.

Kurth, B. 1996. Computer partners program bridges generations. *Leadership for Student Activities* (March): 44–45.

Lafee, S. 1998. A sporting chance for home-schoolers? *School Administrator* (November): 18–22.

Laird, J., and L. Laird. 1998. Celebrating awareness activities. *Leadership for Student Activities* (February): 26–29.

Langdon, C. A. 1997. The fourth Phi Delta Kappa poll of teachers' attitudes toward the public schools. *Phi Delta Kappan* (November): 212–20.

———. 1999. The fifth Phi Delta Kappa poll of teachers' attitudes toward the public schools. *Phi Delta Kappan* (April): 611–18.

Langdon, C. A., and N. Vesper. 2000. The sixth Phi Delta Kappa poll of teachers' attitudes toward the public schools. *Phi Delta Kappan* (April): 607–11.

Lannert, G. 2000. Academics, activities, attitude. *Principal Leadership* (October): 24–29.

———. 2001. Leadership class prepares students for success. *Leadership for Student Activities* (January): 10–13.

Lapchick, R. 1996. School sports: A safety net for youths. *Sporting News* (March).

Leddo, J. 1997. A virtual schoolhouse: Creating on-line resources for schools. *NASSP Bulletin* 81, no. 592 (November): 39–45.

Lee v. Weisman, 505 U.S. 577 (1992).

Lemon v. Kurtzman, 403 U.S. 602 (1971).

Lenz, B. 1997a. Academy X develops leaders for the 21st century. *Leadership for Student Activities* (April): 20–21.

———. 1997b. Block scheduling and student activities. *Leadership for Student Activities* (November): 27–28.

Levine, B., and L. A. Courier. 1996. A community leadership experience. *Leadership for Student Activities* (April): 20–22.

Lewis, A. C. 1989. The not so extracurriculum. *Phi Delta Kappan* (May): 1–8.

Lickona, T. 1988. How parents and schools can work together to raise moral children. *Educational Leadership* (May): 36–38.

———. 1993. The return of character education. *Educational Leadership* (November): 6–11.

———. 1997. Becoming a school of character: What it takes. *High School Magazine* (November–December): 6–15.

———. 2000. Developing democratic character. In *The fourth and fifth Rs: Respect and responsibility*, 2–6. Cortland: SUNY Press Cortland.

LoCastro, S. A. 2000. Student magazine fosters useful skills. *Schools in the Middle* (January): 4–7.

Lounsbury, J. H. 1996. Personalizing the high school: Lessons learned in the middle. *NASSP Bulletin* 80, no. 584 (December): 17–24.

Loupe, D. 2000. Community service: Mandatory or voluntary? *School Administrator* (August): 32–39.

Lundt, J. C., and T. Vanderpan. 2000. It computes when young adolescents teach senior citizens. *Middle School Journal* 31, no. 4 (March): 18–22.

Mac, M. R. 1998. Managing the risks of school sports. *School Administrator* (November): 42–46.

MacGregor, M. 2001. Engaging emerging leaders: Working with young non-traditional student leaders. *Leadership for Student Activities* (March): 13–15.

Mahon, J. P. 1990. Mergens: Is the equal access issue settled? *Journal of Law and Education* 19, no. 4:543–47.

Mahoney, J. L., and R. B. Cairns. 1997. Do extracurricular activities protect against early school dropout? *Developmental Psychology* 33, no. 2:241–53.

Males, M. 1998. Five myths, and why adults believe they are true. *New York Times*, April 29, at www.nytimes.com/specials/teens/male.html (accessed April 29, 1998).

Mann, D. 1999. The future of schooling: More of the same? *School Administrator* (December): 21–22.

Manning, M. L. 2000. Letting all young adolescents participate. *Schools in the Middle* (May): 19–21.

Marano, R. 1983. Inside views. *Student Advocate* 25 (March).

———. 1999. Foreword. In *Organizing an inter-club leadership conference* by Earl Reum. Reston, Va.: National Association of Secondary School Principals.

———. 2000a. "Extracurricular" is out of date. *Education Week* (November 15): 43.

———. 2000b. Student activities are not extra. *Principal Leadership* (October): 8.

Marshak, D. 1995. Reconnecting with students: How to make our schools communities. *High School Magazine* (March): 30–33.

Mavrelis, J. 1998. Understanding differences in cultural communication style. *Leadership for Student Activities* (February): 18–22.

Mawdsley, R. D. 1998. The principal and religious activity. *NASSP Bulletin* 82, no. 599 (September): 10–17.

———. 1999. Legal issues involving field trips. *School Business Affairs* (September): 28–31.

———. 2001. Let us pray? *Principal Leadership* (April): 20–25.

McCracken, R. 1998. Volunteerism and service learning. *Leadership for Student Activities* (December): 35–36.

McEwin, C. K., and T. S. Dickinson. 1997. Interscholastic sports: A battle not fought. *Schools in the Middle* (January–February): 17–23.

McKowen, H. C. 1952. *Extracurricular activities*. New York: Macmillan.

McLaughlin, M. W. 2001. Community counts. *Educational Leadership* (April): 14–18.

McNeal Jr., R. B. 1998. High school extracurricular activities: Closed structures and stratifying patterns of participation. *Journal of Educational Research* 91, no. 3: 183–91.

McPartland, J. M., and W. J. Jordan. 2001. Restructuring for reform: The talent development model. *Principal Leadership* (February): 28–31.

McPherson, K. 1997. Service learning: Making a difference in the community. *Schools in the Middle* (January–February): 9–15.

Megyeri, K. 1999. Serving for credit. *Leadership for Student Activities* (March): 19–23.

Meier, D. W. 1996. The big benefits of smallness. *Educational Leadership* (September): 12–15.

Melchior, A. 2000. Costs and benefits of service learning. *School Administrator* (August): 26–31.

Merrow, J. 2001. Understanding standards. *Phi Delta Kappan* (May): 653–59.

Miley, C. 1998. Build a strong foundation for activities. *Leadership for Student Activities* (September): 35–36.

Miller, F. A., J. H. Moyer, and R. B. Patrick. 1956. *Planning student activities*. Englewood Cliffs, N.J.: Prentice Hall.

Mills, R. P. 1998. School violence. *Memo to District Superintendents, Superintendents of Public and Nonpublic Schools, and Presidents of Boards of Education* (June). Albany: New York State Department of Education.

Montano, J. 1998. Marketing scholastic sports. *School Administrator* (November): 30–31.

Morgan, P. L., and C. J. Hertzog. 2001. Designing comprehensive transitions. *Principal Leadership* (March): 10–16.

Morrison, S. 1998. A corporate pitch for athletics. *School Administrator* (November): 23–28.

Morrissey, P. A. 1998. The Individuals with Disabilities Education Act Amendments of 1997: Selected observations. *NASSP Bulletin* 82, no. 594 (January): 5–11.

Murphy, M. 1997. Student council as an educational tool. *Leadership for Student Activities* (April): 24.

Murray, K. T., and C. S. Evans. 2000. U.S. Supreme Court revisits school prayer. *NASSP Bulletin* 84, no. 620 (December): 73–82.

Mutter, D. W., E. Chase, and W. R. Nichols. 1997. Evaluation of a 4 x 4 block schedule. *ERS Spectrum* 15, no. 1:3–8.

Namey, J. 2000. Raising spirit, building pride. *Leadership for Student Activities* (September): 8–11.

National Association of Secondary School Principals. 1976. *How to run an efficient and effective student activities program.* Reston, Va.: National Association of Secondary School Principals.

———. 1988. *The changing shape of students' rights—A legal memorandum* (June). Reston, Va.: National Association of Secondary School Principals.

———. 1992. *Student publications and distribution issues: Rights and responsibilities—A legal memorandum* (May). Reston, Va.: National Association of Secondary School Principals.

———. 1996. *Breaking ranks: Changing an American institution.* Reston, Va.: National Association of Secondary School Principals.

National Collegiate Athletic Association. 2001a. *2001–2002 NCAA guide for the college bound student athlete.* Indianapolis, Ind.: National Collegiate Athletic Association.

———. 2001b. www.NCAA.org. June 14, 2001, 1–5.

National Commission on Excellence in Education. 1983. *A nation at risk.* Washington: U.S. Department of Education.

National Federation of State High School Associations. 1998. *The case for high school activities.* Indianapolis, Ind.: National Federation of State High School Associations.

Nebgen, M. K., and K. McPherson. 1990. Enriching learning through service: A tale of three districts. *Educational Leadership* (November): 90–93.

Neel, M. M. 1996. To become an effective leader . . . get involved in the arts. *Leadership for Student Activities* (December): 17–18.

New York State Education Department. 1991. *Assessing student achievement in home economics education.* Albany: New York State Education Department.

———. 1999. *The safeguarding, accounting and auditing of extra classroom activity funds: Finance pamphlet 2.* Albany: New York State Education Department.

———. 2001. *Regulations of the New York State Commission of Education.* Albany: New York State Education Department.

———. n.d. *The career development and occupational studies resource guide.* Albany: New York State Education Department.

New York State School Boards Association and School Administrators Association of New York State. 2001. *A comprehensive guide to developing student handbooks for New York State schools, 2001–2002.* Albany: New York State School Boards Association and School Administrators Association of New York State.

New York State School Boards Association and the New York State Bar Association. 2000. *Information about the New York State education law regulations and decisions of the Commissioner of Education and other laws and legal opinions relating to education for the guidance of school boards and school administrators in New York State.* Albany: New York State School Boards Association and the New York State Bar Association.

Niestemski, J. 1996. A letter to the principal: Student activities and you. *High School Magazine* (September–October): 30–31.

No child left behind: A special reprint of President George W. Bush's education plan with relevant discussion questions education leaders should ask. 2001. Arlington, Va.: Educational Research Service.

Noguera, P. A. 1999. Confronting the challenge of diversity. *School Administrator* (May): 16–18.

O'Brien, E., and M. Rollefson. 1995. *Extracurricular participation and student engagement* (June). Washington D.C.: National Center for Education Statistics, U.S. Department of Education.

O'Neil, J. 1995. On preparing students for the world of work: A conversation with Willard Daggett. *Educational Leadership* (May): 46–48.

———. 1996. On emotional intelligence: A conversation with Daniel Goleman. *Educational Leadership* (September): 6–11.

O'Neill, M. 1996. Service x 2: Service learning benefits both students and community. *Leadership for Student Activities* (October): 23–25.

O'Reilly, J. M. 1992. Did the kids win or lose? The impact of the "no pass/no play" rule on student achievement. *ERIC Document Reproduction Service*, 357–410.

Odell, S. J. 1990. *Mentor teacher programs*. Washington, D.C.: National Education Association.

Office of Technology Assessment. 1990. *Competing in the new international economy*. Washington, D.C.: Office of Technology Assessment.

Okun, S. J. 1996. Religion in the public schools: What does the First Amendment allow? *NASSP Bulletin* 80, no. 581 (September): 26–35.

Olson, L. 2000. Sweetening the pot. *Education Week* 13 (January): 28–30.

Olson, S. 2001. Student council grading chart. *Leadership for Student Activities* (January): 52.

Omizo, M. M., S. A. Omizo, and M. R. Honda. 1997. A phenomenological study with youth gang members: Results and implications for school counselors. *Professional School Counseling* 1, no. 1 (October): 39–42.

Otto, L. B. 1982. Extracurricular activities. In *Improving educational standards and productivity*, edited by H. J. Wahlberg. Berkeley, Calif.: McCutchan.

Palting, C. 1999. When gangs come 2 town: Youth gangs aren't just a big-city problem. *American School Board Journal* 186, no. 5 (May): 53–55.

Pantleo, S. 1999. Making connections to ease transition from eighth to ninth grade. *High School Magazine* (January–February): 31.

Papagiotas, A. 1998. How to encourage student participation in cocurricular activities. *Tips for principals* (September). Reston, Va.: National Association of Secondary School Principals.

Pardini, P. 2001. Extended school days. *School Administrator* (August): 12–15.

Permuth, S., and R. S. Permuth. 2000. Legal dimensions of school activities. *Principal Leadership* (October): 34–37.

Perrin, K. 1999. Banishing the bully. *Leadership for Student Activities* (January): 26–27.

Pickeral, T. L., and J. Bray. 2000. Service learning in an age of standards. *School Administrator* (August): 6–11.

Poinsett, A. 1996. *The role of sports in youth development* (March). New York: Carnegie Corporation of New York.

Portner, J. 2000. Teens' risky behavior tied to school troubles. *Education Week* (December 6): 5.

Pottgen, 40 F.3d at 929 citing Davis, 442 U.S. at 413, and Arline, 480 U.S. at 287n.17.

Powell, C. 1999. Self-fulfillment through service. *Leadership for Student Activities* (March): 12–15.

Pressley, J. S., and R. L. Whitley. 1996. Let's hear it for the "dumb jock": What athletics contribute to the academic program. *NASSP Bulletin* 80, no. 580 (May): 74–83.

Promoting pluralism. 1998. *Leadership for Student Activities* (February): 17.

Prothro, M. S. 1993. Involving your faculty. *Leadership for Student Activities* (October): 34–35.

Putnam City Schools. n.d. Oklahoma City, Okla.

Randall, E. D. 2000. A former Boy Scout leader speaks. *On Board* 1, no. 21 (December 11): 5.

Rasmussen, K. 1999–2000. The changing sports scene. *Educational Leadership* (December–January): 26–29.

Ravitch, D. 1996. The case for national standards and assessments. *Clearing House*. 69: 134–36.

Reeves, K. 1998. Athletic eligibility: Right or privilege? *School Administrator* (November): 6–12.

Reid, K. S. 2001. U.S. census underscores diversity. *Education Week* (March 21): 1.

Reith, K. M. 1996. New NCAA academic standards: Will your student-athlete make the cut? *High School Magazine* (September–October): 13–17.

Rewick, J. 2001. Off campus: Private virtual universities challenge many of the assumptions long held by educators. Their own challenge: Survival. *Wall Street Journal*. March 12, R10.

Rhoder, C., and J. N. French. 1999. School-to-work—Making specific connections. *Phi Delta Kappan* (March): 534–42.

Richardson v. Brahan, 249 N.W. 557 (Neb 1933).

Richardson, A. M. 1995. Teaching tolerance to middle school students. *Schools in the Middle* (November–December): 39–40.

Riley, K. W. 1991. *Street gangs and the schools: A blueprint for intervention*. Bloomington, Ind.: Phi Delta Kappa Educational Foundation.

Riley, R. W. 1995. Getting families involved at the high school level. *Leadership for Student Activities* (March): 17–20.

Riley, R. W., and H. Wofford. 2000. The reaffirmation of the declaration of principles. *Phi Delta Kappan* (May): 670–72.

Robinson II, D. M. 1999. Student group helps kids attack the causes of school violence. *Middle Ground* (October): 35–37.

Robinson, T. R., S. W. Smith, and A. P. Daunic. 2000. Middle school students' views on the social validity of peer mediation. *Middle School Journal* 31, no. 5 (May): 23–29.

Rogers, S., J. Ludington, and S. Graham. 1988. *Motivation and learning*. Evergreen, Colo.: Peak Learning Systems.

Rogers, S., and L. Renard. 1999. Relationship-driven teaching. *Educational Leadership* (September): 34–37.

Roland, M. 2001. Commitment to cocurricular excellence. *Leadership for Student Activities* (May): 11–13.

Rose, L. C., and A. M. Gallup. 1998. The 30th annual Phi Delta Kappa/Gallup poll of the public's attitudes toward the public schools. *Phi Delta Kappan* (September): 41–56.

———. 1999. The 31st annual Phi Delta Kappa/Gallup poll of the public's attitudes toward the public schools. *Phi Delta Kappan* (September): 41–55.

———. 2000. The 32nd annual Phi Delta Kappa/Gallup poll of the public's attitudes toward the Public Schools. *Phi Delta Kappan* (September): 41–58.

Rose, L. C., A. M. Gallup, and S. M. Elam. 1997. The 29th annual Phi Delta Kappa/ Gallup poll of the public's attitudes toward the public schools. *Phi Delta Kappan* (September): 41–56.

Rosen, J. 1999. Kentucky offers statewide virtual high school. *CNN*, November 29, at www.cnn.com (accessed April 11, 2001).

Rough, J. 1994. High school: What do students want? *Leadership for Student Activities* (February): 10–15.

Rourke, J. 2000. From peaceniks to serviceniks: The new face of student activism. *Leadership for Student Activities* (October): 5–8.

Rowley, J. B. 1999. The good mentor. *Educational Leadership* (May): 20–22.

Ruggero, E. 2001. *Duty first—West Point and the making of American leaders*. New York: HarperCollins.

Sabatino, M. 1994. A look back at the no pass/no play revision. ERIC Document Reproduction Service. ED 379 304.

Sammon, G., and M. Becton. 2001. Principles of partnerships. *Principal Leadership* (February): 32–35.

Sapon-Shevin, M. 2000–2001. Schools fit for all. *Educational Leadership* (December–January): 34–39.

Savard, J. 1993. Student council advisers: Let the students shine. *High School Magazine* (December): 22.

Scales, P. C. 1999. Care and challenge—The sources of student success. *Middle Ground* (October): 21–23.

Schellenberg, S. 1998. Loss of credit and its impact on high school students: A longitudinal study. Paper presented at the meeting of the American Educational Research Association, April, New Orleans, La.

Schlechty, P., and V. Vance. 1983. Recruitment, selection and retention: The shape of the teaching force. *Elementary School Journal* 83, no. 4:469–487.

School failure, choice of friends are major factors in teenage risk behaviors. 2001. *News Leader* 48, no. 5 (January): 1.

Sergiovanni, T. J. 1995. Small schools, great expectations. *Education Leadership* (November): 48–52.

Shaller, G. 1999. Cowabunga. *Leadership for Student Activities* (March): 24–25.

———. 2000. Defy your limits: Recipe for boosting self-esteem. *Leadership for Student Activities* (May): 25–29.

Shanahan, L. 1997. Survival of activities in a block-scheduling format. *Leadership for Student Activities* (November): 28.

Shelton, C. M. 2000. Portraits in emotional awareness. *Educational Leadership* (September): 30–32.

Sherrill, J. 1997. Student activities: What are they and what is their place in the middle level curriculum? *Schools in the Middle* (January–February): 6–8.

———. 1998. Student activities included in new assessment guide. *Leadership for Student Activities* (February): 32–33.

———. 1999. Student leaders: The youngest partners in excellence. *Schools in the Middle* (March): 20.

Shoffner, M. F., and R. D. Williamson. 2000. Facilitating student transitions into middle school. *Middle School Journal* 31, no. 4 (March): 47–52.

Shoop, R. J. 1999. Sexual abuse of children by teachers. *High School Magazine* (May–June): 8–12.

Shore, R. 1995. How one high school improved school climate. *Educational Leadership* (February): 76–78.

Shumer, R. 1997. What research tells us about designing service learning programs. *NASSP Bulletin* 81, no. 591 (October): 18–24.

———. 2000. Service and citizenship: A connection for the future. *High School Magazine* (April): 34–39.

Slotz, D. F. 1984. Athletics and achievement—Making the grade. *Interscholastic Athletic Administration* (Winter): 4–7.

Smith, D. W. 2000. Ten rules for daily living. *School Administrator* (December): 53.

Smith, L. 2001. What are schools for? We should seize the moment to define our purposes. *Education Week* (October 3): 44–45.

Smith, M. 1998. In our America: A dream for the 21st century. *Leadership for Student Activities* (February): 32.

———. 2001. The leadership dilemma. *Leadership for Student Activities* (March): 10–12.

Snyder, E. E., and E. Spreitzer. 1992. High school athletes' participation as related to college attendance among black, Hispanic, and white males. *Youth and Society*:390–96.

Snyder, H., and M. Sickmund. 1999. *Juvenile offenders and victims: 1999 national report*. Washington, D.C.: U.S. Office of Juvenile Justice and Delinquency Prevention.

Solter, D. 2000. How to avoid adviser burnout. *Principal Leadership* (October): 81.

Solter, D., and M. A. DeFamio. 2000. Wall of support. *Leadership for Student Activities* (February): 32–33.

Sommerfeld, M. 1998. Parity on the playing field. *School Administrator* (November): 32–36.

Spady, W. G. 1970. Lament for the letterman: Effects of peer status and extracurricular activities on goals and achievement. *American Journal of Sociology* 75, no. 4:680–702.

Spreitzer, E. 1994. Does participation in interscholastic athletics affect adult development? A longitudinal analysis of an 18–24 age cohort. *Youth and Society* 25, no. 3:368–87.

Stader, D. L., and F. J. Gagnepain. 2000. Humanizing the high school: The power of peers. *ERS Spectrum* 18, no. 2: 28–33.

Starratt, R. J. 1994. *Building an ethical school: A practical response to the moral crisis in schools*. London: Falmer Press.

State University of New York. 1995. *College expectations: Knowledge and skills—Recommendations of the SUNY task force on college entry-level knowledge and skills*. Albany: State University of New York.

State University of New York and the New York State Education Department. 1996. *Learning standards for career development and occupational studies* (July). Albany: University of the State of New York and the New York State Education Department.

———. n.d. *Career development and occupational studies resource guide*. Albany: University of the State of New York and the State Education Department.

———. n.d. *New York State learning standards*. Albany: University of the State of New York and the New York State Education Department.

Stegman, M., and L. J. Stephens. 2000. Athletics and academics: Are they compatible? *High School Magazine* (February): 36–39.

Steinberg, A. 2000. Community-connected learning. *School Administrator* (August): 40–44.

Steinberg, J. 2000. Skeptic now sees the virtue in teaching children online. *New York Times*. December 28, B1.

Stemmer, P., B. Brown, and C. Smith. 1992. The employability skills portfolio. *Educational Leadership* (March): 32–35.

Stephens, R. D. 1994. Planning for safer, more effective schools: School violence prevention and intervention strategies. *High School Magazine* (September): 4–8.

Sternberg, B. J. 2000. The right stuff of schools: How our high schools can become better communities for our children. *NASSP Bulletin* 84, no. 613 (February): 61–75.

Sternberg, R. J. 1996. IQ counts, but what really counts is successful intelligence. *NASSP Bulletin* 80, no. 583 (November): 18–23.

Sternberg, R. J., L. Okagaki, and A. S. Jackson. 1990. Practical intelligence for success in school. *Educational Leadership* (September): 35–39.

Strope, J. 1998. The law and student activities: Answers to ten frequently asked questions. *NASSP Bulletin* 82, no. 599 (September): 34–41.

Student pledge against gun violence. 1998. *Leadership for Student Activities* (September): 42–44.

Student Press Law Center. n.d. At www.splc.org.

Sullivan, K. A., P. J. Lantz, and P. A. Zirkel. 2000. Leveling the playing field or leveling the players? Section 504, the Americans with Disabilities Act, and Interscholastic Sports. *Journal of Special Education* 33, no. 4:258–67.

Swaim, J. H., C. K. McEwin, and J. L. Irvin. 1998. Responsive middle level sports programs. *Middle School Journal* 30, no. 2 (November): 72–74.

Sylwester, R. 1994. How emotions affect learning. *Educational Leadership* (October): 60–65.

Tam, Pui-Wing. 2001. Tools of the future—Thanks to technology, K–12 will never look the same. *Wall Street Journal*. March 12, R28.

Tanaka, G., and K. Reid. 1997. Peer helpers: Encouraging kids to confide. *Educational Leadership* (October): 29–31.

Taylor, E. 1999. Bring in "Da Noise": Race, sports, and the role of schools. *Educational Leadership* (April): 75–78.

Taylor, K. R. 2000. Equal treatment for student clubs: Do you have the answers? *Principal Leadership* (October): 68–71.

Tenenbaum, I. M. 2000. Building a framework for service learning: The South Carolina experience. *Phi Delta Kappan* (May): 666–69.

Tewel, K. J. 1996. Vision and beliefs: Critical to successful high schools. *High School Magazine* (June–July): 43–46.

Thomas, L. G. and D. G. Knezek. 1999. National educational technology standards. *Educational Leadership* (February): 27.

Thomas, O. S. 1999. Legal leeway on church-state in school. *School Administrator* (January): 12–16.

Thomas Sr., L. R. 1999. One school, one groove. *High School Magazine* (January): 44–46.

Thomson, S. D. 1983. *Statement on student activities* (December). Reston, Va.: National Association of Secondary School Principals.

Tompkins-Seneca-Tioga Area Vocational Center-BOCES. 1995. *Employability progress report*. Tompkins-Seneca-Tioga Area Vocational Center-BOCES.

Totty, M., and A. Grimes. 2001. The old college try—Traditional universities are taking to the net with a wide range of strategies. *Wall Street Journal*. March 12, R10.

Township High School District 211. 1989. *Position description*. Palatine Township High School District 211 (Illinois), 1–2.

———. 1997. *Activity handbook*. Palatine: Township High School District 211.

———. 1998. *Sponsor handbook*. Palatine: Township High School District 211.

REFERENCES

Trotter, A. 2001a. Census shows the changing face of U.S. households. *Education Week* (May 23): 5.

———. 2001b. Cyber learning at online high. *Education Week* (January 24): 28–33.

Trump, K. S. 1998. *Practical school security: Basic guidelines for safe and secure schools.* Thousand Oaks, Calif.: Corwin Press.

Tungate, D. E., and D. P. Orie. 1998. Title IX lawsuits. *Phi Delta Kappan* (April): 603–4.

Udry, J. M. 1986. *How I faded away.* Chicago, Ill.: Albert Whitman.

U.S. Department of Education. 1992. *Longitudinal study, second follow-up.* Washington, D.C.: National Center for Education Statistics.

———. 1995. *The condition of education.* Washington, D.C.: National Center for Education Statistics.

U.S. Department of Education; U.S. Department of Justice. 2000. *Working for children and families: Safe and smart after-school* programs (April). Washington, D.C.: U.S. Department of Education; U.S. Department of Justice.

U.S. Department of Labor. 1991. *What work requires of schools: A SCANS report for America 2000* (June). Washington, D.C.: U.S. Department of Labor.

Upton, J. 1995. Getting parents to assist. *Leadership for Student Activities* (March): 21–23.

Urban, V. D. 1999. Eugene's story: A case for caring. *Educational Leadership* (March): 69–70.

Vail, K. 1998. Give peace a chance: Peer mediators in Cleveland choose nonviolence. *American School Board Journal* 185, no. 8 (August): 22–24.

Van Dyk, P. 1997. Coordinating a cocurricular program through an organizational homeroom. *Leadership for Student Activities* (March): 37–39.

Van Til, J. 1997. Facing inequality and the end of work. *Educational Leadership* (March): 78–81.

Vessels, G. G., and S. M. Boyd. 1996. Public and constitutional support for character education. *NASSP Bulletin* 80, no. 579 (April): 55–62.

Viadero, D. 2001a. Getting serious about high school. *Education Week* (April 11): 1.

———. 2001b. U.S. urged to rethink high school. *Education Week* (January 24): 1.

Visher, M. G., and P. M. Hudis. 1999. *Aiming high: Strategies to promote high standards in high schools—Interim Report* (October). Berkeley, Calif.: MPR Associates.

Volp, R. 1995. The difference between leaders and managers. *Leadership for Student Activities* (January): 34–35.

Vornberg, J. A. 1998. How to administer student activities programs. *Tips for Principals* (October). Reston, Va.: National Association of Secondary School Principals.

Wagner, C. 1999. Improving the prospects for poor children. *Futurist* 33, no. 4.

Wagner, M., C. Knudsen, and V. Harper. 1999–2000. The evil joker. *Educational Leadership* (December–January): 47–50.

Wallace v. Jaffree, 472 U.S. 38, 75 (1985).

Wallinger, L. M. 1999. World-class standards in education: Are we there yet? *NASSP Bulletin* 83, no. 611 (December): 80–86.

Walsh, M. 2000a. Judge's approval of club for gay students leads to protest. *Education Week* (February 16): 1, 10.

———. 2000b. Scouts' ban on gays is prompting schools to reconsider ties. *Education Week* (October 25): 6–7.

———. 2001a. Appellate Court rejects extracurricular drug testing. *Education Week* (March 28): 7.

———. 2001b. Court boosts school access for religious groups. *Education Week* (June 20): 1.

———. 2001c. Former Education Secretary starts online-learning venture. *Education Week* (January 10): 7.

———. 2001d. Graduation season means commencement of prayer flaps. *Education Week* (June 6): 10.

Wanko, M. A. 1996. Lights, cameras, pro-action: How one school raises additional funding for activities. *High School Magazine* (June–July): 38–39.

Waters, C. S., and D. L. Waters. 1997. Cocurricular activities and the restructured high school. *Leadership for Student Activities* (November): 20–23.

REFERENCES

Watson, R. 1995. A guide to violence prevention. *Educational Leadership* (February): 57–59.

Watters, C. 1996. A middle level leadership class. *Leadership for Student Activities* (March): 21–23.

Weasmer, J., and A. M. Woods. 2000. Shifting classroom ownership to students. *Middle School Journal* 32, no. 2 (November): 15–20.

Webb, D. L. 1997. Home-schools and interscholastic sports: Denying participation violates United States constitutional due process and equal protection rights. *Journal of Law and Education* 26, no. 3 (July): 123–132.

Web-based education commission issues urgent call-to-action to harness Internet's power for learning. 2001. *NASSP NewsLeader* (February): 1.

Weiner, B. 1979. A theory of motivation for some classroom experiences. *Journal of Educational Psychology*, no. 71:3–25.

Wessler, S. L. 2000–2001. Sticks and stones. *Educational Leadership* (December–January): 28–33.

Westerberg, T. 1997. Developing and implementing essential learnings: One school's experience. *High School Magazine* (March–April): 4–11.

Whitaker, T., and C. Hays. 1998. Parent/student computer class: Teaming with technology. *Schools in the Middle* (January–February): 15–16.

White, G. A. 1994. Empowering students to resolve conflict through peer mediation. *High School Magazine* (September): 50–52.

White-Hood, M. 1993. Taking up the mentoring challenge. *Educational Leadership* (November): 76–78.

———. 1994. Enriching adolescent lives: Focus on changing family structures. *Schools in the Middle* (November): 9–12.

Wiggins, G. 1991. Standards, not standardization: Evoking quality student work. *Educational Leadership* (February): 18–25.

Williams, S. B., Jr. 1971. Student activities: Financing of programs. *Encyclopedia of education*. Vol. 8. New York: Macmillan Company, 500–505.

Wilson, D. M. 2001. Educational standards: Too far too fast? *Empire State Report* (February): 28–30.

Wolff, B. 1998. Campaign for respect. *Leadership for Student Activities* (October): 22–25.

Wolff, B., S. Cummins, and L. Fiscus. 2000. It doesn't have to be us against them: Establishing positive faculty relations. *Leadership for Student Activities* (April): 16–21.

Worona, J. 2000. Must Boy Scouts be permitted to use school facilities? Answer depends on school policies. *On Board* 1, no. 14 (August 14): : 17.

———. 2001a. Can outside religious groups use school facilities? *On Board* 2, no. 3 (February 12): 14–15.

———. 2001b. High court widens access of religious groups. *On Board* 2, no. 12 (July 2): 1.

Yell, M. L. 1998. The legal basis of inclusion. *Educational Leadership* (October): 70–73.

Yurek, S. R. 1996. Courts and cocurriculars: Is your school out of gavel's reach? *High School Magazine* (September–October): 25–27.

Zaugg, H. 1998. Academic comparison of athletes and non-athletes in a rural high school. *NASSP Bulletin* 82, no. 599 (September): 63–72.

Zill, N., C. W. Nord, and L. S. Loomis. 1995. *Adolescent time use, risky behavior, and outcomes: An analysis of national data*. Report prepared for the Office of the Assistant Secretary for Planning and Evaluation, U.S. Department of Health and Human Services. Rockville, Md.: Westat.

INDEX

ABOUT THE AUTHOR

Edward Klesse graduated from Chatham High School in Chatham, New Jersey; Rutgers The State University of New Jersey (B.A. in sociology); and The Pennsylvania State University (M.Ed. and D.Ed. in counselor education). He also holds a Certificate of Advanced Study (CAS) in school administration and supervision from the State University of New York at Cortland.

He has worked as a junior high school guidance counselor, college career counselor, director of pupil personnel services/high school counselor, and assistant superintendent of schools. Most of his professional career has been spent working in the Windsor Central School District, Windsor, New York.

In addition, Dr. Klesse has been an adjunct lecturer at the State University of New York at Oneonta, teaching graduate courses in the Department of Educational Psychology and Counseling. For thirteen years, he was the administrative codirector of the Maine National Leadership Camp, an intensive, five-day, summer leadership training program for high school students, sponsored by the National Association of Secondary School Principals (NASSP).

Dr. Klesse has also served on numerous scholarship and award committees for NASSP and has regularly been a staff member for the National Association of Student Councils' annual conference.